Selected Film Essays and Interviews

New Perspectives on World Cinema

The New Perspectives on World Cinema series publishes engagingly written, highly accessible, and extremely useful books for the educated reader and the student as well as the scholar. Volumes in this series will fall under one of the following categories: monographs on neglected films and filmmakers; classic as well as contemporary film scripts; collections of the best previously published criticism (including substantial reviews and interviews) on single films or filmmakers; translations into English of the best classic and contemporary film theory; reference works on relatively neglected areas in film studies, such as production design (including sets, costumes, and make-up), music, editing, and cinematography; and reference works on the relationship between film and the other performing arts (including theater, dance, opera, etc.). Many of our titles will be suitable for use as primary or supplementary course texts at undergraduate and graduate levels. The goal of the series is thus not only to address subject areas in which adequate classroom texts are lacking, but also to open up additional avenues for film research, theoretical speculation, and practical criticism.

Series Editors

Wheeler Winston Dixon – University of Nebraska, Lincoln, USA
Gwendolyn Audrey Foster – University of Nebraska, Lincoln, USA

Editorial Board

David Sterritt – Columbia University, USA
Valérie K. Orlando – University of Maryland, USA
Thomas Cripps – Morgan State University, USA
Robert Shail – University of Wales Lampeter, UK
Catherine Fowler – University of Otago, New Zealand
Andrew Horton – University of Oklahoma, USA
Frank P. Tomasulo – City College of New York, USA

Selected Film Essays and Interviews

BRUCE F. KAWIN

FOREWORD BY HOWIE MOVSHOVITZ

ANTHEM PRESS
LONDON · NEW YORK · DELHI

Anthem Press
An imprint of Wimbledon Publishing Company
www.anthempress.com

This edition first published in UK and USA 2013
by ANTHEM PRESS
75–76 Blackfriars Road, London SE1 8HA, UK
or PO Box 9779, London SW19 7ZG, UK
and
244 Madison Ave. #116, New York, NY 10016, USA

Copyright © Bruce F. Kawin 2013

The author asserts the moral right to be identified as the author of this work.
All rights reserved. Without limiting the rights under copyright reserved above,
no part of this publication may be reproduced, stored or introduced into
a retrieval system, or transmitted, in any form or by any means
(electronic, mechanical, photocopying, recording or otherwise),
without the prior written permission of both the copyright
owner and the above publisher of this book.

British Library Cataloguing-in-Publication Data
A catalogue record for this book is available from the British Library.

Library of Congress Cataloging-in-Publication Data
Kawin, Bruce F., 1945-
  [Selections]
  Selected film essays and interviews / Bruce F. Kawin ; foreword by
       Howie Movshovitz.
    pages cm. – (New perspectives on world cinema)
  Includes bibliographical references and index.
  ISBN 978-0-85728-304-7 (hardback : alk. paper) – ISBN
      978-0-85728-305-4 (pbk. : alk. paper)
 1. Motion pictures. 2. Motion pictures–Reviews. 3. Gish, Lillian,
1893–1993–Interviews. 4. Hawks, Howard, 1896–1977–Interviews. I.
       Title.
   PN1995.K347 2013
   791.43–dc23
   2012045244

ISBN-13: 978 0 85728 304 7 (Hbk)
ISBN-10: 0 85728 304 9 (Hbk)

ISBN-13: 978 0 85728 305 4 (Pbk)
ISBN-10: 0 85728 305 7 (Pbk)

This title is also available as an eBook.

In memory of Ernest "Chick" Callenbach

Also by Bruce F. Kawin

Telling It Again and Again: Repetition in Literature and Film

Faulkner and Film

Mindscreen: Bergman, Godard, and First-Person Film

To Have and Have Not (ed.)

Faulkner's MGM Screenplays (ed.)

The Mind of the Novel: Reflexive Fiction and the Ineffable

How Movies Work

A Short History of the Movies (co-author, Gerald Mast)

Horror and the Horror Film

Love If We Can Stand It

CONTENTS

Foreword by Howie Movshovitz   ix

Preface   xiii

PART I. VIOLENCE AND POLITICS

1. Me Tarzan, You Junk   3
2. The Whole World Is Watching   13
3. Violent Genres   22
4. Wild Blueberry Muffins   31

PART II. HORROR AND SCIENCE FICTION

5. The Mummy's Pool   35
6. Time and Stasis in *La Jetée*   50
7. *Carnival of Souls*   57

PART III. REVIEWS

8. *Welcome to L.A.*   63
9. *The Fury*   66
10. *Piranha*   69
11. *The Elephant Man*   72

PART IV. INTERVIEWS

12. Lillian Gish   81
13. Howard Hawks   89

PART V. LITERATURE AND NARRATION

14. The Montage Element in Faulkner's Fiction	131
15. Horton Foote	149
16. An Outline of Film Voices	153
17. Dorothy's Dream: Mindscreen in *The Wizard of Oz*	167

PART VI. GETTING IT RIGHT

18. Creative Remembering and Other Perils of Film Study	175
19. Late Show on the Telescreen: Film Studies and the Bottom Line	180
20. Video Frame Enlargements	187
21. Three Endings	196
Acknowledgments	203
Index of Names and Titles	205

FOREWORD

by Howie Movshovitz

As readers of this volume are about to see, over the course of his still-stellar career, Bruce Kawin regularly has committed two sins, for a film scholar. The first is that his ideas and insights stress that the ultimate purpose of cinema is to enlighten human beings about the nature of actual life, not merely to enhance the careers of film teachers. This book reminds me of a medical humanities meeting a few years ago at the University of Colorado's med school, when Rita Charon of Columbia University described getting members of the Columbia English Department up to the teaching hospital to work with patients, nurses and doctors. As she put it, the literary scholars who made that journey discovered why they'd studied literature in the first place—because they cared about people, not because they cared about theory. Kawin has known that all along. Kawin's second sin, a cousin of sin number one, is that his writing is utterly, utterly clear. You don't have to belong to a club or be an initiate to understand what Bruce Kawin writes about; you simply have to care enough about film to read and think along with his fine prose. In fact, it might be more accurate to say that Kawin is simultaneously scholar and critic, which makes him a teacher. He brings to his work the love of cinema and brightness of insight and discovery that mark the best criticism, but backed by the scholar's discipline, depth of knowledge and willingness to look at films and ideas that have not attracted attention before.

These dual principles of engagement and accessibility show themselves together in the very first essay in the collection. "Me Tarzan, You Junk" gets to its subject in the first sentence. The issue is catharsis and what gets "catharted." It's a moral argument about violence in movies, but not a moralistic discussion. I know for a fact that Bruce Kawin rather likes movie violence, when it isn't a cheap and easy sell-out of a tough conflict, when the film is smart about its violence. As he does regularly, with this article Kawin gets inside the common, the official version, to look at what's actually in a film, instead of what even generations of commentators have allowed. He goes into the issue of what questions are solved by violence, and the answers to the questions expose the paltry aims of some revered favorites, like *McCabe & Mrs. Miller*, *A Clockwork Orange* and *Straw Dogs*. So *High Noon* isn't necessarily what it looks to be, and in one fine sentence Kawin rearranges the terms of the argument: "Hollywood is a great believer in the Just War, but it lacks the respect for peace that makes such an attitude supportable." Therefore, the discussion is not only moral; it also does what good film criticism has to do. It opens up the film, makes you see it clearly, and also highlights the difference between what a film is and what it says it is.

Another example comes in the sensible and observant "An Outline of Film Voices," which looks at the all-important question of the ways in which the cinema signals narration in first, second or third person. Early in the essay, Kawin makes the crucial observation, which runs contrary to popular opinion, that first-person narration does not need what Kawin calls the "forced analogy" of the subjective camera. The essay continues to explain in clear, direct language how film articulates the three voices.

This volume shows the range of Kawin's thinking, and his insight into the kinds of approaches that enhance the understanding of cinema. His interviews with Howard Hawks and Lillian Gish allow the voices of actual filmmakers into the conversation, where they are crucial, but in the academic world are too rarely heard. Aside from the information that comes from the two selections, the two interviews demonstrate how artists think and talk about different questions, and in different terms, from critics and scholars. Most published interviews—and I myself have published and broadcast hundreds like this—are directed to one or two central ideas. Much of the conversation is cut out for the sake of efficiency, a limited kind of clarity, and space, but here Kawin includes his questions and lets Hawks and Gish have their say, regardless of the "inefficiencies," with the result that the reader comes away with a feel for how the two speak, their rhythms, their thought processes, their digressions—their humanity. The result is not an "answer" to some question; it's a picture of who these people are.

The Hawks interview provides a rare look at how William Faulkner got on in Hollywood, his friendship with Hawks and his occasional need for a Hollywood paycheck. Hawks died not long after he spoke with Kawin, and you can hear his own frailty when he says about Faulkner, "Bill died about five years ago, didn't he?" And after Kawin says that Faulkner had died thirteen years before, the sigh in Hawks's voice as he replies, "It's hard to believe," brings you right into the room where the two men conversed. After reading this interview, and with Hawks's voice in your head, the restraint of feeling in the Hawks films no longer seems like a fault. The tight-lipped characters in *Air Force* or *Only Angels Have Wings* make a new kind of sense, and even the screwball comedies gain emotional depth.

I too once spoke with Lillian Gish, and, frankly, I'm not sure she ever reveals much, but her voice is unique and charming, and shows the surface sweetness of early Hollywood and Gish's own impenetrable veil of Victorian manners. Maybe in private conversations, Gish really did call Louis B. Mayer "Mr.," and maybe she really did just write to "the women's clubs and the churches" that objected to a production of *The Scarlet Letter*, but while I don't believe her account of making the film for a second, I think the interview shows exactly the kind of perfectly proper and implacable naif Gish presented herself to be in public.

One of the many strengths of Bruce Kawin's work is his drive for accuracy. Since he took over Gerald Mast's *A Short History of the Movies* some years ago, it has become a far more accurate and trustworthy film history than it had been. In the essay "Creative Remembering," Kawin worries about being pedantic—which he is not. It should be obvious that it makes a load of difference for intelligent, accurate and useful discussion of films to know (among other things) what happens when. The argument for precision becomes even more urgent when you see how often mistakes are simply copied from generation to generation. Kawin notes correctly that with the convenient use of video copies of films, the problem of accuracy has lessened, but it has not gone away. The recent Susan Orlean biography of Rin-Tin-Tin has already been criticized for its obvious inaccuracies.

The two essays "The Montage Element in Faulkner's Fiction" and "The Mummy's Pool" are straight-out two of my favorite pieces of film history and criticism. While the Faulkner essay makes and illustrates the contradiction that Faulkner's fiction is profoundly cinematic, but his film scripts tend to be novelistic, the essay also opens up the discussion of what the terms *cinematic* and *novelistic* might actually mean. It's a fine description of the difference between film and literature, an obvious and crucial identification which has often been garbled and labored. With elegant and commonsensical precision, "The Mummy's Pool" uses horror and science fiction film to discuss the similarities between cinema and dream, and in turn uses cinema and dream to separate horror from science fiction and to define the two expressions of experience. The essay shakes up and re-frames the terms of discussion to bring clarity out of confusion, uncertainty and the clouds of obfuscation that can plague academic writing. After invoking Frazer's *The Golden Bough*, Kawin writes, "The parallel with horror films should be immediately obvious: one enters the Land of the Dead, gives death temporary dominion in order to emerge reborn and refreshed." The sentence is wonderfully succinct and it nails the issue dead on.

The essays in this collection show that Kawin is constantly aware that the cinema unfolds in the actual world and that he understands history in terms of the kinds of lived moments that define and determine how a nation's mindset can be altered. These are often events that vanish from memory as history is organized and written. So, in "The Whole World Is Watching," Kawin "remembers" for us the repressive chaos of the 1968 Democratic Convention in Chicago, with Mayor Richard Daley screaming "Kike" at Abraham Ribicoff, and some of the other critical events in late-1960s America that destroyed optimism and drove many to avoid political and social engagement. That historical context then shapes his discussion of how the cold ironies of Stanley Kubrick and his film *Full Metal Jacket* buffaloed two of America's major magazine film critics at the time because they didn't know how to read recent American history. This is an angry piece of writing, which makes obvious the fact that Kawin writes from a position of genuine commitment to political and social awareness.

He also makes the reader feel the life in individual people. The two short pieces on Horton Foote give loving tribute to that fine and talented man. In "Late Show on the Telescreen," Kawin's principled, rigorous argument in favor of using actual film to teach film, he talks about Adam Reilly, the only director of the too-short-lived Denver Center Cinema. Both of us loved impish and resolute Adam, and reveled in the glorious prints he presented to the public day after day for nearly ten years.

As a critic myself, I much appreciate Bruce Kawin's reviews of individual films. He has what Stan Brakhage longs for at the start of *Metaphors on Vision*— "an eye unprejudiced." In my experience, even good critics get taken over by various kinds of group-think, often initiated by often smart publicists. Kawin is not quite an instinctive contrarian. But his eye is not easily led astray by things like commonly held attitudes. The pieces on *Welcome to L.A.*, *The Fury*, *Piranha* and *The Elephant Man* consistently find what others have missed, overlooked or dismissed, which makes the essays exciting and rewarding. They can change how one sees.

A film scholar friend once told me that when her father died, she felt that she had lost her audience. She said that he was a smart man, interested in film, but in no way expert, and, she said, that if he didn't understand something she'd written, that was a sign that it wasn't written well enough. That immediate accessibility—without surrendering a whiff of meaning and complexity—is part of Bruce Kawin's genius. If one is interested enough to read these essays, as payment one will receive great insight. As he notes in the lovely short manifesto, "Wild Blueberry Muffins," the world of film theory is frequently a place of convoluted language with no substance and nothing really at stake. None of the essays in this book commits those offenses. For me, this is the best kind of scholarly criticism—observant, alert, committed to understanding, and profoundly informed. These smart, coherent essays make difficult ideas clear. They do what D. W. Griffith supposedly said to Lillian Gish: "Above all, my dear, I'm trying to make you see." Bruce Kawin makes us see.

PREFACE

I put this book together because I thought people should have a chance to read these articles and reviews, most of which are out of print and not available online, as well as the unpublished interviews with Lillian Gish (1978) and Howard Hawks (1976). Some of what is in the interviews is old news, but much is not.

The pieces have been grouped by topic and type. "Violence and Politics" considers the uses of violence in American film and its relation to sexual politics as well as national and international politics; the section also takes up academic politics. "Horror and Science Fiction" looks at the two genres, sometimes in relation to each other, and offers both a close reading of *La Jetée* and an overview of horror based largely on the Mummy films. "Reviews" includes four early reviews, but not the review of *Full Metal Jacket*, which is more a political essay and appears in "Violence and Politics" as "The Whole World Is Watching." "Interviews" contains the complete transcriptions of my interviews with Gish and Hawks. All that's missing is the last half hour of the four-hour Hawks interview, when the tape recorder seized up. "Literature and Narration" covers the relations between literature and film, the art of screenwriting, and the uses of first-, second-, and third-person narration in cinema; it ends with a close reading of the beginning of the dream sequence in *The Wizard of Oz*. "Getting it Right" takes the reader through the coming of video and then of digital cinema (these essays were written between 1978 and 2011) and their impact on film as well as on film scholarship. It also examines the differences among film, video, and digital frames, and it takes strong exception to film books, especially reference books and textbooks, that don't get their facts straight.

In spite of these groupings, the book has been arranged to be read in order. The Hawks interview leads directly into the article on Faulkner, for example, and Faulkner both overlaps and contrasts with Foote. The last paragraph of "Late Show on the Telescreen" concerns an excellent film print and implicitly raises the issues researched in "Video Frame Enlargements," and so on.

The title of the final section addresses a running theme in all the essays: the attempt to understand and present a subject correctly—the attempt, for example, to establish whether Faulkner was influenced by the movies or not, or to find in the course of several essays what I want to say about film and video or about movie violence. In the case of the interviews, getting it right means getting down exactly what Gish and Hawks said and the way they said it. In film theory, as in the discussions of mindscreen cinema, it means coming up with a valid idea and testing it in different contexts. In film history, it means seeing how, in a film like *La Roue*, Abel Gance got it right. In film scholarship, it means standing up for accuracy and encouraging readers to call factual errors in film books to the attention of the authors and publishers of those books. I don't mean to suggest that I got everything right, but I did continually try to.

For anyone who is interested in tracing my development as a writer, the earliest pieces in this volume are the interview with Hawks, the review of *Welcome to L.A.*, and "Me Tarzan, You Junk." "Wild Blueberry Muffins" and "Horton Foote" are roughly halfway. The most recent are "Dorothy's Dream" and "Three Endings."

Variations from the original wording are enclosed in square brackets and have been kept to a minimum. Typos have been fixed silently. The different house styles have been left to clash.

I am grateful to my editors, especially the late Ernest Callenbach at *Film Quarterly*. I am also grateful to Lise Menn, who suggested that the essays have individual introductions, and to Howie Movshovitz for writing the Foreword.

Boulder, Colorado
May 2012

Part I
VIOLENCE AND POLITICS

1

ME TARZAN, YOU JUNK

This was published in 1978 by the Canadian film magazine Take One. *It was written at the height of the Hollywood Renaissance (mid-1960s to late '70s) when nobody knew it would be called that; it just seemed that there were a great number of powerful new films that commanded attention. What bothered me was not that there was more sex and violence in the movies but that violence was being endorsed in preference to other solutions and in a notably sexist context. Over the years I came to terms with* A Clockwork Orange *and some of the other films in this article (and lost my enthusiasm for the Billy Jack pictures), but I still agree with what it says about how certain movies set out to manipulate audiences and reinforce systems of values. Although the majority of violent films today are not as sexist as they used to be, they continue to take violent solutions for granted. I regret that I forgot to describe the final gunfight in* High Noon, *where the wife claws at the villain to free herself and to allow her husband to shoot him. While the points of the last two gunfight scenes are similar (she is again responsible for a death and is again working with her husband), she grows in the audience's estimation because this time she attacks a man in the face with her hands instead of shooting a man in the back.*

One of the most effective ways a movie has to teach us its view of the world, its system of values, is to control the thematic energy of catharsis. Many of the most widely distributed American films of the last 25 years have been pushing the message that violence can be justified in terms of some "higher" system of values, and have been making the point in terms that are not so much violence-oriented as they are sexist. In the most juvenile of these films—*McCabe & Mrs. Miller*, for instance, or *Straw Dogs*—the apparent enemy is a cluster of violent men, but the important enemy is a selfish woman. To get a handle on this slippery, stupid, and dangerous message, I'd like to reopen the question of how catharsis works and what it does.

Drama in general appears to work by creating tension in the audience, increasing that tension, and then releasing it. This tension is usually attached, by the artist, to some kind of issue or emotion, theme or dominant mood, so that at the moment of climax one has an intense experience of thematic energy. In a "triumph of love" movie like *Intolerance*, for instance, the audience is supposed to be washed through with a pure sense of joy-at-the-triumph-of-love when the Dear One saves the Boy from the hangman. Dramatic climax is like sexual climax: at the moment we surrender to the energy and let it flood us, the energy is dispersed. In that moment of release, the accumulated tension and its attendant emotions—and ethics—are profoundly and personally felt. The question is, does this purgative process, which purges only what it introduces to our systems, free us from the aroused emotions or deeply teach them to us? Were the Greeks more stable for having watched *Medea*, the Victorians more sensitive to the pains of the poor for having read Dickens—and what is it, exactly, that makes Americans associate violence and heart-wrenching with directorial competence—in *Little Big Man*'s snowy Indian massacre sequence, for example?

A violent climax floods us with violence. A love climax floods us with love. After deeply experiencing the release of violence (attacking the Other) we are not left full of love (accepting the Other). We are left relaxed. What we have accepted is our violence.

Peckinpah has argued that his violent films, because they are cathartic, release his audiences from their inside violence. I think it more likely that *Straw Dogs*, anyway, can *make* people violent, deeply teach them violence. The compromise position—that catharsis helps us live with an emotion we have been led through—makes sense too. The rest of the point, however, is that cathartic violence is often the vehicle of an ethic, and that it is really the ethic that is learned, that is applied, that affects both the self-image and the politics of the audience.

I am not saying that we should not be exposed to violence, or that we should be out of touch with anger. I am saying that catharsis reinforces as it disperses; it teaches acceptance of the energy it releases, gives us a guided tour of that emotion. Anger, of course, is not the same thing as murder. Yelling at the students who demand all her energy and give nothing back, Jean, the heroine of *The Trial of Billy Jack*, teaches us how to accept and release an extraordinary anger. Beating the rat-catcher to death like a rat, David, the hero of *Straw Dogs*, teaches us how to enjoy murder. In fact, he does more: he teaches the one thing we must believe if we *are* to murder—that the enemy is not as human as ourselves, but merely some kind of inconvenient animal. And *The Trial of Billy Jack* (despite the unfortunate fact that Laughlin's film is so incompetently directed and flabbily cut that it makes Peckinpah's look like the Elgin Marbles) insists that an enemy can behave like an animal—that is, brutally—without *being* an animal, and teaches that even enemies, when loved—when accepted as human beings—can slowly learn to love back. Allen Ginsberg once said, "You only get hostile when somebody says that you don't exist."[1]

---

1 [Bruce Kawin, unpublished interview with Allen Ginsberg, October 1964, New York City.]

What I'm interested in talking about here is the kind of film, epitomized by *High Noon*, in which judgment is passed on the value of the hero's decision to become violent. This judgment is keyed to the world view of the film, to the issues it associates with violence.

Like *Straw Dogs*, *High Noon* teaches both that nonviolence is irresponsible and that a woman should back up her husband. *A Clockwork Orange* teaches that one is not human without freedom, that freedom necessarily includes the option to do evil, and that male freedom matters more than female freedom. The violence these movies present and justify is most consistently related to their sexual politics and to their fear of the Other.

This is not to suggest that these movies are made only for men, but that they reflect the central attitude of our selfish and patriarchal culture: that the Others are less than human, be they Viet Cong or female or rival Mafia faction. Female audiences participate in this fantasy much as male audiences do, by identifying with the values of the central character (of whatever sex) and celebrating his success against his enemies.

One of the characteristics of the modern humanist, and often feminist, picture is that it attempts to present both Self and Other as comprehensible human beings, even when the Other is an "enemy." (In *A Woman Under the Influence*, for instance, the violent double-binding husband is Other but not Object.) Violence does not preclude humanism, but the sense of the-enemy-as-subhuman does; in that way, among others, sexism emphatically precludes humanism, and can be taken as a useful indicator of a particular movie's "violence rationale."

"War is evil, and it is often the lesser evil," said George Orwell in reference to the fight against Franco. Hollywood is a great believer in the Just War, but it lacks the respect for peace that makes such an attitude supportable. Witness some of the causes for which it is willing to endorse violence:

—male supremacy (do not forsake me, o my darling),
—self-defense (my death would be more important than yours),
—territory- and property-defense ("I will not allow violence against this house"),
—consolidation of power (we can't let things get out of hand),
—existential freedom (ultraviolence),
—revenge (I'll hurt you the way you hurt me) […].

The list goes on, but by this point two central anxieties appear to predominate: the fear of others' freedom (the need to control) and the fear of others' control (the need to be free). It's all one pendulum, and the message at either extreme of the swing is: fight for your self, against your other self. Friends, it's a mess.

Before it was made into a movie, *Friendly Persuasion* was about Quakers. This movie teaches there is always something more important than the integrity of one's beliefs—the lives of loved ones, or patriotic duty. I am questioning not the importance of these other values, but the tokenistic way in which nonviolence is "endorsed." In the occupation scene, for instance, no serious attempt is made to show what might happen, or how the Quaker wife might feel, if the soldiers had their way; no nonviolent *strategy* is allowed to suggest itself to her. Worse, her bashing the soldier with her broom when he grabs for the goose is comical violence; she looks like a ridiculous woman. (Her husband's violence has more serious consequences; he's a man.)

The audience of *Friendly Persuasion*, because it has been given no reason to take nonviolence seriously, is encouraged to consider the wife unrealistic (however sympathetic) and is waiting for the moment when she will crack—and behave like "one of us," a person.

After *High Noon*, of course, *Friendly Persuasion* couldn't do much damage. The value structure of *High Noon* is remarkably sexist. The sheriff loves his Quaker bride, and has agreed to give up his guns, but first he has to shoot Frank Miller dead. If he doesn't, the craven town will be overrun by the bad guys. Like the paranoid America of 1952, he perceives himself as the only power brave enough to defend the Right, even if no one appreciates or helps him; if he doesn't stand fast, his world and all that he values will go under. (The Commies—or McCarthy, depending on your point of view—are coming on the high noon train.) His violence is justified by appeal to a value higher than nonviolence and higher than marriage: Duty. Duty in this case is a variant of Work, but includes honor, toughness, self-sacrifice, protectiveness and political judgment. These aren't bad values, but in opting for them the sheriff opts not against pacifism, but against *cowardice*. (He changes the subject.) He chooses male value over female value: it would be sissy to leave town at this time, especially for life with a woman. Another way to put this is to say that he chooses work-duty over love-duty.

As is well known, the sheriff gets all the bad guys but one; it remains for the wife to throw over her convictions and shoot the bad guy who's about to shoot her husband. This is the big surprise, and the climax of the picture (triumph-of-love-and-justice). Why does she do it? Simple: her duty to her husband is more important than what she originally considered her duty to herself. To a woman, then, marriage is more important than philosophy. In this context it has to be observed that the Grace Kelly character has probably given Quakers as bad a name as Nixon has. One version of *High Noon* that I play over in my head has her save his life, then annul the marriage; that seems both better drama and better politics. In the film as we have it, she totally surrenders. But of course, that is the point.

In other words, the film endorses marriage as the highest female value and work as the highest male value. The word "duty" applies with equal rigor in both value structures: she has a duty to him, he has a duty to Right. For each character, the question is rephrased in terms of violence; they both dramatize their decisions by shooting a bad guy. He shows that Right is more important to him than she—or himself—is; she shows that he is more important to her than Right—or herself—is. (She made that promise when she wed.) We're a long way from *Straw Dogs*, but it's down the same track; the train that stops here at noon stops there at midnight.

With or without its sexist aspects, the justification of violence goes on in film after film, always with reference to some higher system of values, and appealing to a variety of emotions. One of the most common appeals made is to fear. Since people do not usually go to the movies in a state of fear, the film must first convince them there is something to be afraid of. A large number of our most popular and critically acclaimed films appeal to a lurking understanding that we are besieged, doomed, misunderstood, nice people—who are right to be afraid.

Take Alex, for instance, in *A Clockwork Orange*. He is the center of sympathy; we in the audience are his "only friends." The violence he inflicts on others is stylized; the pains he feels are real. He attacks in slow motion, in fancy lighting, with music on the soundtrack and arty weapons in his hands—it's fun and games, intellectual storm-troopery. For a while I didn't know how to take the movie. I knew I walked out of the theater feeling nauseated (Alex-sympathy). Thinking about the scene where Alex is forced to watch violent films and is made sick, I constructed a "moral" rationale for the picture, in which Kubrick shows us a violent film (*Clockwork Orange* itself) and makes us—or me, anyway—sick. To take it further: the worst thing anyone does to Alex is to change the way he feels when he hears Beethoven; Kubrick decisively changed my associations with "Singin' In The Rain," a happy, loving song if ever there was one. Instead of seeing Gene Kelly dancing down the street, I began to see Alex kicking and raping his way down his kind of street. When Gene Kelly, rather than Alex, sang the song under the final credits, I felt sure that Kubrick was hoping to alert his audience to the power of conditioning (by reinventing "Singin' In The Rain") and, hammering in the irony that is his basic tone, trying to make us sick of violence. When I saw the film again, two rows behind a happy gang of thugs who had shoved their way past an usher and were having the time of their lives, I gave up on at least the last half of the idea. The film's practical effect, at least, is pro-Alex all the way. I had hoped that the fierce, even heavy-handed moralist who had ground out *Paths of Glory* and much of *Spartacus*, and the war-mocker who had given us the brilliant *Dr. Strangelove*, had finally homed in and attacked the violence in his own back yard—i.e., the movies.

Instead I became convinced that the cliché is correct: Kubrick's main concern is, and has been, the way people make "machines" more powerful and resourceful than themselves—especially the unique tendency of bureaucratic control to co-opt or pervert sexual expression (strange love, copulating bombers, P.O.E., HAL, etc.). The point about Alex seems to be that he is in danger of being made to respond like a machine (clockwork) and therefore of ceasing to be human. (The people he kills, of course, cease to be anything.) His restoration to a state in which he can "appreciate" Beethoven and women is supposed to be a happy one.

A Clockwork Orange, then, if my reading is right, sets out to make its audience afraid—not of violence and anarchy, but of conditioning and government control, and endorses both sexism and violence, as freedoms, in preference to such control. Its humanism is flatly contradictory. The woman whom Alex murders with the phallic sculpture, for example, has our admiration for being free, standing up for herself, and living the way she wants to; on the other hand, Kubrick not only does nothing to make us care about her death, but in fact does all he can to make her look ridiculous. He keeps our sympathies entirely with Alex, who is having trouble making his escape. Granted, the film is limited to Alex's point of view; even so, the ironic mechanisms do nothing to suggest that his point of view is deficient. Alex's violence, and our sympathy with him in it, free all concerned from the fear the film has aroused. The viewer is reassured, along with Alex, that he is the most important person in the world, and that no one will take away his cocky peenie.

It seems to me that these fear of freedom/fear of control films amount to a minor genre: the paranoia film. It isn't just that they're about people who are fearful, and who perceive their attackers as having infinite power and guile—it's that the films make those people appear correct in their judgments. Everybody *is* out to get the hero; he can't win, he can't relax, and he'll probably lose in the end. The most straightforward example of the genre from last year's crop of films was *Looking for Mr. Goodbar*; director Brooks drastically rearranges and interprets the elements of the original novel, converting it into a hopelessness thriller, a film not about sexual compulsiveness and pre-feminist isolationism but about the randomness of urban violence. (The most significant change he makes is to move the murder scene to the end of the story and introduce a number of knife motifs, so that what used to be part of a comprehensible character design becomes just a series of scare tactics; for a perceptive and moving response to the "ethics" of this film, see Gene Youngblood's column in the January issue of *Take One*.)

This is, I think, as consistent a phenomenon in the last ten years as *film noir* was in the forties; it may even be an outgrowth of *film noir*, with contributions from the anti-communist horror films of the fifties (*Invasion of the Body Snatchers*, etc.), from the adult western with its deliberate de-romanticizing of the myth of outdoor freedom and danger (*Lonely are the Brave* and *The Misfits* in particular), and from new attitudes toward political change and sexual freedom. The notion of freedom seems to frighten these filmmakers; they seem comfortable only with failure, with depression, and with negativity, and express this by bringing their plots around to unhappy endings that *pretend* to inevitability. The prototype was *Bonnie and Clyde*; by the time *Easy Rider* and *Medium Cool* came around (even though the latter is grounded more in real politics than in the kind of fantasy space under discussion here, that toys with hope before settling into hopelessness and carnage) it was clear that the movies were going to be a different kind of experience for several years—that moments of peace would be set-ups for unmotivated disasters, and that the experience of community-in-the-theater that Tolstoy thought would be the best thing about the movies would be replaced by isolationist conditioning—fear, aloneness, an end to hope—not because things in the world or even in the stories were hopeless, but because it was an easy way to get a strong response from the audience. But as these fantasies became more common, the response became harder to evoke; the audience gave up on its hopes, to protect itself against the films' set-'em-up-and-knock-'em-down flat betrayals. A film like *Chinatown* looks backward to *film noir* and forward to the paranoia film; *McCabe & Mrs. Miller* is a definitive example of the latter.

McCabe is like the frog he talks about, who bumps his ass so much because he doesn't have wings; at least, that's what we're encouraged to think. The important question is, why doesn't he have wings?—and the answer is that he does, but they aren't allowed to make any difference, since the movie aspires to a sense of fatality. Take the case of the kid with the socks (played by Keith Carradine). Remember how easy it was to dislike, even to abominate, the fat-boy gunfighter who tricked him into "drawing" his gun, then shot him down? The point is that the Carradine figure was created *only* so that we could feel upset when he was murdered; he has no other function in the world of the film. Altman built on our anger and shock, and channeled our sadness into the satisfactions of McCabe's attack; before we could get mad at the script, we got mad at the bad guys. We were made to feel that violent revenge was good, and that sneaky murder by unattractive people was bad. We were not encouraged to consider that we were being manipulated into a vengeful state of mind, and then being taught that revenge is a good release. This is paradigmatic of the way violence and negativity reinforce each other in the paranoia film; they pretend to add up to the Code of the West while insisting on an ethical vacuum. It is only a false hope—a falsely *entertained* hope—that righteous violence and good sex will restore the moral order in politics, religion, and the bedroom; what Altman wants to demonstrate is that nothing does any good in this mess of a world.

Altman's most distinctively fashionable gesture here is to isolate McCabe and kill him off, and to lay the blame for this on everyone in the picture (a sure sign that the disaster is gratuitous). McCabe has killed all the bad guys but is not allowed to win. Just when he has saved his empire, he loses everything; how ironic. And how manipulative this hopelessness is—how phony to appear to denounce Mrs. Miller for being in an opium fog (when she ought to be out saving McCabe, like the good little woman in *High Noon*), when she has been put in that fog precisely to increase the audience's sense that one's best efforts *are* always doomed, and that one's friends (especially women) cannot be depended on. Mrs. Miller, in other words, is being attacked for believing that it does no good to struggle, one will certainly lose—when the logic of this paranoia film is precisely that crazy disaster lurks everywhere and that nice guys lose. This is not just a directorial contradiction, and certainly not a deliberate irony; it is manipulative, destructive, and double-binding. From this perspective, the fascism of *Straw Dogs* feels clean.

The hero of *Straw Dogs* has come to the "innocent" wilderness, like McCabe, and is similarly assaulted by the nasty primitives. He is an intellectual, on the run from urban violence and even from—or bearing—international violence. (In its first sentence, the novel on which the film was based makes explicit the connection between the U.S. in Vietnam and David in Cornwall.) Like McCabe he is frightened and retreats to a private dream, then fights back. Like McCabe he wipes out many bad guys. Unlike McCabe he survives; he enters a new and powerful manhood, in which he is sexy and powerful and [can see through his broken] glasses. He is liberated into this satisfying life by mass murder—but not even the implicit connection with Vietnam can render this point ironic. "The sage is ruthless and treats the people as straw dogs," says Peckinpah, taking his cue from Lao Tze, who meant something entirely different. As Pauline Kael has observed, David is a "real man" now that he has secured his cave and won his woman. In the happy ending, David defends the helpless (Henry Niles) and shoots Frank Miller dead. Not only that, his wife, who has learned her place (Me Tarzan, You Junk), blasts the last bad guy to hell when her husband is in danger, and thereby intensely relieves the audience. (Although it looks for a while as if *High Noon* has been turned around, with David the runner and Amy the toughie, it becomes clear on reflection that Amy is a coward and David only dormant in his fascist violence.) The Law of the Jungle is the Law that Lasts.

A Clockwork Orange and *Straw Dogs* are comedies. Each ends with the promise of a happy ending and celebrates both cunt submission and the successful resolution of a phallic crisis. Perhaps the clearest way to point out the perversity of all this, the sheer needlessness of it, is to observe that *Modern Times* makes the same points about freedom, law, and machines as *A Clockwork Orange*, and that *Tol'able David* turns on much the same issues and situations as *Straw Dogs*, even to the David and Goliath number. Each of the earlier films ends hopefully, shows respect for life, praises courage, and celebrates love. Each of the later films celebrates murder and rape, and reinforces our sense of embattlement, isolation, and self-righteousness. To paraphrase Gertrude Stein's "Composition as Explanation," nothing changes except the way you see things.

The upshot of all these manipulations is a confusion bearing a message. Going into a paranoia film, we know we'll be shocked and hurt, that we'll feel betrayed by the unhappy ending, that we'll be made to want to do something to fix the world, and that we'll be made to feel that there's nothing we can do. We take two things away from the theater: the conviction that we are not safe, and the immobilizing fear of freedom/fear of control. Paranoia films disseminate a fear of life, a fear that is most evident in the filmmakers' *lack of ideas*; they don't know how to fix their worlds, and their knee-jerk reaction is to kill off the characters rather than to let them grow and risk. It is possible that this fear of life connects with a hatred of women; certainly Capra or Hawks would never make films like this, and clearly there is no room for a Jean Arthur in *Straw Dogs* or *The Sailor who Fell from Grace with the Sea* or *Chinatown*. But there is a Jean Arthur of sorts in the Billy Jack films (the third of which is significantly an update of Capra's *Mr. Smith Goes to Washington*). Billy Jack starts off as Tarzan and grows out of it; at no point is Jean considered to be junk.

All one need do is compare the ending of *Butch Cassidy and the Sundance Kid* with the ending of *Billy Jack*, to appreciate how a bloodbath not only does not settle anything but in fact demoralizes the audience while giving the impression of dramatic resolution. Butch and Sundance [are slaughtered together], while Billy and Jean go from trial to trial, making love, not war. The Billy Jack films get their audiences furious at the bad guys, then eventually channel their anger into nonviolent *work*, just as Jean educates Billy beyond the satisfactions of violent revenge. Anger and hope are primary here; vengeance and a sense of outraged isolation are not. This is all the more remarkable because the Billy Jack films have a subject that is worth getting paranoid about: the racism, sexism, fascism, and violence that reinforce each other throughout our culture. (As preoccupations go, this makes more sense than confusing life with death.) The purge toward which these films build has a clean feeling. All the aroused emotions find coherent resolution, without a lingering sense of contamination. One of the major reasons they succeed is that they take Jean seriously, allow her to be strong; another is that they are genuinely involved in the world and are aware of the role movies play in shaping the goals and self-image of the audience.

"The sage" neither treats the people as straw dogs nor does he encourage them to think of themselves in that fashion. The subject of the Billy Jack films is the spiritual education of a violent man; their mission is the spiritual education of an audience assaulted on all sides by violence and by object lessons on the necessity of violent response. It's about time they were joined in this effort, as well as in their (however tentatively) non-sexist investigations of autonomy and dependence. It's taken a long time, but we've finally seen past the muddle of *High Noon*. Regardless of what violence is threatened, Billy Jack is not forsaken by his darling—but neither does his darling forsake herself.

Near the end of *Steelyard Blues*, when Donald Sutherland, Peter Boyle, and friends are stealing part of an airplane from a military stronghold, one of the guards unties himself and runs toward the alarm. Boyle has given Sutherland a gun; the question is whether he will use it before the guard reaches the alarm box. The audience asks itself what it wants to happen. Sutherland doesn't shoot. The guard reaches the box, but the alarm doesn't sound. Boyle holds up the alarm-box fuse—and the clip of bullets. "Just wanted to see what you were made of," he smiles.

2

THE WHOLE WORLD IS WATCHING

"The whole world is watching" was chanted outside the 1968 Democratic Convention in Chicago when TV cameras broadcast live images of the police beating up demonstrators. About 19 years later, I wrote this review of Full Metal Jacket *in the ferocious mood that that film and some of the response to it had aroused in me. It seemed the right time to remind readers, or inform younger ones, of what the idealism of the 1960s and early '70s had felt like and been about, at least for me and the people I knew. The piece was published in the* American Book Review *in 1987. I respect its passionate writing and continue to agree with it, allowing for the fact that its present day was set deep in the time of Reagan. Younger readers may want to relate the discussion of nuclear war to what we currently know (but fail to act on) about global warming. Note that when the article brings up terrorism in its discussion of one radical perspective, it does not endorse terrorism. Like "Me Tarzan, You Junk," this article brings the peace movement into the conversation about violent movies.*

If any single hope characterized the American sixties, it was that oppression and hypocrisy would be vanquished, like a vampire in the sunshine, by an appeal to reason and official—i.e., Constitutional—laws and values. A radical could be defined, in those days, as one who found such idealism naïve, who saw plainly that those ideals were *not* respected and that, like the proverbial mule who needed to be whacked with a 2 × 4 before being told what to do ("First, you've got to get his attention"), the ruling elite would respond only to violence and terrorism. That elite has always denounced such violence as uncivilized and unfair (rather like my mother, who said hitting was wrong no matter who was right)—and has also, with exasperating consistency, patronized if not ignored any and all attempts at rational discourse and responsible, nonviolent argument.

The last major attempt at carrying the idealistic program forward took place outside the 1968 Democratic Convention. That was the last time any serious faith was placed in the democratic process—not to mention the Democratic Party—to behave according to its word and set things right. Who could forget Mayor Daley calling Senator Ribicoff a "dirty kike" on camera? Who could forget Humphrey's incredible, fervent acceptance speech, "We must never see again what we have seen tonight!"—which could be taken two opposite ways: we should never see cops bashing kids/we should never see such disruptive demonstrations—and which got a standing ovation. After that, meaning didn't have quite the *base* it had had before, say during the Enlightenment. (And the buzzword for what followed is, I'm sorry to say, postmodernism: the cult of multiple coherence.) Liberals dropped out, radicals were murdered (Fred Hampton in bed, and my friend Sam Melville in the yard at Attica), Nixons were elected, and the machinery ground on unopposed. By the eighties, under the government's new control system, inflation, most Americans refocused on money—not on cutting the military budget, and with it, deficit spending, but on personal financial security, a parachute for me and mine and to hell with everyone else ("Erst kommt das Fressen, dann kommt die Moral!" [...¹] And now we hear, from every side, wailing and gnashing of teeth: our kids don't respect values; they don't know what values are; they're turning into punks! Hey, they don't even respect *us*—and if what's left of the Left turns up in a movie, it's often as "Professor Berkeley," the quintessentially irrelevant and out-of-touch teacher in *River's Edge*. But of course it isn't *values* whose disappearance the Right laments; it's particular values, like the rights of the unborn and of the Born Again. Talk Tom Paine to these guys and see how far it gets you.

The Watergate break-in, and Nixon's responsibility for it, was broadcast on an AM newscast I had the good fortune to tune in, the day of the break-in. McGovern knew all about it too, and decided, like a gentleman of honor, not to push it. *Years* later, when Nixon had hanged himself in public—it had to get that blatant—you could hear from every hamlet and rag in the country the baffled outrage, the betrayal and confusion: How could this happen? How could we not have known? But it was all there to know, on that afternoon newscast (Cronkite himself, if I remember correctly)—and the rest of it was plain, to anyone who paid attention, when that same story did *not* appear on the evening TV news, nor in the next day's papers. What drives me to distraction is the breast-beating of those who took so damn long to acknowledge the obvious. The same thing happened with Vietnam, whose follies were pointed out loudly and precisely throughout the sixties, and which now has been accepted as an unfortunate, baffling national tragedy. Tragedy my foot; baffling my ass. Do you think that the discussions will be any different after an atomic war? Do you think anyone will remember that we knew—in 1963, when Bertrand Russell was in jail and Stanley Kubrick was shooting

---

1 [This line from *The Threepenny Opera* roughly translates, "First comes the grub, then comes morality."]

Dr. Strangelove; in 1968, when world politics exploded and Kubrick gave us *2001*; and in 1987, when North's Contra-diction won over the TV public and Kubrick fired a *Full Metal Jacket* at us—that war is not healthy for children and other living things? And if they remember that we knew, do you think they will forgive us for our complacency, our materialism, our refusal to follow through on our convictions?

You want to know why people drop out? Because hypocrisy and stupidity reign. In the July 14, 1987 *Denver Post*—a Knight Ridder News Service item, so I'm sure it isn't just weird local information like that Watergate AM newscast—it's reported that a Salvadoran death squad is active in Los Angeles, and full details are given of the abduction, torture, and rape of a woman who was on the way to a political meeting. Now catch this:

> U.S. Rep. Don Edwards, D-Calif., chairman of the subcommittee on civil and constitutional rights of the House Judiciary Committee, said Monday he thought there was enough evidence of death squad involvement to warrant an FBI investigation. The FBI has declined to get involved in the case, citing lack of jurisdiction.

It should not have to be pointed out—but apparently does—that if a communist outfit had kidnapped, beaten, burned, cut, and sexually assaulted a young woman on the way to a DAR meeting, the FBI would have found jurisdiction. To notice something like this and want to make a big deal out of it is sixties; to realize that the government does no more than pay lip service to "American values" and is truly in the business of supporting death squads abroad and not interfering with them at home, and therefore to sit back and just watch the Kooky Franco and Ollie show in a mood of evil black humor—that's eighties. It is the demonic look of the maddened recruit in *Full Metal Jacket*, the look that says "OK, if the party is to be on your terms, then Let's Party!" It's what the father in *The Shining* said to the [hotel]. It's what *Dr. Strangelove* said to Kennedy and Johnson. It's what *Barry Lyndon* said to the "new age." If there is an escape from the space station in *2001*, with its air-conditioned, lying politicos, its AT&T billing card, its Howard Johnson's, and especially that perfectly drawn attaché-case cold-fish bastard who is the first since the Dawn of Man to touch a monolith—if there is an escape from the ways men use learning to kill, then it is *away*, to a higher order.

There were two films that laid out the basics of the nuclear age. The very best was Peter Watkins's *The War Game*; it was understated, well researched, and morally intense. It was also banned. The other was *Dr. Strangelove*, which one B. Crowther recommended be withdrawn from international distribution because it made us look like destructive fools. (No doubt he just couldn't take the line, "Our source was the *New York Times*.") Well before that, Kubrick had made a powerful, sentimental, right-minded antiwar movie, *Paths of Glory*; it didn't work. What did work was Losey's *King and Country*; that offered an ironic, bitter, virtually hopeless look at military "thinking," like a *Paths of Glory* by the later Kubrick, and it came out in the same 1964 as *Dr. Strangelove*, whose special brilliance was its acceptance of ordinary, venal, stupid, human being—a status quo of dangerous idiots, mirrored like Narcissus in a pool of atomic sludge. It was a film that knew there was no hope and no reason to assume that, confronted with truth and reason, people in power would relinquish or at least redirect their power. About ten years from now, I expect that to be a fairly common point of view; what I am sure of is that Kubrick saw plainly, in 1968 and *2001*, that engagement with the stupid bad guys was hopeless and that "turn on, tune in, drop out" was the next *political* wave. If idealists were offended by *A Clockwork Orange*, if they could not see how dark things really were, tough. But by then Kubrick had outthought the majority of the audience; he was *way* ahead. Most people had no idea what *Barry Lyndon* was about or why it was so desperately funny and sad, but as that vain pre-yuppie went down, as his nonfictional cohorts are sinking now, so the family followed—in *The Shining*. What every Kubrick film since *Spartacus* has done is to improve the cinematic mechanism for the transmission of extreme irony, and the most ironic of them have been *Dr. Strangelove*, *A Clockwork Orange*, and *Full Metal Jacket*.

The attacks on *Full Metal Jacket*, notably those by Pauline Kael in the *New Yorker* and David Denby in *New York*, are worth dissecting. Both of them accuse Kubrick of coldness, of putting technique over emotion, and of expatriatism. They also attack the film's structure, calling it a mess. They seem to be reviewing the picture they expected to see, and not to have forgiven Mr. Wizard for becoming Mr. Iceman. The rhetorical manipulations of Kael's review are typical of her best and worst work:

> What is emotional in the book is made abstract. The movie has no center, because Kubrick has turned his hero into a replica of himself; his Joker is always at a distance—he doesn't express his feelings. So the movie comes across as not meaning anything. But it has a tone that's peculiar to Kubrick. His cold-sober approach—the absence of anything intuitive or instinctive or caught on the wing—can make you think there's deep, heavy anti-war stuff here. The gist of the movie, though, seems to be not that war makes men into killers but that the Marine Corps does. (In "2001," we were told that it was enough to be a man to be a killer.) Here's a director who has been insulated from American life for more than two decades, and he proceeds to define the American crisis of the century.

He does it by lingering for a near-pornographic eternity over a young Vietnamese woman who is in pain and pleads "Shoot me! Shoot me!" This is James M. Cain in Vietnam.

Now I will freely grant that Kubrick is, quite happily, not Spielberg—while insisting that emotion is not the only way to communicate an idea in the cinema—nor Capra, nor Fuller, nor Milestone. The breast-beating of *Paths of Glory*, which leaves me cold, in any case proved long ago to be inadequate to the job at hand, which is to change public attitudes toward oppressive institutions commandeered by the selfish and the stupid. "Feelings," that mush-word, has been irrelevant to Kubrick since *Lolita*; this is nothing new. And it has nothing to do with politics, no real effectiveness. What was devastatingly effective in *Dr. Strangelove* was its plainly saying, "Sure, go ahead and blow up the world!" It was, of course, all about sex, and it said plainly that the new human sexuality is impotence. In *2001*, the clearest joke was that Hal had more sexual presence than his operators; it was an extension of the head-credit sequence in *Dr. Strangelove*, where the planes tried a little tenderness. For Kael, Hal is a real character; for me, Hal is a joke, and much of what's good in the film is that there *are* no humanistic presences, no deep folks, while the closing image of the Überkind is a rich unknown (blown utterly into the stupid, the emotive, the "feeling," in the godawful *2010*, a movie as negatively symptomatic of our "culture" as any I can think of). But Kael's missed the point, the reason coldness works, the reason that irony cannot always be kind, or that a Jonathan Swift may find it difficult to live a happy life or sit down to a hearty meal with others, or respect people at all; she continues:

> It's very likely that Kubrick has become so wrapped up in his "craft"—which is often called his "genius"—that he doesn't recognize he's cut off not only from America and the effects the war had on it but from any sort of connection to people. (The only memorable character in his films of the past twenty years is Hal the computer.) What happened to the Kubrick who used to slip in sly, subtle jokes and little editing tricks? This may be his worst movie.

This is more than a series of cheap shots, and more than a plea for a cinema of nice emotions, the kind that don't change your life; it's also an imprecise appeal to some common understanding of the effects the war had on Americans, which anyone who was here at the time could see. What I've tried to show, so far, is what the effect of the war was on me and those around me, something I consider true and clear and ubiquitously forgotten, buried under the hindsight rhetoric of those who finally decided, after years of denying it, that the war was a bad idea from the start, misrepresented by the government and canonized by the media. (The media also canonized the postwar sense that somehow the war was an incomprehensible national tragedy, for which conscientious objectors and the veterans who actually fought in Vietnam—rather than Kennedy, Johnson, the Trilateral Commission, and the Pentagon—were somehow responsible.) If you opposed the war at the time, you were unpatriotic and a coward; but if you took 20 years to wake up and smell the coffee, then you had some kind of right to your anguish. I think that all that was *perfectly* obvious to Kubrick, and that he made *Dr. Strangelove* instead of *Fail-Safe* on purpose; I think, in fact, that he was politically brilliant to attack in that manner rather than to bemoan and warn. There was simply no reason to fall in with the bad guys and tell them an *On the Beach* story they could easily ignore (with lines such as "Of course nobody wants a nuclear war; that's why we have nuclear weapons"). The movie of "feelings" is nothing but well-meant; it is a humanistic appeal to shared values, and it ignores—in any nuclear context, at least—the real power relations in this country and the fact that values and priorities are not at all shared between those who are apparently willing to be the last generation and those who would rather see their children grow up. The story of how "people" were affected by the war is, OK, a good story, but that's all. But here I'm anticipating Denby, who says:

> Instead of dramatizing what Vietnam did to people, he tries to impress us with how poetically wasted everyone was, which is an adolescent's idea of cool… Kubrick doesn't make the sniper a character either. Only the mocking, antagonistic joke on American futility interests him. *Full Metal Jacket* is a large-scale, exciting, and audacious movie, but it has an impotent and malicious spirit. Whose complacency is Kubrick attacking with his nasty ironies? The two kinds of idealists who fought in Vietnam—the ones who thought they were saving the South Vietnamese and the military enthusiasts who believed in the invincibility of the American forces—have long been disillusioned. Apart from them, many people remain saddened by the moral confusions of Vietnam, but Kubrick would seem to be indifferent to such people. His annihilating wit denies any obligation to make sense of what it tells us. The movie is a case of intellectual laziness passing itself off as bitter truth: Stanley Kubrick has created a chaos out of his own demoralized and alienated state and called it Vietnam.

Denby's review, which is sincerely and carefully meditated—and quite wrong—is at pains to rule out of consideration anything like a sixties perspective ("Years after the war, Kubrick cultivates the awestruck mood of a stoned hippie exclaiming 'Hea-*vy*!'"); what he's leaving out, along with the idealists who did *not* fight in Vietnam, is the value of the uncontaminated perspective of the adolescent, the one who has not yet bought into the system and can see many of its aspects plainly from the outside.

What Denby appears truly to be objecting to is simple cold hard irony, Kubrick's refusal to wring his hands over the war or to give us another *Dr. Strangelove* now that America might finally be ready for it; rather than pay lip service to what we say we believe, Kubrick is making us pay for that lip service, rubbing our noses in it. Those who were in America at the time and who did oppose the war, like those who were aware of Watergate and astounded at how flagrant an evil must be before Americans get off their butts and react to it (accompanied by that damned national-tragedy rhetoric, the infuriating, self-righteous "How could this *happen?*" dreck), were ignored then and have been rewritten in the history books as "stoned hippies." The rhetoric of the official version was the enemy then, and it is the enemy now, for it has managed to absorb and deny horror, to sweep the dust under the ever-more-lumpy rug, to say that we, as Americans, are always right and have always defended the true, the good, the democratic, and the private. But we haven't, and we still don't, and even if there is a replay of Vietnam down Mexico way and further south, no one will do anything to stop it; and after it is over, when someone points out that in 1987 we knew all that, yet somehow "incomprehensibly" let it happen, that person will be accused of, say, not being a team player, while the ones who "remain saddened by the moral confusions" will look like the good guys. "Saddened" and "confusions" are vague words for a muddle. But I do not share in that muddle, and I am obviously not free of emotion, and I have been here all along, and I think that Kubrick has, once again, hit the nail on its groaning little head.

Full Metal Jacket is not cold. It is not bitter. It is not distanced from its subject. It does not suffer from too many retakes, nor from an excess of directorial control. It is moving. It is angry and fast. It is, at times, hilarious ("M-I-C, see you real soon, / K-E-Y, why, because we like you, / M-O-U-S-E / Mickey Mouse, Mickey Mouse / Forever will we hold your banner high high high high!"). While the war-tempered soldiers urge us to come along and sing their song and join the jamboree, I can just hear Kubrick bouncing up in the screening room yelling "Donald Duck! Donald Duck!"

And OK, sometimes it's bad. It has a *lousy* voice-over, probably courtesy of Michael Herr but who can tell; it is all utterly unnecessary, obvious, self-righteous, dumb—nothing remotely like the first-person narration of *A Clockwork Orange*, not even as witty as the unnecessary V-O in *Apocalypse Now*, and in fact about as vapid and bald as the lecture at the end of *Platoon*.

But what is *not* bad about this film is its structure. In the interest of improving the level of discourse on this important movie, let me close by offering a reading of its structure; perhaps that will give viewers and critics a handle on what is, admittedly, difficult about the film. For *Full Metal Jacket* is the first picture since *The Green Berets* to make people angry about the war and the way it's presented—no mean accomplishment, and a clear indication that Kubrick is not taking cold pot-shots at an America he fails to understand and empathize with, but is precisely hitting all the right nerves.

Kubrick has never been casual about his titles. The paths of glory lead but to the grave. Alex, like his culture, is a clockwork orange. Atomic engagement is a strange love. And a full metal jacket is a complete array of ammunition worn into combat, the arsenal as suit; in the context of Gomer Pyle's mad scene, its synecdoche is the magazine loaded with live, steel-jacketed rounds (the shell's own "metal jacket" keeps it intact until it hits the target). In the first act, the magazine is loaded: the recruits are trained, turned into killers (and anyone who finds the soap-beating scene, Joker's role in it, and Gomer Pyle's reaction lacking in emotion and pain and horror is, I'm sorry, just missing something). For a bullet to be fired, there must be a strong casing for the powder to explode against, so that good old Newtonian thermodynamics will propel the shell forward. This movie is a magazine loaded with live ammunition, and the first act is the tight one, the tough one, the well-organized one, driving and driven, ruthless and absolutely coherent. It is the shell casing. Back to Denby for a minute:

> Structurally, the movie is bizarre, a failed experiment that makes one aware of how conventional other movies are—and of why those conventions are necessary. It begins with a stunning 45-minute prologue…

This is a three-act picture, like the majority today (the three acts in *Platoon* were each 40 minutes). The second act, rather like the "Time Passes" section in *To the Lighthouse*, is diffuse, a series of vignettes and blackouts. Here the bullet is flying through the air, and one doesn't know where it will, as the new executives say, "impact." This lasts about half an hour. In the third act, which lasts about 35 minutes, there is a clearly organized and highly effective battle sequence, and it is in this act that the shell reaches its target; it is tighter than act two, but necessarily less tight than act one. For one thing, compare a bullet before and after it's been fired. For another, "good structure" or a "well-wrought urn" can't mean or be the same after the Vietnam experience as before; it's a war that changed our ideas (and the characters') about why and how things are done as well as our expectations of meaning; what is launched in a compulsive and driven world flies through the unstructured air until it hits as the postmodern.

The magazine is loaded with the recruits. The first one hits where the Marine Corps doesn't intend it to: in the chest of Sir Yes Sir, the drill sergeant;

Gomer Pyle is, then, a misdirected bullet. Every other recruit is followed, through the film, to the point where he either is killed or kills somebody else; each is a shell, and we trace each to its target. Joker, "Born to Kill," is the main bullet, and the movie follows him until he hits that praying, female sniper. The movie becomes a tunnel down which echo the words, "Shoot me! Shoot me!"—and Joker, the round, strikes home. Sir Yes Sir would have been proud. "Hard core," says one of the soldiers at that moment, and it certainly is.

3

VIOLENT GENRES

This was written for Ron Gottesman's encyclopedia Violence in America, *which appeared in 1999. The manuscript was called "Violent Film Genres," but in the encyclopedia the article appeared under the "Film" heading, so the title was changed. I mention this because I don't want the reader to expect some attempt here to cover all violent genres in all countries and all media; there's enough here as it is. I am grateful to Ann R. Cacoullos for helping me organize this piece, an attempt to update and summarize my thinking on violence in film despite its being limited to American movies from the twentieth century. For what it's worth, I have not seen anything in the twenty-first century that disproves what is said here.*

> I'm different from other people—pain *hurts* me!
> —Daffy Duck

Murder and bloody death are everywhere. In the Hollywood movie as surely as on network TV, hardly a crime is worth solving that doesn't involve a murder. Without the killings of an ape, an astronaut, and a computer, *2001: A Space Odyssey* would have no plot. By the end of *Oklahoma!*, poor Jud *is* dead.

Since the 1960s, a decade that began with *Psycho*, American filmgoers' tolerance for onscreen violence has steadily increased. The camera looks at awful things instead of looking away, the sounds are sharper and louder, and the makeup and explosions and optical effects are ever more convincing. Even considering two films in the same subgenre (killer lovers on the run), both of which were perceived as shocking and irreverent when released, *Natural Born Killers* is far more violent than *Bonnie and Clyde*.

The body count in *Halloween*—the number of people killed or corpses shown onscreen—is 4; in *Halloween II*, 11; in *Henry: Portrait of a Serial Killer*, 16; and in *Lethal Weapon*, which is not a horror film but a cops-and-robbers action buddy picture with an upbeat ending, 26. In *The Steel Helmet*, an outright war movie, it's 40. An earlier mystery, *Vertigo*—as citywise as *Lethal Weapon* but far more obsessive and charged end to end with death—made do with 3, and each of them, from the policeman to Madeleine to Judy, mattered. If *Halloween* feels more violent and disturbing than *Lethal Weapon*, that is not because it shows more violence. If *Lethal Weapon* is more frightening, as an event in American culture, than *Halloween*, that is because it shows such indifference to death and suffering—unless it wants us to care, in the case of certain favored characters whose pain matters—and because everybody knows that in a movie like this, the "action" isn't real and nobody takes it seriously, so lighten up.

Throughout the 1960s and '70s the representation of violence had its breakthrough films, and in many of them the action was, to say the least, not to be taken lightly. Like *Bonnie and Clyde* and *The Wild Bunch*, Coppola's *The Godfather* and *The Godfather Part II* managed the trick of being bloody and profound, charging the world with violence and confronting it with tragic, romantic guts. If they raised the ante of onscreen violence, making it more vivid and direct, they presented it in the fullness of its pain, its long-term implications, and—in unflinching spectacle—its beauty. In contrast, the James Bond pictures, with their soft-core sex and hard-core effects, led the way for the contemporary action film: the spectacle of deaths whose pain is not explored, of victims who are blown out of their shoes or through plate-glass windows but mainly out of the way, cipher obstacles nobody cares about after they are gone and whose passing is fun. In the post-*Psycho* horror film, *Night of the Living Dead* and *The Texas Chain Saw Massacre* broke all boundaries of taste in an assault on the gut that evolved (notably in Romero's *Dead* sequels and in the films of David Cronenberg) into an assault on mindless society as well as on the mind's conventional understanding of limits—not just the limits of behavior, but the limits of what can be shown or categorized or understood, the limits of experience, of identity, of being. These limits were likewise stretched in the family melodrama and the romantic comedy, primarily by David Lynch (*Blue Velvet*). Physical comedy has always been violent, but the traps set for the villains in *Home Alone* go beyond any banana peel. All these films set new standards, broken by others, as the American cinema became ever more graphically violent, carnal, and foul-mouthed—and as its occasionally deep look into the darkness got it somewhere, to a new and terrible vision whose politics is *Alien*, whose rite of passage is *Apocalypse Now*, and whose revelation is *Se7en*.

The amount of violence and its onscreen presentation vary with the times, as Production Codes and ratings systems come and go, and as public acceptance of violence as a part of life rises and falls. Reading genre-analogous films across the decades uncovers not only the development of commercial and artistic strategies, but also the symptoms of social change (*Lost Highway* has its roots and double in *The Lady Eve*). If *Natural Born Killers* includes more murders and is more casual about them than *Bonnie and Clyde*, the significant difference is not in the violence but in the attitudes toward it and in fact toward anything: the difference between a world in which everything matters and a world of surfaces whose truth of the day is the image of the day. After Mickey and Mallory have killed her parents (a grotesque sequence in *Natural Born Killers* that demands comparison with the realistic murder of the heroine's father in *Badlands*), Mallory tells her brother that he's free. No matter how difficult it might be for him to go on with his life after this, how hard any real person in his situation would have to work to deal with the murder of his parents, *Natural Born Killers* never again shows the brother or says anything about him. Even a scene of his following Mallory's exploits in the tabloids would have helped. [Bonnie and Clyde at least visit family.] There is continuity in that earlier world, and with it a sense of consequences and relations, of the human mess and glory that continue to unfold.

The Uses of Violence

To choose violent means of dealing with another person is to put one's project or desire or life above the other's suffering or death. It is also to put everything in physical terms, which are convenient to the motion picture. You can see it, and it moves. By far the easiest way to dramatize conflict for the movies—to make it visual—is to show people hitting each other. And to allow the viewers to enjoy the violence, all the film has to do is allow them to ignore or deny the full reality of the Other; that makes slapstick comedy possible, but it also can provide an excuse to dodge the work of creating characters.

There are countless cases where the use of violence indicates a failure of dramatic invention, where nothing more interesting or revealing could be imagined, no scene that would allow a character to grow or fester or do anything more than kill or die. In the deeper films, the Michael Corleones survive all the way to the silent scream (*The Godfather Part III*), the abyss of self-knowledge. Much the same thing happens—this going to the bitter end, eyes open—in the extremely violent Western *Heaven's Gate*, the gory mystery *Se7en*, and the thriller *Blow Out*, whose reflexive ending fuses tragic awareness with the absolute horror of violence.

There are, of course, equally serious films that take violence to its logical conclusion and celebrate it, from the Western *The Wild Bunch* and the coming-of-age melodrama *Tol'able David* to the horror movie *The Hills Have Eyes*. And for every one of these pictures, there can be found in the same genre or subgenre a picture that takes violence for granted, as a simple and irrefutable motivator and as a spectacle demanded by the genre as inexorably (and, in the largest sense, neutrally) as a Western demands a gunfight: the horror film has its *Friday the 13th*, the action film its *True Lies*.

If any film can adopt any attitude toward violence, from acceptance to abhorrence, it would obscure matters to say that in an action film the violence isn't "serious," but in a war film it is. This is a question not of genres but of films within genres. Any violent-genre film achieves its vision of violence in its own terms, which it works out in relation to and engagement with the terms of the genre. The genre provides a framework and a set of expectations, not a mandatory formula and attitude. Within any genre, one film may be more violent than another, may use violence for more spectacular or more conceptual ends, and may work with or against audience expectations of violence.

It may be useful, then, to introduce a distinction that applies across genres: between films that make the audience *feel* the violence, much as they might if confronted with the same event in real life (*Henry: Portrait of a Serial Killer*, *The Last House on the Left*, and the TV movie *The Burning Bed*), and films that urge the audience not to feel or respond to the violence as they would in real life (*Home Alone*, *Die Hard 3*, and the Road Runner cartoons). In the first group, violence hurts; in the second it is fun, a spectacle not meant to be taken seriously. Either extreme, or any position between them, may occur in any "violent genre." It is not that the action picture presents violence as a fast-paced, enjoyable ride— that the genre has perfected painless death and ought to notify the medical community—but that *True Lies* does this while *Deliverance* does not.

A related distinction worth introducing is between films, in any genre and in the terms of that genre, that *teach* violence, presenting it as the only solution to the character's or culture's problems as defined by the film (*High Noon*, *Straw Dogs*), and films that offer other, more creative solutions (*The Boy With Green Hair*, *The Shawshank Redemption*).

Some genres do include violence more readily than others, or are known for it: action, adventure, atrocity, boxing, cops-and-robbers, disaster, gangster, horror, prison, road, science fiction, and war pictures, Westerns and mysteries and thrillers. An adventure or science fiction serial without fistfights and certain-death cliffhangers would be rejected because it failed to deliver not just as a genre piece, but as a ritual. But many genres usually considered peaceable are rife with violence, decorated and motivated and crammed with it, from the family melodrama (*The Color Purple*, *Affliction*) and the musical (*West Side Story*, *Zoot Suit*) to the animated fairy tale (*Snow White and the Seven Dwarfs*) and cartoon comedy (*Duck Amuck*). Griffith set an enduring pattern for the family melodrama in 1919 with *Broken Blossoms*, in which a drunken boxer beats his daughter to death, and the genre has continued to bring its threat of violence within the family to the many genres it has intersected (as *Psycho* is a horror film as well as a gothic family melodrama, and *Mildred Pierce* is a family melodrama plotted as a murder mystery), but there has never been any expectation or requirement that it be violent. There can easily be a romantic comedy in which no one is murdered, and even a romantic tragedy (marrying the wrong person is bad enough), but it is almost impossible, if not perverse, to make a boxing picture without fights or a gangster picture without guns. The difference appears to be that violence is considered a familiar or essential element of certain genres, but one among many optional elements in others.

The Genres

There is no room here to detail all of the terms of any genre as complex as the gangster film, let alone of all violent genres, even when the discussion is confined, as it is here, to films made in the United States. But it may be possible to indicate some of the characteristic ways violence is dealt with, and what might be called the generic expectations of it, in some of the most routinely violent genres.

The Western demands a showdown. It is the scene in which the values for which the major antagonists stand are tested, and its roots are medieval, in the trial by combat—to the death, and let God be the judge. As in many other genres and indeed other narrative arts, it is simple to attach to the good guys the values an artist endorses, and to turn the audience against the bad guys—and the values they are made to represent—by having a bad guy do violence against a good guy or an unfairly easy target (*Shane*). This familiar manipulation works in films that argue for violence (*The Birth of a Nation*) and that argue against it (*Broken Blossoms*).

Genres that pit criminals against each other and against the forces of society—from the cops-and-robbers pictures to the gangster and caper films—are, like the Western, arenas in which personal qualities and social values, united in codes of conduct and degrees of skill, are tested. These standards apply with equal rigor in the original *Scarface* and in *The Godfather Part II*—and in numerous films that cross genres, such as *Mad Max 2* (released in the U.S. as *The Road Warrior*, an Australian road-movie/Western that is also a foundation epic, like a prequel to the *Aeneid*, set in the future) or the horror/adventure/social-criticism/cop-Western *Jaws*.

If these trial-by-combat genres of outlaws, settlers, and wanderers, of enforcers and rebels, carry expectations, codified if not born in literature hundreds of years ago, that God will be on the side of right (as in *Ivanhoe*), to play on and even frustrate those expectations is part of the art of working in a genre and a vital way to express the moods of the artist or reflect those of the culture, where the right may not turn out to be blessed (*Prince of the City*). These codes of honor and visions of the way the world works, or ought to work, are tested from their dark sides in the darker genres, which include not only horror (*Cat People*) and take-no-prisoners satire (*Natural Born Killers*), but also dystopic science fiction (*A Clockwork Orange*, *Brazil*), radical docudrama (*Salt of the Earth*), atrocity documentary (*Night and Fog, 4 Little Girls*), and, at the heart of darkest Hollywood, *film noir* (*Out of the Past, Gun Crazy*)[. *Noir*] characters kill to express their love and power and values, to insist that and why they exist, even if all concerned know that they are, as [in some of the novels of Jim Thompson], already dead.

The gunfighters of the West, like the gangsters, police, soldiers, outlaws, and knights, as folklore, pop history, and the genres have chosen to remember them, carried weapons—or were supposed to (*The Man Who Shot Liberty Valance*)—and used them. To the extent that the genres are built around these figures, as the war film might be said to fit itself to the soldier and the mystery to the detective, they take on the figure's weapons and his or her reasons for using them. Thus the war film and the soldier use violence to survive, to win, and to defend a position (*The Bridges at Toko-Ri, The Steel Helmet*). Malicious, personal violence may intrude in the war film (*Platoon*) but belongs properly to those genres, led by the mystery, in which the people who kill each other know each other.

Most mysteries revolve around at least one murder, and someone always turns out to have a compelling reason to commit it. The murder climaxes an earlier, [often] unshown story while starting another, motivating the tale of detection. The decision to murder is followed or uncovered rather than questioned; the genre demands blood. The mystery deploys violent events not only to keep the plot moving, but also to uncover the secrets of the heart and mind and will whose violent expression created the story's world along with its terms and logic, like an evil foundation tale that remains to be translated, a masked and twisted *fiat ego* (let there be me) that in the case of a movie is a literal *fiat lux* (let there be light). The key murder, finally unraveled and revealed, is frequently presented as the climax to the present story. Thus the world returns to its point of origin—as it usually does in horror when the threat has been annihilated—and the social and personal fractures brought about by the crime are overcome. Unless it is an exposé film (often a real-world mystery solved partly by journalists, as in *All the President's Men* or *Z*), a mystery [rarely] solves anything but a mystery; in this it is a pure art but rarely a vehicle of political or social change. The courtroom drama, however, sets out to tell the culture how to think about an issue; if it gets moving with a crime, it climaxes with a debate (Lang's German *M* and American *Fury*). Here violence focuses an issue (*To Kill a Mockingbird*), as in the murder mystery it heightens a conflict while reducing it to brutal essentials (*Frenzy*) and in a thriller is the preferred language of danger and romance (*Niagara*).

The prison picture, a claustrophobic morality play, pits good against evil under pressure, with anger and violence constantly erupting and being suppressed. Evil may take the form of a corrupt penal system (*I Am A Fugitive*

From A Chain Gang), a sadistic official (*The Hill*), a brutal roommate or gang of inmates (*American Me*), or a dishonorable rat (*The Criminal Code*). Some prison pictures sincerely denounce violence and present viable alternatives (*The Hill*), but the violence happens anyway; it is the genre's almost invariable means of dealing with evil.

The adventure film challenges its heroes to survive violence and unknown danger (*King Solomon's Mines, The Most Dangerous Game, The Man Who Would Be King*) as they explore the farthest reaches of the world and the limits of their own resources. In addition to the spy adventure (*North by Northwest, Dr. No*)—taking the spy film proper, from the fact-based *The House on 92nd Street* to the fictional *The Spy Who Came In from the Cold*, as a [different subgenre]—the kin of the adventure film include the fantasy adventure (*The Wizard of Oz*) and the road movie (*Easy Rider*), so bloodily combined in *Wild At Heart*. And the fantasy adventure, the thrilling visit to the world of impossible realities, of dreams and nightmares, is, like the romance and the thriller, deep kin to the horror film (*A Nightmare on Elm Street*).

Categories of understanding are always shifting in the horror film; things one thought were one way turn out to be another, to answer to another paradigm. What would be a peaceful event in real life or in some other genre may well turn deadly in a horror film (visiting a parent's grave in *Night of the Living Dead*, leaving the bedroom to get a beer in *Halloween*) or put the soul in danger (renting a terrific apartment in *Rosemary's Baby*). In horror movies, violence is the most common way the monster or threat expresses itself, and the violence is usually repeated (Dracula kills in his own way, over and over; so does Norman Bates) until the evil is expelled or destroyed—after which the culture licks its wounds and attempts to return to stability, which formulaically includes romance and reproduction; hence the heterosexual couple that so often survives. Violence—attacking it with *something*, whatever works (shoot them in the *head!*)—is the almost mandatory but not exclusive means of vanquishing the horror: ritual, including prayer and magic, is as effective in this genre as it is in the Biblical spectacle, and the best way to get rid of a ghost may be to stop being afraid of it (*The Uninvited*).

While the literature of science fiction is often free of violence, as reconceived for the movies it almost always demands death—at the hands of a bug-eyed monster (*This Island Earth*), an intriguing technology (*The Fly, Forbidden Planet*), the hazards of space travel (*Rocketship X-M*), things from outer space (*Invasion of the Body Snatchers*), and even close-minded humans (*The Day the Earth Stood Still*). Linked decisively to the genres of romance and adventure as well as to both fantasy and science (unlike fantasy and horror, it must make a scientifically credible case for what it imagines), science fiction is concerned with much more than angry bacteria and mad scientists. But as practiced in Hollywood, the science fiction film may be difficult to distinguish from the horror film (*Tarantula*). Even pictures that belong squarely within the genre, like *Gog* or *Star Trek II: The Wrath of Khan*, are full of violence, enhanced—appropriately, since it is a genre in which technology counts—by sophisticated, vivid effects.

Realistic violent effects are rampant in the action film (*First Blood*), and even in the subgenre of the disaster movie (*Earthquake*) they are meant to be enjoyed. As in the thriller, sex and violence advance together, reinforcing each other in converging, adrenaline-fueled drives to climax (*Speed*).

The action film depends on athletic and mechanical spectacle. Sex, in that context, also becomes spectacle. (It does in other genres too, but the reasons vary.) The viewer's reaction to the sex as well as to the violence becomes a montage of distanced voyeurism and engaged identification: an explosion is enjoyed from a safe distance, as an embrace is imagined up close. Good-looking actors, embodying characters who desire each other and act on their impulses, authorize the desires of the viewer who has lusted after them, wanted to be like them, and identified with them. The same is true of violent impulses, authorized by characters who use violence effectively, attractively, and for such compelling reasons as survival and revenge. If this complex of voyeurism, identification, and authorization applies, with modifications, to most sex-and-violence pictures and finally to most bourgeois narrative films, it may be most clearly at work in the action picture, where the enjoyment of violence as thrilling spectacle—like the enjoyment of sex in pornography—is not just authorized, but essential.

The Viewer

The desire to enjoy the spectacle of violence, brought to the theater by the genre fan who expects that desire to be reinforced and satisfied, may be traced to the pleasures of adrenaline. Or the action and disaster pictures may let a caged audience blow off revolutionary and criminal steam in a dream of destruction, where banks are bombed, officials are idiots, smashing somebody in the face solves a problem and really feels good, and right prevails—while outside the theater, of course, nothing changes.

In "The Work of Art in the Age of Mechanical Reproduction," Walter Benjamin wrote that mankind's "self-alienation has reached such a degree that it can experience its own destruction as an aesthetic pleasure of the first order." That may be one more reason it is fun to watch our world blow up. Violence not only keeps viewers entrenched in the ideology, entertaining them with fantasies of blasting away every enemy from the bad guy to the system—so that they will go out into the real world in a post-climactic calm, an energized sense of release and well-being—but also entertains those whose sole rebellious impulse is to watch the house burn down around them, identifying only with the carnage.

Some viewers have deadened themselves to all this violence as a condition of going to the movies; others enjoy it in the first place and, as genre enthusiasts, seek it out. Many have just learned to take it—taking the punches thrown by *Raging Bull* in order to make it through a great film and in the process growing calluses, so that watching the later *GoodFellas* is easy.

It is not that people used to care and no longer do. They can still get upset when the good die young (*Titanic*) or when the painful consequences of violence are left onscreen for a long time (*Unforgiven*). They care when they are given performances and images that reveal what they share with the victim—mortal being, the potential to be in an equally perilous situation, and in some contexts gender[, race,] and class—and what they recoil from sharing (that wound, that behavior) or see clearly in its Otherness (the monster, from Godzilla to the State). They care when they hate the villain. They care when they feel that the victim hurts and matters.

This caring is not necessarily a matter of getting to know a character, for one can recognize the humanity in a group and empathize with the suffering of many to whom one has not been formally introduced (the slaves who are chained and drowned in *Amistad*). Nor is it a matter of the camera's distance from the violence or the amount of time devoted to the event; in *Open City*, the sudden death in long shot of the woman gunned down in the street is at least as affecting as any of the killings shown at length in that film, close up. It is a matter of what is considered and presented at all. A bloody murder can be a second of action—bang, they got me, clunk. Or it can hurt, and take a long time, and be a humiliating mess and a shock, and leave people behind, things undone, everything undone, with pieces to be put back together that can never again be put together right.

4
WILD BLUEBERRY MUFFINS[1]

The title has a footnote—a parodic gesture; it now quotes the relevant dialogue from The Thing, *when the reporter implies that the scientist is "stuffed absolutely clean full of wild blueberry muffins." This article was written for a special issue of* Film Criticism *called* Interpretation, Inc.: Issues in Contemporary Film Studies, *which appeared in 1993. Those invited to participate were asked to respond to the recent work of David Bordwell and to indicate what they thought were the important current issues in film theory as well as what kind of work they would like to see in the future. Most people wrote long articles; I wrote this short, frank manifesto. Bordwell later told me it was the only pluralistic piece in the issue. In tone, attitude, and content it was way out of sync with where the field was going.*

Film theory is a philosophical discipline, logical and intuitive as well as abstract and linked to a physical phenomenon. Its primary job is to define the ontology and phenomenology of cinema. At its worst, it may be no more than a self-justifying set of biases appealed to in the course of making hash of a text. At its best, it creatively and demonstrably defines and enlarges the field, showing what film is and can become.

As a member of numerous search committees, I have read hundreds of dissertations about nothing, usually expressed in the same terms, with appeals to the same key players of the same academic discussion game. The discipline has installed the sociopolitical and psychoanalytic nonscience of poststructuralist theory at the entryway to as well as the pinnacle of film study, and not much else is deemed relevant to The Discussion.

Academic survivors learn the punishing vocabulary of the dominant mode even if The Discussion is dry and fruitless, even if it has valid political concerns but no political impact, and even if offbeat ideas are often ruled irrelevant—and badly argued, casually researched work applauded—by the clique that

---

1 *The Thing From Another World* (1951). [In that film the reporter says to the chief scientist, "Dr. Carrington, you're a man who won the Nobel Prize. You've received every kind of international kudos a scientist can attain. If you were for sale, I could get a million bucks for you from any foreign government. I'm not, therefore, going to stick my neck out and say that you're stuffed absolutely clean full of wild blueberry muffins. But I promise you my readers are going to think so."]

decides what is worth talking about. They learn it because they want jobs and because the alternative is a recalcitrant humanism that has lately been seen as politically conservative and analytically sloppy.

In academics anything can become exclusive: the rules of a club and a reason to exclude. Stanley Cavell, an actual philosopher, is paid little attention to—largely because of his apparent indifference to the work of other film theorists, whom he almost never cites, and his independent use of terms. Cavell has much to add to our deepest conversations concerning the nature of film, but he has been dismissed from the dominant trajectory of thought; the in crowd of inquiry has found his questions laughably out of touch. And Cavell is by no means the only one to have been snubbed, patronized, prevented from publishing, or ignored for failing to set arguments in the terms framed by the critical elite.

Critical fads eventually become the ruts of discourse. I'd like to see critical theory endorse a carefully researched historical poetics, much as David Bordwell has suggested—I just don't want to see that, or anything, take over the joint. I'd like to see more work on acting, screenwriting, genre, narrative structure, and the intuitive in film, and to encounter more writing by critics and theorists who got their facts straight, wrote more lucidly, and read more widely.

And for Christmas, I'd like our discourse to affect the real world of political struggle and oppressive visual rhetoric.

If I had a polemical motive when writing *Mindscreen*, it was to demonstrate that film could do something that critics and producers lazily assumed it couldn't—namely, speak in the first person, not only in the third. The argument behind that, and [behind] the related discussion of reflexivity, was and remains that film is capable of a full narrative field. Films on the order of *Citizen Kane*, *Faces*, and *Days of Heaven* demonstrate this practically, but the argument can also be made on a purely theoretical level. Some critical theorists have gone on to tackle voice-over, POV structures, and "I/Thou" address in the cinema, and naturally I think there's room for more of this and for even bolder examinations of the narrative field itself.

What has to *vanish* from the scene is a certain snobbish, ignorant, and downright nasty attitude that has poorly masked its rudeness and narcissism behind a set of rhetorical and ideological conventions. On the headstone of this phase of theory I believe should be graven the translators' footnote to the first sentence of *The Imaginary Signifier*,[2] which refuses to define that sentence's key terms (especially "the imaginary," without which that sentence and that expensive book make no sense) and refers the uninitiated reader to the Lacanian entries in an obscure dictionary of psychoanalysis.

---

2 Christian Metz, *The Imaginary Signifier: Psychoanalysis and the Cinema*, trans. Celia Britton, Annwyl Williams, Ben Brewster, and Alfred Guzzetti (Bloomington: Indiana University Press, 1982), 81.

Part II

HORROR AND SCIENCE FICTION

5

THE MUMMY'S POOL

This article appeared in the experimental journal Dreamworks *in 1981, has been reprinted in several anthologies, and was slightly revised in 1984. (This is the revised version.) Many years later, it led to my book* Horror and the Horror Film. *From this distance, I think it contains too many Freudian readings. I also have a few corrections:*

The reference to "the color section of The Wizard of Oz*" should say that it is part of Dorothy's mindscreen, which also includes some sepia shots (see "Dorothy's Dream," later in this volume). The discussion of* The Last Wave *is based on the U.S. release print; the director's cut, which I saw much later, implies that at the end the lawyer, rather than becoming the first victim, is having a vision. And in the discussion of* The Day the Earth Stood Still *and* The Thing From Another World, *"the military" should be substituted for "the army."*

Most horror movies made since this was written have refused to wrap things up neatly and reclose the system at their conclusions. Instead they have had open endings in which the horror is reasserted. Before that happens, however, a climax usually leads, even if briefly, to some kind of resolution. These open endings may be more radical than conservative, unless their message is to close down immediately, to try to be safe. Either way, they remain quite different from the more positive open endings so often found in science fiction.

HELEN: Have I been asleep? I had—strange dreams. Dreams of ancient Egypt, I think. There was someone like you in them.

ARDETH BEY: My pool is sometimes troubled. One sees strange fantasies in the water. But they pass, like dreams.

—*The Mummy*

SIR JOHN TALBOT: All astronomers are amateurs. When it comes to the heavens, there's only one professional.

—*The Wolf Man*

Figure 5.1. *The Mummy*: The Mummy, Helen, and the pool.
© 1932 Universal Pictures Corp. All rights reserved. From the library of the Academy of Motion Picture Arts and Sciences.

Karl Freund's *The Mummy* (1932), George Waggner's *The Wolf Man* (1941), Reginald LeBorg's *The Mummy's Ghost* (1944), and Peter Weir's *The Last Wave* (1978) point to some very interesting connections among horror films, nightmares, and prophetic dreams—connections that might help explain what horror films do and why they remain interesting to viewers who probably stopped believing in Dracula along with Santa Claus. To clarify some of these points—such as the relations between displacement and reflexivity, prophecy and the attractions of being the "first victim," catharsis and the Land of the Dead, reincarnation and repression—it is necessary to define the elementary ways in which films are like dreams and the broad characteristics of horror film as a genre.

Watching a film and having a dream are both passive and active events. The dreamer/audience is physically cushioned in a darkened room, most of his movements restricted to slight shifts of position in a bed or chair, and mentally in various degrees of alertness, watching a visual process that often tells a story and often masks/presents some type of thought. In both cases the eyes move and the mind exercises creative attention. The dreamer might be considered more creative since the dream manifests his own thought processes, but the role of the film audience is also an active one since the viewer creates his own experience of the work: we all have different interpretations of *Persona* (1966) not because the film is difficult, but because we interact with the signs in the generation of meaning and because our attention is selective. Although the dreamer is completely responsible for the dream, he usually avoids this awareness and casts himself in the role of participant or spectator; although the filmmakers are responsible for the movie, the viewer decides which film to attend and so chooses the general content of his experience. Thus dreamer and filmgoer approach a middle ground of pseudo-responsibility for what is watched. Both dreams and films include verbal and visual information but are effectively dominated by the limits of pictorialization. Film is primarily a visual medium, and the stories and symbols in dreams are subject not only to condensation, displacement, and secondary revision, but also to translation into pictorial and concrete representability, according to Freud.[1] In *Mindscreen*[2] I have attempted to show how the visual fields of film and dream are analogous, particularly in the ways each field [may indicate] the "off-screen" activity of a consciousness. In a film this "narrating" mind may be that of the artist, of a character within the fiction, or of the work's self-awareness; "mindscreen" generally refers to the visual and sometimes aural field of such a consciousness, as opposed, for instance, to [the POV shot, also called] "subjective camera," which imitates the visual field of the physical eye of a character. A dream is the mindscreen of its dreamer, as the color section of *The Wizard of Oz* (1939) is the mindscreen of Dorothy and as *Persona* is the mindscreen of its own systemic self-consciousness. A film like [Val Lewton]'s *The Curse of the Cat People* (1944) plays with the question of whether the ghost is "real" or an aspect of the mindscreen of the child.

One goes to a horror film in order to have a nightmare—not simply a frightening dream, but a dream whose undercurrent of anxiety both presents and masks the desire to fulfill and be punished for certain conventionally unacceptable impulses. This may be a matter of unconscious wish-fulfillment, following Freud; of confronting a hidden evil in the culture, as in *Alien* (1979) or *The Stepford Wives* (1975); or of voyaging through the Land of the Dead and indulging a nostalgia for ritual, as we shall see when we turn to Frazer. Horror films function as nightmares for the individual viewer, as diagnostic eruptions for repressive societies, and as exorcistic or transcendent pagan

---

1 Sigmund Freud, "The Dream Work," *The Interpretation of Dreams*, in *The Basic Writings of Sigmund Freud*, ed. and trans. A. A. Brill (New York: Random House/Modern Library, 1938), 319–68.
2 Bruce Kawin, *Mindscreen: Bergman, Godard, and First-Person Film* (Princeton: Princeton University Press, 1978).

rituals for supposedly post-pagan cultures. They can be analyzed in all these ways because they represent a unique juncture of personal, social, and mythic structures and because each of these structures has a conscious/official and an unconscious/repressed dualism, whose dialectic finds expression in the act of masking.

The clearest way to define the horror film genre is to compare it with that of science fiction, since the two are regularly confused with each other and often draw on the same materials (*Alien*, for instance, is a monster movie set in outer space). In what may seem like an unnecessarily long digression, I would like to show how horror and science fiction tend to present radically opposite interpretations of what may look like comparable situations, because the closed-system worldview of horror may be a key to its personal and societal dreamwork.

Genres are determined not by plot elements so much as by attitudes toward plot elements. Horror and science fiction are different because of their attitudes toward curiosity and the openness of systems, and comparable in that both tend to organize themselves around some confrontation between an unknown and a would-be knower. To lay to rest the usual assumption that a film is science fiction if it has scientists in it and horror if it has monsters, let us look quickly at a science fiction film, *The Day the Earth Stood Still*, and a horror film, *The Thing*, both of which are 1951 Cold War American studio films about flying saucers with highly intelligent pilots.

The Day the Earth Stood Still (directed by Robert Wise) is the story of a spaceman, Klaatu (Michael Rennie), who sets down his flying saucer in Washington, D.C., with the intention of putting Earth on notice: anything resembling nuclear violence will be punished by the obliteration of the planet, courtesy of a race of interstellar robot police. The spaceman has three forces to contend with: the army, which wants to destroy him; the scientists, who are willing to listen to him; and a woman (Patricia Neal), who understands and helps him. The central scientist (Sam Jaffe) is a kooky but open-minded and serious figure. Although it is suggested that earthlings understand violence better than most kinds of communication, they do respond to a nonviolent demonstration of Klaatu's power, and he does manage to deliver his message—perhaps at the expense of his life. The film's bias is in favor of open-minded communication, personal integrity, nonviolence, science, and friendship. The major villain (Hugh Marlowe) is a man who values personal fame and power more than integrity and love; he is willing to turn Klaatu over to the army, which shoots first and asks questions later—even if it means losing Neal, his fiancée.

The Thing [or *The Thing From Another World*] (directed by Christian Nyby with considerable assistance from the producer, Howard Hawks) is deliberately formulaic, and so it is valuable as a key to the genre. It is the story of a team of military men sent to an Arctic station at the request of its scientists, to investigate what turns out to be the crash of a flying saucer. The saucer's pilot (James Arness) is a bloodsucking vegetable that is described as intelligent but spends most of its time yelling and killing and leaving evidence of plans for conquest. The minor villain is a scientist (Robert Cornthwaite) who wants to communicate with the Thing rather than destroy it and who admires the alien race for its lack of sexual emotion. The Thing, however, has no interest in the scientist, and the human community (from which the scientist wishes to exclude himself), led by an efficient, hard-headed, and sexually active captain (Kenneth Tobey), manages to electrocute the "super carrot." The film's bias is in favor of that friendly, witty, sexy, and professionally effective—Hawksian—human community, and opposed to the dark forces that lurk outside (the Thing as *Beowulf*'s Grendel). The film also opposes the lack of a balanced professionalism (the scientist who becomes indifferent to the human community and whose professionalism approaches the fanatical, as opposed to the effective captain and the klutzy but less seriously flawed reporter), and what was meant in that paranoid time by the term *Communism* (we are all one big vegetable or zombie with each cell equally conscious). This is how the oppositions between these two movies stack up:

Army versus Scientists. In both films the army and the scientists are in conflict with each other. The army sees the alien as a threatening invader to be defended against and, if necessary or possible, destroyed. The scientists see the alien as a visitor with superior knowledge, to be learned from and, if possible, joined. In *The Thing*, the army is right and the scientist is an obsessive visionary who gets in the way of what obviously needs to be done. In *The Day*, the scientists are right and the army is an impulsive force that is almost responsible for the end of the world (hardly a far-fetched perspective).

Violence versus Intelligence. The Thing is nonverbal and destructive; Klaatu is articulate and would prefer to be nonviolent. The army, which meets violence with violence, is correct in *The Thing* and wrong in *The Day* because of the nature of the alien, but what I am suggesting here is that the alien has its nature because of each genre's implicit attitude toward the unknown. The curious scientist is a positive force in *The Day* and a negative force in *The Thing*, for the same reasons.

Closing versus Opening. Both horror and science fiction open our sense of the possible (mummies can live, men can turn into wolves, Martians can visit), especially in terms of community (the Creature walks among us). Most horror films are oriented toward the restoration of the status quo rather than toward any permanent opening. *The Day* is about man's opportunity to join an interstellar political system; it opens the community's boundaries and leaves them open. *The Thing* is about the expulsion of an intruder and ends with a warning to "watch the skies" in case more monsters show up; in other words, the community is opened against its will and attempts to reclose. What the horrified community has generally learned from the opening is to be on guard and that chaos can be repressed.

Inhuman versus Human. Science fiction is open to the potential value of the inhuman: one can learn from it, take a trip with it (*Close Encounters of the Third Kind*, 1977), include it in a larger sense of what is. Horror is fascinated by transmutations between human and inhuman (wolfmen, etc.), but the inhuman characteristics decisively mandate destruction. This can be rephrased as Uncivilized versus Civilized or as Id versus Superego, suggesting the way a horror film allows forbidden desire to find masked expression before it is destroyed by more decisive repression. The Id attempts to include itself in the wholeness of the dream-picture but is perceived as a threat [or a monster] and expelled from the community of what is human. It is not too heavy a borrowing from *The Republic* to observe that the Gestalts of an artwork, a person, and a society are comparable. *The Wolf Man* expresses and exorcises the Id-force of uncontrolled aggression in its own system (the werewolf), in Larry Talbot (his werewolf phases), and in the community (the destabilizing forces of rape, murder, gypsy liminality, and aristocratic privilege—Talbot often behaves as if he had *droit du seigneur* when courting the engaged Gwen). In *Invasion of the Body Snatchers* (1956), the egoless, emotionless[, inhuman] attitude of the "pods" is as undesirable in Becky as it is in the culture.

Communication versus Silence. This links most of the above. The Thing doesn't talk; Klaatu does. (Or: Romero's Living Dead are [at first] completely nonverbal, while the climax of *Close Encounters* is an exchange of languages.) What one can talk with, one can generally deal with. Communication is vital in *The Day*, absurd in *The Thing*. The opened community can be curious about and learn from the outsiders, while the closed community talks only among itself. Horror emphasizes the dread of knowing, the danger of curiosity, while science fiction emphasizes the danger and irresponsibility of the closed mind. Science fiction appeals to consciousness, horror to the unconscious.

In Gestalt terms, any dream (or fantasy or artwork) involves the projection of aspects of the self and the arrangement or interplay of those projections in a structure that corresponds to the whole self; the therapist's task is to help the dreamer re-own the projections. If I dream that I am walking in the desert and see a flower, a therapist might have me speak in the voice of the flower and then in the voice of the desert, to help me realize that they are as much myself as that image of the wandering observer and that the whole scene is a display of my wholeness. In this sense, the science fiction Gestalt features a split-off creative hope that, once re-owned, can lead to an open, growthful, positive system. The horror Gestalt features a split-off destructive element that will be feared until it is re-owned, at which point the system can become stable. In most horror films, however, the negative projection is not re-owned but rejected and repressed: the Blob is frozen but can never be killed, the Mummy is burned but reappears in sequels, and in *Alien* the monster is destroyed but the corporate evil survives. Repression solves nothing, but (coupled with the momentary wish-fulfillment) gives a temporary sense of relief. Henry Frankenstein (leaving the novel out of this) may attempt to reverse the Original Sin and re-enter the community by acquiescing to the horror cliché that "there are things we are not meant to know"—except that his initial hubristic motive was not just to figure out eternity but to create life without the help of any Eve (he wants to "be as God" in a double sense), and when in the sequel he manages to get married it is a sure bet that some Dr. Pretorius will "force" him into an all-male effort to create a bride for the monster, Henry's split-off rejected/rejecting child-self.

In the dreamworld of movies, horror movies come under two headings: in the Freudian sense, they are anxiety dreams or nightmares; anthropologically they express a nostalgia for contact with the spirit world. In his *Introductory Lectures on Psycho-Analysis*, Freud observed that "the attitude of the dreamer towards his wishes is a peculiar one: he rejects them, censors them, in short he will have none of them. Their fulfillment, then, can afford him no pleasure, rather the opposite, and here experience shows that this 'opposite,' which still has to be explained, takes the form of *anxiety*."[3]

In *The Wolf Man*, this process is extremely clear. Larry Talbot (Lon Chaney, Jr.) is a big, Americanized engineer who is being groomed by his short and controlling father, Sir John (Claude Rains), to take over Talbot Castle and the role of village Baron. Larry meets Gwen (Evelyn Ankers) and comes on like a "wolf," despite her being engaged to his father's gamekeeper (a model of controlled animal aggression, who is suited for the civilized institution of marriage). After he is bitten by a gypsy werewolf (Bela Lugosi), Larry splits into a wolf and a man. The man experiences pain and anxiety at the prospect of acting out his unconscious desires; at the climax, the wolf begins to attack

---

3 Freud, "The Psychology of the Dream Processes," *The Interpretation of Dreams*, 520n.

Gwen and then abandons her for more pressing game, Sir John. Larry insures he will be punished for this, for although he has given Gwen his own protective medallion, he has given his father the silver-headed wolf cane that can kill him. *The Wolf Man* is a transparently Oedipal nightmare, a full playing out of castration anxiety, and a clear example of how some horror films are analogous to one kind of dream. Although it can be said that *The Wolf Man* is the dream of the screenwriter (Curt Siodmak, who went on to dream the similar *Bride of the Gorilla*, 1951), it could also be analyzed as Larry's dramatized dreamworld—or, taking a cue from *Beauty and the Beast*, as Gwen's projection of the two sides of her sexuality, werewolf and gamekeeper[. But it is also] the dream of the audience, which has decided to let its own unconscious desires find as-if expression, with the scariness of the film carrying the dream's anxiety quotient and the killing of the beast appearing to vindicate repression.

There is yet another side to all this. Sir John (a prize-winning researcher) believes in God, the universal "professional"; his religious sense is conventionally patriarchal, and Larry's Oedipal rebellion includes his participation in an erupting/repressed religion, gypsy superstition. (Recall the scene where Larry is too upset to join his father in church.) Whereas Sir John believes that all this is in Larry's mind and that werewolfery can be explained as a split between "the good and evil in a man's soul," with the evil finding expression in a fantasy of animality, the film attempts to prove him wrong. Sir John finds that all of this is not a dream, that the wolf he has killed is his son. In this sense, the horror film asserts the survival of "paganism" (the gypsies are right) and the inadequacy of science ("all astronomers are amateurs," a theme recognizable in *The Thing*)—a return to magic. Judaeo-Christianity represses, in this sense, the mystical unconscious that the horror system allows to be expressed. (All this opens the possibility of a Jungian reading as well.) We may recall Van Helsing's pronouncement in *Dracula* (1931) that "the strength of the vampire is that people will not believe in him."

In *The Golden Bough*, Frazer observed that dreams are often considered instances of contact with the spirits of the dead and that such dreams may serve as keys to the future and (through the symbolism of mistletoe, placed under pillows to induce prophetic dreams[4] and, as "the golden bough," an illuminating open-sesame) to the Underworld. Freud, too, mentions the ancient concept of "true and valuable dreams which were sent to the dreamer as warnings, or to foretell future events,"[5] and there is [a] considerable surviving literature [on] dreaming as genuine out-of-body travel, usually on the astral plane.[6] A medieval poem like *Pearl* (in which the poet mourns the death of his

---

4 Sir James George Frazer, *The Golden Bough* (New York: Macmillan, 1963), 818–19.
5 Freud, *The Interpretation of Dreams*, 184.
6 For [an example], see John-Roger, *Dreams* (New York: Baraka Press, 1976).

daughter and then has a dream of her full-grown in heaven) can be [analyzed and cleverly explained] by any number of Freudian readings, but its appeal and point are clearly in the way it presents itself as a genuine visionary experience.

Horror films appeal to this kind of dreaming through the figures of seer and "first victim," and thus to the audience's desire to glimpse the truth, no matter how horrible. (A Freudian might translate this into the desire to learn about sex and be punished for it, which is often a legitimate reading.) In science fiction, the visionary is usually rewarded; in horror, punished. Peter Weir's *The Last Wave* (one of the few great horror films of the decade, perhaps matched only by *Spirit of the Beehive* and *Don't Look Now*, both 1973) is the story of an Australian lawyer named David (Richard Chamberlain) who defends a group of Aborigines involved in a ritual murder, one of whom (Gulpilil) begins to appear in his dreams. These dreams put him in touch with a parallel world ("the other side," in Western terminology) and remind him of his childhood experiences of night travel and prophetic dreaming. Eventually David discovers that he is a member of a race of priests and that the Aborigines are expecting a great wave to destroy the intruding white civilization. As soon as he accepts his true vocation, David sees the wave and becomes its first victim. The wish such a horror film fulfills is that of *seeing*, and the worldview it confirms is that "the other side"[—and, for Aborigines, the Dreamtime—]is real. In other words, David is a surrogate for the audience's desire to have, through watching a horror film, a spiritual vision. The satisfaction of being "the first victim" is that one knows the hidden truth.

In the greatest of all horror films, Dreyer's *Vampyr* (1932), the world and "the other side" continuously overlap, and a dream within this dreamworld reveals to the hero the identity of the vampire. It is within this dream—of nearly being buried in a coffin whose window is clearly a reference to the frame of the movie screen, so that the audience is cast as the victim/dreamer of the film-as-horror-object—that the hero is most in danger. The survival of Dreyer's dreamer and the death of Weir's visionary show that the crucial issue is not the destruction of the seer, but the threat of victimization. They also show that, although the more common impulse in the horror film is to exorcise the demon and save the community (*Vampyr*; *Jaws*, 1975; *The Thing*; *Tarantula*, 1955; *The Blob*, 1958; *Frankenstein*, 1931, etc.), there is a parallel track in which the community is rightfully destroyed (*The Last Wave*; *Dawn of the Dead*, 1978 [...]).

"The other side" may be a parallel spirit-world or it may be the Underworld, the Land of the Dead; in horror films these are usually comparable. At the climax of *The Last Wave*, David finds that he is a reincarnated priest, in a sense his own ghost. In *Apocalypse Now* (1979), which advertises its indebtedness to *The Golden Bough*, the possibility of the community's being restored by the exorcism of Kurtz is overwhelmingly ironic, since the truths of the Underworld have more integrity than the lies of the conscious Establishment, and the transfigured seer can never rejoin "their fucking army." So although there are many horror films that play on the dangerous attractions of prophecy and spirit-contact, the cathartic journey into the Land of the Dead presents itself as the larger category and as the key to all the patterns observed so far, especially if one makes the link between death and the rigidity of unconscious fixations. Freud's work on the relations between compulsive repetition and the death instinct (*Beyond the Pleasure Principle*) is very useful here, but the more luminous juncture is that between the Mummy films and *The Golden Bough*.

The Mummy opens with the best "first victim" scene I know of. An expedition has discovered a mummy, Imhotep (Boris Karloff), and with him a sealed casket bearing a formidable curse. While two senior Egyptologists (one a straight scientist, one superstitious) discuss whether to open the box, the junior researcher, left alone, opens it and finds the Scroll of Thoth. Mouthing an impromptu translation under his breath, he inadvertently raises the Mummy from the dead. Imhotep takes the scroll and exits, leaving a terminal madman in his wake. Here the desire to discover what is forbidden is related to the thrills of danger and self-destruction that are part of the cathartic masochism of attending horror films and having nightmares, and the mechanism of releasing an unconscious deathless force is tied into the legend of Isis and Osiris.

According to Frazer, the spell of Thoth was first used by Isis to raise her son Horus from the dead. When her brother/husband Osiris was murdered and dismembered, Isis had the aid of several gods and relatives in reassembling the body parts (except for his genitals) and raising him from the dead. Revived, Osiris became the King of the Underworld, Lord of Eternity, and Ruler of the Dead. The rituals Isis practiced were imitated in Egyptian burial ceremonies so that the deceased might be born again in the Underworld [...].[7]

In Freund's film, this is condensed into Isis's using the Scroll of Thoth to revive Osiris from the dead. The story is that Imhotep had tried to read the scroll over the body of his beloved Anckesenamon, a priestess of Isis and daughter of the Pharaoh; for this attempted sacrilege, Imhotep had been buried alive along with the scroll, which could thus never again be used. Revived and in possession of the scroll, however, Imhotep (now calling himself Ardeth Bey) sets out to find the reincarnation of Anckesenamon, who turns out to be Helen Grosvenor (Zita Johann). He nearly convinces her to die and be reborn as a living mummy like himself, but at the last moment Helen decides to live rather than to let her ancient identity dominate her (i.e., she chooses health over neurosis) and appeals to Isis to teach her again the spells she has forgotten

---

7 Frazer, *The Golden Bough*, 422–6.

over the ages. The statue of Isis responds to the spells and kills the Mummy; this implies that it was not enough for Helen simply to reject Imhotep, that she had to integrate her Helen and her Anckesenamon aspects in order to come into her full power. This is very similar to what Imhotep wanted her to do, except that he would have had her proceed from that integration to a fuller Anckesenamon rather than to a fuller Helen.

What this shows is that there is no safety in ignoring the Id/Underworld/monster (the attitude of the ineffectual patsy in most horror films, e.g., the mayor in *Jaws* and [the] modern boyfriend [(David Manners)] in [*Dracula* (1931) and] *The Mummy*), but that there is considerable strength in confronting the danger and surviving that deeply acknowledged contact—in other words, re-owning the projection. In this sense, horror films are valuable and cathartic, for they may offer the possibility of participating in the acting out of an unacknowledged wish or fear in a context of resolution rather than of repression. This is of course what happens to Helen and not to the Mummy. He is a walking repetition compulsion, determined to complete his frustrated sacrilege and consummate his romance (the sexist aspects of all this are quite blatant in the film). He would have her "go through moments of horror for an eternity of love," but what he means by love is the insatiability of unconscious drives (which are, to be fair, often involved in fantasies of eternal romance). There is value, then, not in being Imhotep but in, like Helen and like the audience, *almost* being Imhotep.

We are now back to Osiris and Frazer. One of the major points of *The Golden Bough* is that the agricultural year and the sacred year are closely related in a great many cultures, and that the myth of the death and resurrection of Osiris (like that of Jesus, whose death and resurrection occur in the spring) may have served the Egyptians as an explanation or prompter (through ritual reenactment) of the land's return to life in the spring after its death in the winter. The parallel with horror films should be immediately obvious: one enters the Land of the Dead, gives death temporary dominion in order to emerge reborn and refreshed. Horror films are the Land of the Dead, the visionary/ghost world where shades and demons have power; one goes to the theater as to the Underworld, becomes Imhotep or Helen on an as-if basis, undergoes a catharsis, and steps back into the light of day (if it happens to be a matinee, which is how most children see horror films and form lasting impressions of the paradigmatic content of the experience). For Osiris, this transit left him in a position of power over the Underworld, and it will be remembered that Jesus, too, harrowed Hell when he died; thus for the community, the benefits include an assured sense of the existence of divinity and a reborn economy, and for the god, the benefits include life and power. But not all dreams, not all winters, and not all horror films have such happy resolutions. The stories of

Osiris and Jesus do not depend on repression. A Freudian dream solves little or nothing until it is understood in analysis; simply to allow the unconscious wish to find masked fulfillment does not remodel the psyche. Left to his own devices, the Mummy will simply repeat his compulsive and insatiable project in sequel after sequel, like an incarnation of neurosis itself. So it is valuable to have a character within the film who can, like Helen, acknowledge the unconscious drive and go on from there into an integrated life—or a dreamer who can re-own projections and live a free, healthy, flexible future.

This reduces itself to a question of audience intention, since even a film like *The Thing* or *The Wolf Man*, in which the horror object is simply repressed/killed and the community reasserts its boundaries, can serve its audience as a visit to the Land of the Dead. The overall structure of such a visit may be cathartic in the same way that to dream may promote psychic health regardless of dream content. One could, in any case, go to *The Wolf Man* because one would enjoy participating in a fantasy of uncontrolled aggression and victimization (which is why most people went to *Jaws* and *Alien* and *The Texas Chain Saw Massacre*, 1974). But once there, one has the option of feeling that one's private beast has been purged and will require no further playground, or of enjoying the punishment and anxiety that attend unconscious wish-fulfillment and planning to attend another horror film the next time one feels in conflict about such desires. The latter is clearly more in line with Freud's reading of dreamwork, and with my outline of closed-system behavior, and it is doubtless the more common experience of horror films. Yet the former response is possible and legitimate, and it strikes me as being encouraged in those films that call the viewer's attention to the fact that he is watching a horror film and pretending to believe it, much as the analyst may attempt to engage the patient's ego while interpreting a dream. This is the method of *Vampyr* and of the bizarre, neglected, wonderful *Mummy's Ghost*.

The intervening sequels—*The Mummy's Hand* (1940) and *The Mummy's Tomb* (1942) changed many of the terms of the story. The Mummy, Kharis, [now tries] to raise the Princess Ananka by giving her the fluid from nine tana leaves; his tongue is torn out (Kharis is silent, unlike Ardeth Bey), and he is buried with a box of the leaves and charged with guarding her tomb for eternity. The Banning expedition discovers Ananka and ships her mummy back to the Scripps Museum in America, despite considerable interference from Kharis, who has been revived by a cult of priests (led by George Zucco). Kharis's motives are to keep the dead Ananka with him (neurotic possessiveness) and to defend the integrity of the Ancient Gods (against whom he rebelled in the first place). Therefore in these two films he is fulfilling the curse made against himself and has no strategy for reviving Ananka. The climax of these films comes when the priest (George Zucco in *Hand*, Turhan Bey in *Tomb*) decides to administer tana fluid to himself and the nearest heroine (who is never Ananka), but is foiled or killed, after which the Mummy is burned and the community of Americans restored. So if Kharis represents anything here, it is the deathless persistence of compulsive fixation that may have begun in sexual desire but has become only an undead, rigid, destructive, rejecting anger.

The Mummy's Ghost may be a brilliant parody of the series, a self-deconstructing masterpiece, or simply what used to be called a really good bad movie. It exploits every formula it can, turning them against themselves, right up to the climax where the monster, for once, gets the girl. It begins in the tombs of Arkham (a reference to Lovecraft?), where Zucco explains his role to the new priest, Yusef Bey (John Carradine). When told of his mission, Yusef Bey says incredulously, "Kharis—still *lives?*" His "you've got to be putting me on" tone puts the film in sync with the audience immediately, as the sequel declares its awareness of being a formulaic sequel or its worldly equivalent. Next we see Professor Norman explaining to his college students the legend of Kharis, who was supposedly destroyed in their own town, Mapleton. A student argues, "Maybe it was a man made up as a mummy, to keep the legend alive." The student is of course right, in a way he could not guess but the audience can. The professor, however, insists that he saw the monster (i.e., this is a horror-filmlike world and these dangers are real). [...]

The romantic lead, Tom Harvey (Robert Lowery), has a crush on an Egyptian, Amina Monzouri (Ramsay Ames), who is working on the college staff; he also has a little dog named Peanuts. Whenever Amina thinks of Egypt, she gets a chill, but Tom insists that Egypt is just like any other modern country. Tom is the all-time ineffectual patsy of the formula, blindly confident in the status quo of modern America and uncomplicated marriage, while Amina is in conflict about her destiny, which is called Egypt but means sex and death—"forbidden love." When Kharis is on his way to kill Professor Norman, his shadow crosses her sleeping face and Amina walks in a trance to the site of the murder. When she is found in the morning, her wrist bears the birthmark of Ananka and her hair has a white streak. The next evening, Tom manages to convince Amina to neck with him in his car; while they kiss, Kharis's shadow crosses her face again.

By this time, Yusef Bey has brought Kharis to the museum. Downstairs a guard prepares to relax, hanging his hat on a realistic statue of a woman (i.e., he doesn't believe art is real), opening a crime magazine, and turning on the radio ("This is *The Hour of Death*. The forces of evil stand at the threshold. A man shall die tonight... Did you ever meet a killer, my friend? You will tonight—"). The guard is a surrogate for the horror audience, which enjoys pretending that horrors exist, and a play on and against the suspension of disbelief—because the lies on the radio describe the truth of his situation.

The reflexivity of this picture allows it to disarm the audience completely, since it continually calls attention to the fact that it is just a ghost story and just as continually presents its horrors as *real anyway*.

Upstairs, Kharis finally touches the mummy of Ananka; there is a straight cut to Amina in bed, waking and screaming; straight cut back to a collapsed pile of wrappings. Ananka's soul has been reborn in Amina, again to seek its salvation. (This would frustrate the curse—for in this version of the story, Ananka and Kharis are equally culpable for their forbidden love, and the priests' motives include keeping either of them from working out their karma through reincarnation.) The site of Amina's joining her repressed Ananka is, as usual, implicitly sexual. A friend reassures her that she "must have been having a nightmare." Back at the museum, Kharis kills the guard ("gunshots—crash—," the radio had said; the guard shoots Kharis and then is smashed against a glass door before being strangled).

Kharis finds Amina in bed and takes her away, unconscious, to a shack where Yusef Bey waits. Yusef Bey soon tells her that she is Ananka, and points to Kharis as an example of eternal unfulfillment and restlessness; she faints, and in her sleep her hair turns completely white. Then Yusef Bey decides to give her and himself the tana fluid—the most blatant instance of formula (or compulsive role-playing) in the whole film, coming absolutely out of nowhere—and Kharis kills him. Peanuts has led Tom to the scene, and Kharis knocks him out; then he carries Amina into the swamp (in New England?—again, more formula than "reality"). Tom is joined by the sheriff's posse (which has been digging a pit for the Mummy and burning tana leaves—another fakeout, since the Mummy transcends his compulsive desire for the fluid and walks on with his romantic burden, i.e., the fixed pattern of his [romantic] desire is stronger than the fixed pattern of the movie's formula; [something like] this pit business would have served as a typical solution in many films of the period). A formulaic rush to the rescue ensues—reminiscent of the torchlight parades in *Frankenstein* and *The Mummy's Tomb*—with Peanuts and Tom and the posse all chasing the Mummy. Such cross-cut chase scenes have signified climax and resolution since Griffith, and aside from the St. Bartholomew's Day Massacre sequence of *Intolerance* (1916), there are very few examples of failed climactic chases in the whole history of film. One of the most troubling closes *The Mummy's Ghost*.

Because the chase does fail, and in a masterful way. As Kharis carries her, Amina becomes entirely Ananka: her flesh dries, her frame contracts, but she is still alive. Imhotep's project has been fulfilled (Kharis, too, has returned to his origins): the two lovers are united as living mummies. This rare moment of absolute fulfillment of forbidden love, which Amina has been shrinking from and growing toward, and which Kharis has been yearning after for

3,000 years, is immediately succeeded by their deaths—they drown in the swamp. The posse stands there looking beaten; Tom (who has seen Amina's face) is a wreck; Peanuts is alone on the swampbank cocking his puzzled head. There is a sudden feeling of "what happened!" Suddenly a real horror has asserted itself—Amina has given herself over to her unconscious drives; the Mummy has abducted her and gotten away with it; all the formulas have failed at once. And at this point a George Zucco voice-over intones the curse: "The fate of those who defy the will of the Ancient Gods will be a cruel and violent death." (This is what Derrida would recognize as a good place to begin deconstructing the film, except that the film has already done it for us.) Although it seems that Ananka has repeated her sin rather than sought her salvation, and therefore is properly punished (Freud again), there is no denying the satisfactions of romantic apotheosis. Except if one views it from a feminist perspective, whereby Amina could be seen as surrendering to the deadly obsessions of her abductor, utterly identifying with her state of victimization; the horror of her no-win situation is that her only alternative to Kharis, in this culture, would be to play the role of Tom's wife. Whether Amina is seen as joining her demon lover or as the victim of a cosmic rape, it is still clear that the curse, as formulated, is not in control, and that horror has triumphed.

Behaving according to formula is one aspect of repetition compulsion and of neurosis. In this film, the force of Kharis's and Ananka's unconscious desires is so strong that they at least balance and perhaps make irrelevant the repressive curse. (To say that Amina has these "desires" is to say that she behaves like a Freudian construct of masochistic femininity; if one abandons the feminist reading, one is left with the less complex observation that she allows the aspects of her sexuality that frighten her to find complete expression.) Kharis is so compulsive that he wins, even if briefly, and the formulaic aspects of the genre are turned against themselves; the community is not restored. The audience is unable to take comfort from the expected formulaic resolution and has been made aware of the presence of formula all along, so the possibility exists that this film educates its audience (engages the ego in self-consciousness) rather than encouraging it only to participate in unconscious wish-fulfillment (while, as usual, having it both ways and fulfilling the wish completely). As it reminds the audience that it is a formulaic film, *The Mummy's Ghost* is like a dream, one of whose major strategies has been undermined—since one of the basic functions of displacement and secondary revision is not just to mask the desire but to keep the dreamer asleep, to keep the dreamer from realizing what these masked desires are and that they are his own. Like the most intense nightmares, *The Mummy's Ghost* awakens the audience in a moment of anxious clarity and fulfillment. It may be, to reverse the phrase, that the sleep of monsters breeds reason.

6

TIME AND STASIS IN *LA JETÉE*

I had been teaching La Jetée *for several years when Chick Callenbach asked me to put the gist of what I'd been saying in class into this article, which appeared in* Film Quarterly *in 1982. There is a fuller presentation of the problems of analyzing and intuiting the ineffable in my book* The Mind of the Novel, *which I was completing at the time I wrote this.*

Chris Marker's *La Jetée* [(1963)] is identified as a "*photo-roman*," a photograph-[novel], a term that readily evokes its complex narrative strategies. The visual track consists primarily of still photos connected by straight cuts, fades, and dissolves; the editing rhythms and the variations in camera position are so like those in conventional "moving pictures" that the spectator may feel s/he is watching a movie rather than a comic book, and this impression of flow is reinforced by the soundtrack of the film, whose music, sound effects, dialogue, and voice-over commentary move along at a normal rate. Though the images seldom move, the film has duration and the impression of proceeding. The commentary—the "roman" element—is continuous and self-conscious; the nameless hero is "the man of whom one is telling the story." There is more movement than fixity in *La Jetée*, but the overall impression it leaves, the first thing anyone says about it, is that it consists primarily of stills. It is a reasonable assumption that the world of the story—rather than the world of the narration, or discourse—is one in which conventional movement occurs, and that the stills are an aspect of the storyteller's vantage point outside the diegesis. Run to earth, what this implies is that there is an apparent difference between event time and film time that vanishes into a systemic understanding of first, the stasis of the accessible instant, and second, the ways consciousness transforms what it observes and what it presents. The narrator's summation, that "one cannot escape from time," might without distortion be rephrased "one cannot escape from film."

The film's title refers to the large "jetty" or pier-like structure at Orly airport outside Paris, where the hero, as a boy on a Sunday shortly before the third world war, sees a man killed and is strongly impressed by the face of a young woman who also observes the event. As an adult, imprisoned in a postwar underground camp, he continues to dream of this woman and is selected by his captors to participate in an experiment in time travel. Through a combination of drugs[, hypnosis, and technology] he is eventually able to live in the past he so vividly imagines. Like a ghost or a demon lover he appears to the woman at various times and places, until the satisfied experimenters send him on his true mission, which is into the future, from which he brings back a power source that will allow the human race to get on its feet again. Before the scientists can liquidate their romantic "tool," the people of the future help him return once and for all to the world before the war and to the woman he loves. As he runs down the jetty to join her, he is killed by a man from the prison camp staff (who have had time, of course, to perfect their methods) and realizes that he is the man whose death he observed as a child.

His is not the "jeté" of a dancer—that word is masculine—but that of a projectile, something thrown (from the verb "jeter," to throw or cast), and its symbol is the jetty or concourse. Because time is often described in this film as a series of waves, it is significant that "la jetée" can also mean breakwater, something that extends or projects into the sea. To leap, to make a single weight change or step while in the air, is just what he cannot do; that would be to escape from time, to cheat destiny, to escape narration. He is not a leaper, but someone who is thrown. He has found, in the "air," no real freedom, no defiance of gravity. And yet this romantic apotheosis is what the film somehow suggests, in the transfigurative moment when, at the center of the film, an image of the woman does move. That moment is presented as being perhaps an invention or a dream, and it is set apart from the stasis of the rest of the film, which is another way of saying that it appears to be set outside time. "Le jeté" is the romantic aspiration, "la jetée" the political and scientific set of limits. Fantasy, love, and movement are escape; what is real is the sequence of instants, which are static and which are subject to control.

Time travel depends on the notion that all events are somehow present, that from some viewpoint exterior to what we think of as temporal continuity (one instant after the other) all instants are simultaneous. One of the simplest and most convincing images for this concept of time is the reel of film. On the reel, thousands of frames maintain their images of *potential* instants, all together and retrievable. As the film moves through the projector, the images become "present" or *kinetic* (the root of "cinema"); they give the impression of "happening now," which is the time of projection ("jeter" is the root of "projeter," to project a film).

There is an important difference in this film between memory and time. The hero is not sent into his memory; rather his memory is used as a force that helps him to re-enter the past. When in a peacetime garden, for instance, he "remembers that there were gardens," the subject is not reverie but actual time travel, and his memory functions equally well in past and present times. Over the first shots of the woman's face the narrator says that "moments to remember are just like other moments," and that line is a key to the film. All time is presented, has to be presented, in the same manner; any instant is capable of being remembered, or of being presented as a memory. A memory and an event, then, have to share the quality of being present and storable; presenting and retrieving must look the same. Any instant is a frame, and any frame is capable of being projected or waiting on the reel without changing its nature. The present tense of consciousness is projection, the activity of the projector. For most of us, the projector runs only forward and is outside our control; for the time traveler in this story, whose consciousness can select which frame will be present, the sequencing of instants appears to be less deterministic, until one remembers that all the frames remain in place on the reel and that in the hero's beginning is his end.

But our reality is not composed of stills; even the instant is a mental construct, for as Bergson observed in *An Introduction to Metaphysics* the most simple movement consists of an *infinity* of smaller movements. To chop a flow into discrete elements is the activity of analysis; to move, or to be inside the flow, is the province of intuition. Just as to speak involves chopping a thought into the fragments of words, to shoot a film involves chopping a movement into frames; it is the job of syntax and of the listener to reassemble the words into a complete thought, and the job of the projector and the audience to reassemble the frames into an impression of movement. The complete, the undifferentiated, the perfectly flowing, and the ineffable are all outside the process of signification, which is analytic; it is intuition that renders these absolutes of flow accessible to consciousness. And it is one aspect of a vision of the ineffable that one remains unable to express or analyze the vision; from the perspective of language, there is no escaping from language. From the perspective of a frame of film, there is no escape into movement. And all of this is the point of the woman's moving, because it is love that allows the hero to leave analysis and enter intuition, to have a vision of process that transcends the sequence of stills. And this is also the reason that that movement is presented as perhaps a dream: a dream, because it is not like ordinary reality, and perhaps a dream, because there is no way to analyze an intuition. Love and intuition are processes of entering into the being of the beloved, even if the beloved is a simple movement of the arm.

But film is not reality; film does not move; film is a sequence of stills whose relation to movement is entirely potential and fantastic. It can present any instant, regardless of whether that instant is "earlier" or "later" than the "narrative present," because it makes any instant be the narrative present. In this respect it is like a book, any of whose words becomes present as it interacts with the reader's consciousness (i.e., the read word is in its instant rather like the projected frame, and the reader's attention like the interplay between viewer and shutter mechanism). The closed book is like the reel in its can, or like the temporal universe viewed from the extratemporal vantage point of God or Godot, take your choice: Godot because he can send his emissary into any Act, One or Two, for what will always be the "first" time, and God because it is possible to consider time and space as mutually causative and perfectly interlocked, so that the temporal universe is a "place" where things "happen." This is one reason that intuition and not analysis can claim to touch the absolute, and that any filming of any movement will inevitably be analytic rather than synthetic.

Throughout *La Jetée* there is an overwhelming imagery of stasis: statues, stuffed animals, stills. Over a sequence of statues the narrator says that "other images appear, merge, in that museum which is perhaps his memory." The stills in this film are of course very much like statues, images fixed by the attention of the artist and the process of the medium. The longest meeting of the lovers happens in "a museum filled with eternal creatures"—stuffed animals and skeletons. A shot of a stuffed animal and a shot of a character do not appear markedly different in this museum which is perhaps his memory and certainly this film; all of the images are fixed and are calculated to give the impression of life while insisting on the fact that they are images, art, statues, the product of the interaction between life and the attention of the artist—the medium as Medusa.

The reel of film is the museum full of stills. Film arrests. This is surely the point of Marker's having shot the scenes of the underground prison camp in the basement of the Palais de Chaillot, which is where Langlois set up his great Cinémathèque. (He also cast Jacques Ledoux, curator of the Brussels cinémathèque, as one of the time experimenters.) There are fragments of statuary in the dark corridors, one of them clearly marked "head of the apostle." Most of the statues that appear under the remark about the museum of his memory are headless; the last is simply a head, and it is replaced via a dissolve with the head of the hero, making it clear that he and his memories are subject to similar qualities of fixity in time while suggesting rather bitterly the absence of a Savior. The hero must escape from destiny, from time, from the accessibility of the frames in their potential stillness, and even from the controllers and accessors of the frames (the cinémathèque as prison camp). His escape route is the romantic imagination: "Moments to remember are just like other moments. They are only made memorable by the scars they leave. The face he had seen was to be the only peacetime image to survive the war. Had he really seen it? Or had he invented that tender moment to shield him from the madness to come?"

Figure 6.1. *La Jetée*: She opens her eyes.
© 1963 Argos Films. All rights reserved. DVD © 2007 The Criterion Collection. All rights reserved.

From the very start, the hero is unsure whether his beloved exists as more than an image. The world of the image is the world of time, the museum of accessible stills. The images are entirely real: "On the tenth day, images begin to appear, like confessions. A morning in peacetime. A bedroom in peacetime, a real bedroom. Real children. Real birds. Real cats. Real graves." The real birds, seen in flight, do not move. The only thing that moves is the beloved, waking in bed. The implication is that she [may be], in that moment, either not real or [more than real, transcendentally romantic]. The narrator says: "She calls him her ghost. . . . He is never sure whether he seeks her out or is sent, whether he invents or dreams." The image these lines introduce, of the woman in bed, is more grainy and soft than the rest of the film. At first the sequence is silent. There is a dissolve from one still of her sleeping to another still of her sleeping. Then there are more dissolves, and one begins to hear the sounds of birds. Soon the dissolves are between stills that are very similar to each other, as if each dissolve bridged a painfully slight movement between still positions. The birds become very loud. It is as if she, or the film, wakes up.

She opens her eyes and blinks. The hero is suddenly back in the camp and his eyes are squeezed as if he were not sure whether he had been dreaming.

It is important to note, first, that the woman is presented here, as at the start, in a marginally hypothetical and romanticized manner. She may be his invention in the first place (though we find she is not), and her moving may be a dream. It is a dream of escape from stasis, a dream of movement. To escape from time would be for him to join her in a world where they could move, or where their love would feel as transfigurative and transcendent and romantic as movement would be when compared to a world of stasis and doom. That would be the dream of the leap, of intuition. The second thing to note is the way that her movement is achieved, and this is where the film becomes most simple and most brilliant. It is as if her stills came in quicker succession. The dissolves bridge the positions so slowly that one can almost see the still image change position while one knows that it does not. The intervals become shorter, the positions nearer to each other. Finally, the positions succeed each other at the rate of 24 per second. No dissolves are necessary. The characters and the audience advance together, 24 positions per second. That is normal cinematic movement. But it is not true movement, only the as-if-real succession of selected instants. If one thinks about it in these terms, it is clear that *La Jetée* does not actually break its own rules: there is always fixity, but sometimes that fixity behaves like what we call movement or process. The hero's love has allowed him to enter the being of the beloved or of love itself, to escape analysis for intuition, *perhaps* to transcend the system. But it is only a perhaps because this remains a film, and the movement is simply the more rapid succession of stills. Marker gives us and the characters the impression of a romantic apotheosis—however understated, which is of course why it is so powerful—without actually letting anyone out of the Medusan trap.

The proof that this interpretation of her movement as a bridging of stills is valid comes at the end of the film, when the hero attempts to run down the jetty to the beloved. The rhythm of the editing quickens. The hero's running is presented in a sequence of weight shifts, one still per leg movement, and the shots' durations are approximately those of actual running: one weight shift per cut, and the cuts regular and rapid. The impression this gives is one of turgidity and of an intense attempt to break into movement. But his stills are separated by straight cuts, not joined by dissolves; they do not come close together, as do those of the woman in bed. But he tries. (The character, in event time, is doubtless actually running, while feeling that he might escape from destiny; once presented in the medium of film, where film and time and destiny are so metaphorically interrelated, the symbolic impression is that he cannot break into continuous movement but is locked in a series of stills.) It is then that he [sees the killer and] realizes "one cannot escape from time." And if the romantic imagination appears to be a way out, there is no way to put that escape on film (her movement must be presented as a sequence of stills).

One thing this suggests is that film cannot escape from its own processes and procedures and that there is something inherently oppressive about the controlling of reality via image-making (an interpretation that would link *La Jetée*, perhaps with too much facility, to Marker's SLON films and to *Far from Vietnam*; a simpler link can be found in *The Battle of Chile*, where [director

Guzmán or producer] Marker calls particular attention to a shot of someone's firing directly at the camera, a shot in which the cameraman "filmed his own death"). Another—if not opposite—construction is that any romantic or intuitive communications that do occur do so by transcending their medium, so that "la jetée" can only hint at "le jeté" as the projector's advancing of our consciousness from frame to frame can only suggest the independent leap from here to here.

All of this is reinforced rather than contradicted by the continuous flow of the soundtrack and of the voice-over narration, because these too are characteristic of the physical medium. Although the visual track of a film consists of a series of frames [that] have to remain still while the light passes through them and the shutter is open, the soundtrack must flow smoothly past the photoelectric cell or magnetic head. Film is a medium in which movements are capable of being arrested but sounds are not. We have no concept of a fixed sound, and it is in trying to imagine a sound that is not a series of waves hitting the eardrum over the course of time that we come squarely up against the problem of conceiving absolute stasis. If the hero's problem is that he cannot escape from the medium and from the mortal consciousness that surround and determine him, then the continuity of the soundtrack and the stasis of the shots—which both singly and together signify the processes and systems of sound film—oppress him equally. It is not just the image track that arrests him, but the whole medium of sound film, which is itself a symbol for the activity of consciousness and narration as well as for the nature of time. This is not just a reflexive paradox in which a character in an artwork finds himself unable to escape from the laws and nature of the medium; it is that, of course, but there is more going on than an essay on the problems of characters in artistic systems. It is also an essay on the limits of mortal consciousness and on the relations between politics and transcendence, an essay on the nature of the romantic temperament in a world that seems always to be on the verge of war. It is about the attempt of the loving consciousness to reclaim the sane world of happiness and commitment in the face of those controlling and destructive forces that live underground with statues and that can extend themselves into the brightest of Sunday mornings to demonstrate their control in their favorite language.

7

CARNIVAL OF SOULS

This was published as part of the printed insert in The Criterion Collection's *DVD of* Carnival of Souls, *which came out in 2000.*

Horror movies take place in their own territory. The trick is to get us there. It doesn't matter whether they start with fantastic premises and gothic settings, or with ordinary neighborhoods and daily experience, because the places and assumptions change when they enter and are redefined as horror territory—by the intrusion of crazy violence, for example, or an awful discovery: that the folks in the next apartment are Satanists or that a maniac made a bloody sandwich on the cutting board while you were out of the kitchen. The rules have changed, and it is dangerous to find out how they have changed and why. It is also difficult. It can be hard to realize that one's friends are pods or that they have to be dismembered, hard to find the terms of a world that behaves like a slaughterhouse or a dream.

The world can fill up with angular, scary shadows, lurking with little monsters—or it can look the same but be different underneath. Different in a way you can't define, a perceptible but invisible tonal shift that is the ideal of one kind of horror film, a *Peeping Tom* or *The Seventh Victim*. (At the opposite extreme, the ideal would be the most radical, visible, and namable horror, a *Godzilla* or *Blood Feast*.) This ideal of unsettling horror was best described by Carl Dreyer:

> Imagine that we are sitting in a very ordinary room. Suddenly we are told that there is a corpse behind the door. Instantly, the room we are sitting in is completely altered. Everything in it has taken on another look. The light, the atmosphere have changed, though they are physically the same. This is because *we* have changed and the objects *are* as we conceive them. This is the effect I wanted to produce in *Vampyr* (1932).[1]

---

1 Georges Sadoul, *Dictionary of Films*, ed. and trans. Peter Morris (Berkeley and Los Angeles: University of California Press, 1972), 398.

In *Carnival of Souls* (1962), one place is allowed to be blatantly creepy: the amusement park where ghosts rest under the water and rise to dance. The rest of the world appears both normal and somehow wrong, and part of what is wrong about it—and within it, and encompassing it—is the liminal protagonist, Mary Henry (Candace Hilligoss). For she has gone wrong, and the world with her. It may be her subjective world, as in the Cocteau and Bergman films [that] producer-director Herk Harvey and writer John Clifford admired, but it is ours as long as we are in the theater, and it looks too much like the real world outside the theater for comfort.

Call it *Orpheus* meets "An Occurrence at Owl Creek Bridge"—or an episode of *The Twilight Zone* directed by Ed Wood and Antonioni. After surviving an apparently fatal accident in which she and two girlfriends drove off a bridge into a river, Mary leaves to pursue her career as an organist in another town. Before the accident, nothing about her suggested that she was emotionally cold or even that she played the organ. But after the accident, she plays a church organ without religious conviction and dates without desire; she has no libido and is accused of having no "soul." She feels cut off and doesn't know why. And to find out the reason is to be destroyed: to synchronize with and quite literally meet her fate.

In several of the movie's best sequences, Mary's relation with reality shifts or slips, and no one can see or hear her. She's as out of place in this world as if she were dead—until she touches a magic tree and hears its magic bird (who must have sung as well to David Lynch). In this altered state, the reality she sees is ours. It doesn't include her.

Unless a character turns on a jukebox, all the music in the film, especially the underscoring, is played on an organ. The organ is the music of Mary's mind and of the world in which she finds herself: the world as a gap in the way things are. It may be that she imagines her tale in her own terms, with a soundtrack as cold as she is said to be—or that she "really" lives for a while in a world where the dead intrude. The underscoring and the underwater undead make it likely that what we see and hear is her mindscreen.[2] But the horror film can have it both ways: an alternate world and an imagined one, existing as long as it appears to, because it appears to. Aside from the music, the most artistically daring element of this film—one that defies a central convention of the horror genre—is its flight from romanticism, its concentration not on a foaming monster or on the hammering bosom of a Hammer heroine, but on a cold fish. If she is a magnet for the gothic, there is nothing exciting or sexy about it. The thrills of this carnival are cold ones, bits of death.

Carnival of Souls was shot in three weeks for about $30,000: one week at Saltair, an abandoned amusement park on the Great Salt Lake, and two weeks

---

2 [See "An Outline of Film Voices," later in this volume.]

in Lawrence, Kansas, where the filmmakers (who never made another feature) were based; their Centron Corporation made industrial films. To say the least, it was an independent production—and, like many of the best rock 'n' roll records, a one-shot deal. Its influence on other independent work was huge.

If Mary bears a resemblance to Barbra, the heroine of George Romero's *Night of the Living Dead* (1968), and if Romero's undead sometimes look and move like Harvey's, that is because Romero was lucky enough to see *Carnival of Souls* at the right time—when it first came out and all its inventions were fresh—and the right place, a drive-in. (All he missed was a few minutes of footage, restored when the film was re-released in 1989 and, of course, included on this disc.) But the man whose relation with ordinary reality is severed in the French movie *Life Upside Down* (1965) is enough like Mary for one to argue that *Carnival of Souls* has also had an international influence—appropriate for a film that was influenced as much by Bergman (*Wild Strawberries*, *The Magician*) and Cocteau (*The Blood of a Poet*, *Orpheus*) as by the cheap, raw, ordinary landscape of America, out of which Harvey, Clifford, and Hilligoss constructed the only landscape where Mary, a projection pursued by reflections, can exist: the indefinable space of the horror film.

Part III
REVIEWS

8

WELCOME TO L.A.

This review was published by Take One *in 1977, shortly after Altman and Rudolph appeared in Denver for a preview of the film. I had brought a class to the screening, and one of the students asked about the ways the movie portrayed women. That led to more questions, some from me. Rudolph was calm, but Altman got angry.*

Robert Altman (producer), Keith Carradine (actor), and Alan Rudolph (writer-director) pulled into Denver not long ago with their new film, *Welcome to L.A.*, an extremely well-acted and -photographed piece that is not, finally, worth watching. The question/answer/diatribe session that followed the film, however, was revelatory. By the time this review appears, Pauline Kael will probably have lived up to her role as Altman's circus-barker and hailed *Welcome* as a challenging work by a coming talent; Jay Cocks, in *Time*, has already done so; so I'll ask *Take One* to publicize my two cents. A "personal" film is, after all, entitled to a personal response.

As a native of Los Angeles, I find it silly to call L.A. "the city of one-night stands." As a portrait of life in that city, *Family Plot* is more accurate and *Shampoo* more entertaining, but what is especially off-base here is the notion that the hero's very personal problems are an aspect of the city he happens to be visiting. Carradine here is a creature of one-night stands, encouraged by Rudolph to project his limitations onto the structures—and especially the women—that surround him. This practice makes sense in an Expressionist context, but here is simply the mark of an adolescent and sexist sensibility.

Although Altman made it clear that he has no "authorship" involvement with this film, he defended it in terms that implicated his own oeuvre, and suggested—to me at least—several interesting connections between the two men (who together wrote the script of *Buffalo Bill and the Indians*). Both are gifted directors with a good feel for open-ended structure; both know how to say what they mean; neither one, however, *has* much to say of any interest. Both are educated enough to be worrying about "big" issues, and sophomoric enough to feel they can resolve their films with an ironic, superior pose. *Ars gratia ego* could roar at the starts of their pictures.

"Keith Carradine," says the press sheet (and I appeal to the press sheet so as not to be accused of distorting what Rudolph means to say), "plays Carroll Barber, the film's connecting force, the composer whose return home has been merchandized and who finds his welcome filled with anxious L.A. women." Sally Kellerman plays a "desperate realtor who tries too hard to make up for her emptiness." Geraldine Chaplin appears as "the fragile Karen Hood, whose loneliness is realized in a 'Camille' fantasy." Harvey Keitel's role "runs the gamut of repressed feelings." Lauren Hutton "photographs corners and tries to stay out of them." If a pattern emerges here, it is that men are full and women are empty.

The viewer is expected to take Carradine seriously, and to feel some kind of distanced compassion for him, although what emerges is the portrait of a sensitive punk alcoholic. The "emptiness" of the "anxious L.A. women" is clearly imposed on them by Rudolph, and combatted by the actresses, all of whom try hard to turn these figures back into people. The ones who are most successful at this thankless project are Viveca Lindfors, in an Oscar-quality performance as Carradine's agent, and Geraldine Chaplin, whose Karen is about as "fragile" as a bulldozer. In the film's most typical scene, Lauren Hutton puffs languorously on a cigarette, bare-breasted, in her darkroom—the point being clearly to put Lauren Hutton in a dark room. When I pointed out that a serious photographer (which the character is) would be unlikely to scatter ash in her clean work environment, Rudolph said he was "making a statement about nudity." Presumably this line applies to the full-frontal nude shot of Chaplin too—but Carradine spends more time in bed than any of the other characters, and the most we see of him is his nude back. All right, I said, taking him at his word, your statement is that women have nudity and men don't. "This isn't a documentary," Altman broke in; "the things that would be organized the way you want them wouldn't be art." He went on to tell me that I wanted too much "order" in my fantasies, that this was more openended. "The connections are all emotional," said Rudolph. Fair enough—but the film does have an order. As a piece of storytelling with a moral, it is lucid (considerably more so than *Nashville* or *Buffalo Bill*); as an investigation, it projects a very distinct sexual politics. The order is there, and I object to it—and I further object to being told that a film in which all the women are beautiful and "empty," and most of the men have "serious" problems, isn't politically coherent.

Toward the end of the afternoon, Carradine answered a question about his role in Jeanne Moreau's *Lumière*, an extraordinarily well-made—in fact, brilliant—film that has flopped in Paris and been given a lukewarm press in America. In *Lumière*, he said, he played himself and didn't care much for the part. It strikes me that to portray a sexual fascist/infant with such care, a man would have to be either a feminist or the thing itself. Rudolph may want to take credit, after the fact, for the real things *Welcome to L.A.* reveals about sexual communication in our (?) time, but he seems, more accurately, to be in the equivalent of Carradine's position. What he dramatizes are his own, limited views of the natures of men and women, without any distance, and where the picture succeeds in telling the audience anything useful about art, love, and power, it is in spite of his silly script. *Welcome to L.A.* is visually beautiful, and Rudolph clearly knows how to use the camera; he should leave the typewriter to someone else.

9

THE FURY

This review was published by Take One *in 1978. With the exception of* Blow Out, *which complements the movies covered in this review, De Palma's later career took a different course than the one I hoped for here. What I like about this piece is the way it tries to address aspects of the movie that resist being put into words.*

The trouble with film reviews is that so many of them say the same things, and in similar terms. "The word" is beginning to come out on Brian De Palma's new film, *The Fury*, and the point about that film, what makes it really worth seeing and thinking about, appears to be getting missed.

After seeing *The Fury* I walked into the sunny landscape; I was full of the film, moved and excited and feeling very clear. It was Saturday matinee time, and the movies had finally come up with a good scary horror film; I hadn't had such a good fright on a first-run basis since [*Night of the Living Dead*]. But more than that, the film had done something radical to the visual field, something I could recognize but not analyze; it fell somewhere between the physical luminosity of *Barry Lyndon* and the spiritual clarity of *Vampyr*, and when I got that far in my thinking I realized that my actual point of reference was not Hitchcock or Murnau or whatever "a De Palma film" is supposed to make one think of, but Werner Herzog. Then I had the bad luck to remember a review I had just read, whose point was that *The Fury* was a campy send-up of horror films. Anyone who thinks this film is funny, I said to myself, is permanently out to lunch. There is something extraordinary going on in *The Fury*, something that is both hard to miss and hard to talk about, that goes way beyond Saturday afternoon fever and deserves some kind of response.

In the first place, there are some very inadequate gestures in this film, most of which come near the end. The biofeedback lecture is, from the standpoint of tone, ridiculous; Cassavetes has often been better; the revenge taken by Robin, the boy wonder, against his doctor/lover is grossly overdone, and his grotesque levitation act is as overblown and obvious as most of *The Exorcist*; the concluding explosion (which threatens to turn this film into another *Zabriskie Point*, in more ways than one) mainly tells *MAD Magazine* just how to parody the film, which they undoubtedly will do. These flaws don't make a whole lot of difference, even if they stop *The Fury* from becoming a classic. Now that I've done my duty as "reviewer," let me jump to some larger points.

There are some films that charge the screen, some visual fields that have a clarity almost independent of their subject matter. They manifest, but do not discuss, a mental set that falls between the ineffable and a dream. There are parts of Bergman's *Persona* and *Shame* that pull this off, parts of Kurosawa's *Dersu Uzala*, Kobayashi's *Kwaidan* and *Harakiri*, Bresson's *A Condemned Man has Escaped*, and Hitchcock's *Vertigo*. Herzog does it throughout *Aguirre the Wrath of God*, *The Mystery of Kaspar Hauser*, and *Heart of Glass*. Dreyer does it in his *Joan*, in *Vampyr*, in *Ordet*, and [...] in *Gertrud*. And De Palma does it in *The Fury* [...]. The basic characteristic of this sort of film is that it is inseparably real and dream. There are two ways to get at this amalgam: to be absolutely realistic in *mise-en-scène* but to have a metaphysical subtext (not the plot, but the way you feel *something else is going on*), or to approach the world as if it were a dream in the first place. Examples of the latter approach are *Vampyr* and *Heart of Glass*, and of the former, *The Fury* and Dreyer's *Joan*. The most immediately striking thing about De Palma's film is that it is, where it counts, entirely and surprisingly realistic, but it is realism in the service of the unknown. Telekinetics and the supernatural have nothing to do with this; it is much more a question of Kirk Douglas and Amy Irving, facing each other for the first time in the middle of an American street, in one of the greatest scenes I've ever watched.

Maybe Coppola or Fuller could have gotten this good a performance out of Kirk Douglas; maybe not. But I can't imagine anyone's being able to put it to better use. This is simply one of the great performances, in tone and range the best thing Douglas has done, and it's part of the film's own tone and range that the excellence of that performance is respected, lucidly presented, placed in the kind of integrity-space a great novel makes for its characters, or a dream for its major figures, or *Queen Christina* for Garbo. Carrie Snodgress is as fine here as, say, Ingrid Thulin is in *The Silence*. And Amy Irving is simply and irrefutably perfect, a realistic actress of major proportions. Perhaps the best way to characterize the climax of this film [...]—the few minutes on either side of Douglas's suicide—is to say that it makes *The Fury*'s numerous references to Aeschylus's *Oresteia* feel appropriate rather than pretentious. There are elements here of major tragedy.

On the other hand, the film has virtually no ideas. Zilch. And looking back at De Palma's other films, I'm not surprised. His pseudo-underground work (*Greetings*, etc.) struck me as smartass. *Phantom of the Paradise* paved the way for *Obsession* and *Carrie*, all three of them serious attempts to deal with film history and discover a personal style (a good example of what Harold Bloom calls "the anxiety of influence"). *The Fury* completes this personal education; the style has been realized. I don't yet feel, at De Palma's films, that I'm spending an evening with a wise and clever fellow like Buñuel or Hitchcock or Lang or Hawks; I don't yet feel he has anything important to say; but I know I'm in the presence of something new, a different kind of clarity, perhaps the tone that '70s films will turn out to have been about. I literally think that if he picks his next script carefully, this guy could go anywhere. The highest order of excellence wouldn't surprise me. If he could focus that light of his on a profound screenplay, something on the order of *Vampyr* or *Aguirre* or *Persona* or *La Rupture*, he could really be great. He has already gone beyond the directors that most resemble him, Roman Polanski and Paul Almond (*Act of the Heart*), has more guts than Bertolucci in anything but *The Conformist*, knows how to use music better than anyone but Herzog and Hitchcock.

I keep mentioning Herzog because he and De Palma share this exceptionally clean eye; the metaphysical edge, fully addressed, is all that is missing from De Palma. I feel the two men are inching up opposite slopes of a mountain scaled only by Dreyer and Bresson and maybe Jordan Belson, and the point about that mountain is that the view feels important, clear-sighted, and able to address the center of nonverbal experience. They call it transcendental style, perhaps without seeing that it really is that.

Granted that *Obsession* isn't as good as *Vertigo*, that it isn't as troubling or as arresting or even as interesting, that it just didn't make it. Granted that *Carrie* is less its own film than a working-out of influences from Griffith to Hitchcock. But I almost wrote Herrmann instead of Hitchcock, because that's where the profound influence is going to come from, if it hasn't already. Very much like Herzog, De Palma is creeping up on the power of music and making it work for him in clear visuals; if he could bring genuine vision to that incredible gift of his, he could be out of this world.

Maybe he'll miss it and become some kind of Polanski; maybe he isn't interested in the first place and just wants to keep telling shockeroo stories about underdogs with power; maybe Herzog will make that definitive transcendent film instead; and maybe when that film is made, I'll know better how to talk about it. In the meantime I'll take the chance of looking like a jerk, praising a commercial smartass and his silly movie, calling it a masterpiece and wishing I knew what it had done, and how it could be done again.

10

PIRANHA

This was one of the few positive reviews Piranha *received, as Joe Dante told me when I met him in line at the Telluride Film Festival. It was also my first article on reflexivity in the horror film, a subject on which I'm still writing. It was published by* Take One *in 1978.*

My friends have always told me that I have weird taste, that I like some of the dumbest and strangest movies. I feel I ought to warn you of that, before I suggest to you that *Piranha* is an absolutely dynamite horror movie, a tight old-fashioned hour-and-a-half *movie* with good acting, real villains, sharp editing, bright color, the whole bit. (I did feel that paying four bucks admission was a bit much, but that seems to be part of the legacy of Proposition 13 in California these days; as you'll see, that remark is not a very serious digression.) It's a movie that is easy to take seriously, that is not just right on target but as we used to say, right on. The only thing wrong with it is that it's making money by showing carnage and encouraging people to be afraid of nature, but if you can deal with that, and like horror films in the first place, you'll have a great time.

The genre (and co-producer) is Roger Corman. In other words, it's a send-up from the word go, and also a successful example of what it's sending up. It's directed and co-edited by Joe Dante. The cast list lets you know immediately that Dante and Corman, for all their jumping on the financial avalanche of [*Jaws* and] *Jaws 2*, are oriented first in the sixties horror film: Kevin McCarthy and Barbara Steele were the drawing cards for me. Keenan Wynn does a nice job, and Bradford Dillman is wonderful. Like his co-star, Heather Menzies, Dillman is strong, efficient, emotional and attractive; the two of them move the film along in a professional manner that is a joy to watch. There is also a first-class child performer, Shannon Collins as Dillman's daughter, a little girl who's afraid of the water and up against some very pushy camp counselors.

The first shot of the film: a camera moves slowly down a chain-link fence till it stops on a NO TRESPASSING sign. The first tone on the soundtrack: the ground-bass from *Jaws*. By now you know that this is not an exploitation of the *Jaws* craze, but a film about the legacy of films. You wonder whether they'll make the reference to *Kane* stick, and they do. But first, back to *Jaws*. Nubile young couple goes swimming in spite of the NO TRESPASSING sign, almost exactly as at the start of *Jaws*, and of course they get eaten up by the little darlings in the tank of an "abandoned" Army research station. While they're still OK, however, the guy accuses the girl of having somewhat playfully bitten him. "What do you think I am," she says, "the Creature from the Black Lagoon?" Then the carnage, then the titles. These references to old horror films go on throughout the picture—some of them are on television, some in comic books, some in the dialogue; the point is, they never stop until finally, in the resort sequence near the end, we see a sunbather reading the granddaddy of the genre, *Moby-Dick*. Director Dante and screenwriter [John] Sayles have thoroughly covered themselves against any charge of failure of invention, of imitation, of exploitation. What they are very carefully doing, and with great humor, is showing how horror movies play a part in modern life, how they are part of our basic folk mythology, how we relate our primal fears (mostly of unexplored nature, which includes sex in a lot of these films) to our media encounters with the dark. It is especially fun here, this summer, with *Jaws 2* playing down the block, since the audience of *Piranha* and the cast of *Piranha* are in sync in these terms: both groups are familiar with *Jaws*, enjoy playing with the idea of danger, and are as warned and still as easily victimized as each other. In its own little way, this is a perfect use of self-consciousness, or metatheater, or whatever you feel like calling reflexivity. Brecht would have loved it. Producers and director even have their credits blip on a *Jaws* penny-arcade game being played by Menzies.

Having reassured the audience that they know what they're doing, the filmmakers go on to say something that I think is just fine. They make a good horror film too—one that is, I guess it goes without saying, much better than *Jaws 2* and much more intelligent and humanistic than *Jaws* itself. It may even be as good as *Creature from the Black Lagoon*, though it is not as innocent; this is a late age, and one has to approach the genre through its history. But they also, as I have just suggested, actually *say* something, and it's about the military. If I had to place *Piranha* in the post-*Jaws* movement or the post-Vietnam movement, I'd take the latter, for this is a film that assumes that its audience absolutely distrusts the government. Actually, "distrust" doesn't go the distance; the operative terms here ought to be hatred and contempt for corrupt and stupid and destructive authority.

The point, see, is that the Army has been developing this strain of ubiquitous piranha, a kind that can live in any waters and that were developed originally as a variant of biological warfare, to destroy the river systems of North Vietnam. But the war ended... Well, they kept on developing them, because as Barbara Steele says in her most chilling and villainous manner (she's a government scientist), "There'll be other wars." These are not paper targets, these generals and government scientists, and there is more going on here than simply a horror film's choice of a credible sci-fi premise so [it] can get on with the danger/salvation business. This really *is* a film about the evil Army, and the good guys don't necessarily win.

There's just one more scene to mention, and if I go beyond this one I'll be in danger of giving you too much information and spoiling your first experience of the film. But this one's irresistible. There's a bit of hanky-panky with the Army's closing down a polluting plant—not to save the waters, but so the site can be sold to a chummy real estate developer who funnels back some of the profits to an evil colonel (who, you'll be glad to know, does get gobbled). The developer, Buck Gardner, has just been notified by his assistant that the guests at his resort-opening party are being eaten by the little threat that wasn't there. Buck wanders among the bloody bodies, past a couple of soldier boys carrying a stretcher; the whole scene is of course reminiscent of a battlefield. The audience has known all along that these guests will be attacked; even the Army people have known it (and they're not troubled by it; their main concern is that word of the project does not get out, and they're willing to see many people die). So when the swimmers start screaming, it is my strong feeling that the audience is *not* being encouraged to enjoy [or] thrill at the carnage, but is seeing the fruits of military thinking. How many deaths will it take till they learn that too many people have died—that's what ran through my head, and what I thought they were getting at. Anyway, Buck wanders till he sees the local TV camera crew recording the scene. Buck is modeled on L.A.'s own Cal Worthington, a late-night car salesman who would probably resent the reference and whose politics aren't [part of his image]; the point of the reference is that Buck uses the media to sell, which in his case means to distort information so things look more attractive. Overcome, but not to the point of real self-knowledge or character reform, Buck interferes hysterically with the cameraman, saying "What are you filming!" What he means is, "You use film to tell the *truth*?!" As I said, a post-Vietnam film, and a right-on horror film, and a damn good hour and a half. The things it says about money and power and stupid authority almost make it a pleasure to pay that incredible four-dollar admission. Nip, nip, nip.

11

THE ELEPHANT MAN

> Film Quarterly *published this review in 1981. The term "mindscreen," used in this piece and in several other articles in this volume, comes from my book* Mindscreen *and refers to the audiovisual field of the mind's eye, which might present a dream, an inner tale, a memory, a fantasy, a lie, and so on.*

Not since Shakespeare called for "a muse of fire" in *Henry V* and Olivier provided the light of an arc-rod projector has there been such an interesting opportunity to examine the relations between film and theater as David Lynch's *The Elephant Man*. Since the film was not based on Bernard Pomerance's play of the same name, but draws on many of the same historical materials and case studies, it cannot properly be examined as an adaptation; instead, the specific decisions made by Pomerance and Lynch on how best to tell their respective stories of John Merrick reveal something about the basic terms and strategies of theater and film, and those distinctions in turn provide a clue to what *The Elephant Man*, as a film, is trying to accomplish.

Merrick was a hideously deformed young Englishman who was discovered in a sideshow by the anatomist Dr. Frederick Treves, who arranged for him to live in London Hospital until his death a few years later. In the hospital Merrick was visited by many of the leading lights of Victorian society, who were moved by his rare intelligence and sensitive manner of expression. In both the film and the play, Treves agonizes over whether he has advanced his own professional reputation by putting Merrick on display in what might amount to simply another class of freak show; in both, Merrick's handbuilt model of a nearby cathedral is a prominent symbol of his aspiration, drive, and luminous skill. The play, however, provides its audience much greater insight into and respect for Merrick's extraordinary mind and deals at length with the philosophical parameters of Victorian ethics. The film's critique of the latter is conveyed almost entirely through Freddie Francis's dark, sharp, black-and-white cinematography—a claustrophobic and depressing view of the Industrial Revolution as a circle in Hell; the script (by Christopher DeVore, Eric Bergren, and Lynch) deals in affecting but comparatively oversimplified terms with the nature of man and the power of love.

Both the film and the play force their audiences to consider the relations between inner and outer being, though the film—at least on the script level—does not push much beyond the insight that Merrick is "not an animal" but "a human being... a man." Lynch's only previous film, the cult hit *Eraserhead*, deals like *The Elephant Man* with the problem of the painfully unacceptable child, and in both films Lynch has appropriately had recourse to many of the themes and devices of classic horror film. The Frankenstein monster, for instance, is a paradigm of the rejected child, and the project in many horror films—like that in Aristotelian tragedy—is to interrelate dread of the horror object with a sympathetic recognition of his, her, or its essential humanity. The humanism of *The Elephant Man* is conveyed not through its script so much as through its deliberate echoes of such compassionate horror films as *Island of Lost Souls* ("Are we not men!"), *Bride of Frankenstein*, *Freaks*, and *The Hunchback of Notre Dame*; the spirit of Lon Chaney, Sr. is particularly felt, not just in the eloquently vulnerable performance of John Hurt as Merrick, but in the tone of the entire project. To say all this, and to credit the brilliance of the Dolby Stereo mix, the convincing sets, the editing, the costumes, the thoroughly professional acting by all concerned, and the arty but nevertheless magnificent cinematography—all this would be to give *The Elephant Man* its due, in its own terms, as a sensitive and moving version of Merrick's story that does not wish to be compared with a certain brilliant play. But it is in that comparison that the point of this review and the genius of the film are to be found.

The most significant decision Pomerance made was not to give the central performer "elephant man" make-up. Instead Merrick is played by a "normal" actor who adjusts his posture and gait into an analogue of Merrick's while the audience is shown authentic photographs of Merrick in the nude. The audience, then, is continuously in the process of reminding itself that Merrick is grotesquely deformed, while watching and hearing the evidence that Merrick is a beautiful being. The actor's task is to allude to physical handicaps while projecting directly Merrick's probing intelligence and wit. This play converts the theater into a very private, almost textual space, where the conceptual emphasis natural to language—always the mainstay of Western theater—fits naturally with the emblem of the actor who displays the inner Merrick. For the audience this is a profoundly doubled experience, and it is on this experience that the play's best verbal investigations are constructed.

As an experience in what might be called the theater of compassion, Lynch's *Elephant Man* is precisely opposite to Pomerance's. Here Merrick is presented in (accurate) make-up. Generically, this puts things on the footing of the horror film; commercially, this means the film is liable to appeal to several kinds of audience, including those who like to go to freak shows. But the most interesting level on which this decision operates is this: *cinematically*, this decision was obvious, and was probably made with no consideration of the play whatever.

It often used to be said that film could not attain the complexity of literature, the intimacy of theater, the structure of metaphor, or the abstraction of music simply because it was confined to showing the surfaces of physical objects, including people. Bazin did much to advance the notion of the transcendental landscape, Eisenstein demonstrated the range of several kinds of visual metaphor, Godard found the relations between persons and objects to be entirely problematical anyway (in *2 or 3 Things*)—and few readers of this journal are likely to be biased against the possibilities of film expression. Nevertheless, the fact remains that it is both appropriate and natural for a *film* on Merrick to show Merrick's body. The film audience, then, is in the position of continuously reminding itself that Merrick has a spiritual inner beauty, while watching and hearing the evidence of his deformity. This is in its own way just as humanistic an experience as that offered by the play, pointing to much the same conclusion. But the implication of these opposed poles of audience approach is that theater, like literature, encourages the spectator to generate a visual image of its full world while presenting an inherently conceptual text—[while] film, by presenting a visual world, encourages the spectator to generate a view of the interior and to organize an understanding of the concepts, emotions, and metaphors implied by what is shown.

What is exciting here is not this [familiar] insight but the obvious ease with which the two versions of *The Elephant Man* demonstrate its accuracy and suggest the terms of its expansion. Charles Lamb once observed that *Hamlet* could not be successfully performed but had to be read in private, because the theater was too public a space for such meditations to be expressed or credibly enacted. Pomerance's *Elephant Man* transcends that limitation of theater by radically interiorizing its space. Lynch's film would seem at first to be simply a proof that Lamb was right, but about the limitations of the too-physical space of cinema. Lynch's ultimate project, however, is to demonstrate the interiority of film space (both via analogies to kinds of theater and through an examination of its own cinematic processes). And although Hurt carries the immediate burden of leading the audience past his make-up and into a sense of his essential grace, Lynch and his co-writers are very much in evidence as the creators of a structure in which the film addresses its own potential and guides the audience to examine its own quality of vision. [Lynch's] *The Elephant Man* is most profound in its reflexivity, and most affecting in its use of what in another context I have called "mindscreens." For all that these observations about the inherent qualities of the media announce is not the absolute expressive limits of film or theater but the natural tendencies that demand to be confronted and gone beyond if a great form is to emerge. Rudolf Arnheim said in *Film as Art* that film's limitations make its art possible, but it is further true that to grapple with [...] such limits is to advance the form as well as its canon of possibilities, and the task in this particular film is to assert if not define the quality of what cannot be publicly seen.

This brings us around once again to the problem of the freak show, which is also the problem of the nature of theater. One does not see the "elephant man" clearly until a half hour of film has passed, and this delay teases the audience into an awareness of its desire to see how this freak actually looks. At the point of maximum expectation, when Treves (Anthony Hopkins) is given a private showing in the carnival, one sees not Merrick but Treves's shocked, compassionate reaction to what he sees. When Merrick is finally shown frontally and in the light (via a shock cut, in his hospital bed) and a nurse screams, one recognizes a stock technique from the horror film—one that lets the audience feel comfortable with its own voyeuristic impulses, at least for that instant. The more Treves worries about the moral implications of his putting Merrick more or less on display, and the more the obvious villains in the plot are presented as those who want to make money by luring audiences in for a view of Merrick, the more the audience must ask itself what the moral implications are of making a commercial film that offers as its primary spectacle the grotesque "elephant man." Indeed Lynch goes well out of his way to put Merrick in a French freak show, to have him repeatedly and violently abused, to display his humiliation. There is also a good deal of talk about the nature of theater, which often offers some kind of "spectacle" (film, of course, even more so)—but the implication of this film is that spectacle and the desire to peek at the abnormal are both limited structures of the possibilities of vision.

As the actress Mrs. Kendal, Anne Bancroft introduces to Merrick the notion that "The theater is the most beautiful place on earth; the theater is—romance." Many of the voyeurs who torture Merrick are men who hope that the women with them will be sexually stimulated by the horrific vision (which is a well-recognized function of horror-film dates, especially in drive-ins); this is the level of "romance" encouraged by some aspects of grotesque spectacle, including pornography, and it hardly needs to be observed that love, like any really significant aspect of one's life, is much determined by the parameters of personal vision. Vision must be educated beyond the physical if one is to see the world in its fullness and if love is to become a personal, spiritual, political reality. This notion of love is larger than that of the "romance" of theater, but it is not false to the implications of Lynch's film.

Mrs. Kendal is the character whose role seems most truncated in relation to its parallel in the play; here she brushes into Merrick's room like Billie Burke in *The Wizard of Oz*, and within two minutes she and Merrick are trading a sonnet from *Romeo and Juliet*. It all seems too fast, too easy, until one recognizes that Mrs. Kendal *is* the Good Witch of the Theater, that she does have a magic wand; her vision of the theater of beauty, which is drastically different from the freak show and from the industrialized, oppressive landscape Lynch portrays in most of this film (which is itself a dialectic of "theatrical" possibilities and so cannot be called a theater of ugliness; one would need, like Derrida, to write ~~freak show~~ under erasure). In the play it was most important that Mrs. Kendal was understanding and that she was a woman; in the film the emphasis is on her magic. When she calls Merrick "Romeo" she is addressing not his sexual potential but the transfiguring power of role. In her beauty and her magical acceptance, Mrs. Kendal is most like the figure of Merrick's mother (he sets their portraits together on his night table), to whom we will turn in a moment.

The Elephant Man is a sequence of shows—practically nothing else—and its climax comes when Merrick is, for the first time, a member of a theatrical audience. In a sequence that looks as if it had been edited on video, Mrs. Kendal's fairyland performance is shown (often in multiple exposure, sometimes over Merrick's face, and often hard to follow) as Merrick experiences it. For the first time Lynch offers an example of the theater as a site of fantasy (vs. industrial realism), of beauty (vs. grotesquerie), and of private experience. And it is clear that by now what he says about theater applies to film. This is the only point where *The Elephant Man* offers both objective and subjective events simultaneously, as the performance as seen by Merrick and an objective view of Merrick's watching are integrated. The wholeness of this vision, then, is not in some notion of art's escapist or fantasy value, nor in the grim realism of much of this film, but in that power of integration—especially the integration of interior and exterior realities, which was of course the audience's project in both versions of *The Elephant Man* all along.

At this point irony rears its head—or perhaps the moment is meant to be taken as some kind of apotheosis—and Mrs. Kendal turns the audience's attention to Merrick's presence, dedicating the performance to him. The audience applauds; Merrick is asked to say something or at least to stand—that is, he is once again "on stage." When he rises, the audience gives him a standing ovation. This might be read in two ways, and you will have to decide between them (keeping in mind that this will amount to a decision about the tone of Merrick's subsequent suicide, in which he dies for the experience of sleeping like a normal person): that Merrick can never entirely join the community of an audience but must always be somehow the spectacle, or else that *this* audience, applauding rather than gaping and hooting, is a good audience and sees in him much that is of value. The latter—and even the irony that arises when both these interpretations are credited—offers this film's audience a vision of its own best possibilities under the circumstances, and thus both educates their responses and (by saying that not all audiences are perverse) lets them off the hook.

Lynch has been preparing for this vision of inner theater all along, of course, and the final key to the film can be found in its four mindscreen sequences, which are certainly as powerful as anything in the rest of the film and balance its ruthless exteriority in a disturbing and beautiful way. In the first sequence, which opens the film (after some reflexively flickering credits), a vision is presented of Merrick's metaphorical conception: images of elephants and a thrashing woman, preceded by a view of the mother's face and followed by a billowing mist. The second is Merrick's dream, just after he has seen his own reflection in a window and realized that a hospital worker will soon be exhibiting him: there are images of hellish industry, and then some men force a dark plate toward the screen, which becomes a mirror in which Merrick—perhaps remembering an event in his deep past—sees his own face as a child. (In the following scene Merrick screams at his adult reflection in a mirror held by the hospital worker, but it is clear that he does this because that gross audience expects it.) The third sequence is Merrick's vision of Mrs. Kendal's play. The fourth, which closes the film, is a view of his death, in which he moves toward and into a starry vision of his mother's face. As she softly declares that "The heart beats... Nothing dies," the camera pulls into a white space between her eyes, and the image is for the first time entirely light. Then the credits come flickering back, reasserting the problem of vision.

The opening and closing sequences are not necessarily Merrick's views, though the inner two are; the images of birth and death may well proceed autonomously from the film's own reflexive process; and if they do, that only makes more strong Lynch's affirmation of the power of subjective—finally auto-subjective—film (a power perhaps best realized, as here, in dialectic with radical objectivity). The point is that these sequences balance the freak show, offer a richer possibility for cinema, assert that film can be a "theater" of inner being no matter how much it may appear bound to the surfaces of physical reality. The image of the mother, which for Merrick is a central vision of love and all that love means—including the possibility of rejection, a reminder of that beauty from which his ugliness has separated him, the first person he imagines he "disappointed"—becomes in the final moment an image of love, of acceptance, of transcendence: for Merrick, for the deeply moved audience, and for cinema.

A Postscript

Since the film purports to present Merrick's story factually, and since both film and play are often inaccurate, readers may wish to consult Michael Howell and Peter Ford's *The True History of the Elephant Man* (New York: Penguin, 1980).

Part IV
INTERVIEWS

12

LILLIAN GISH

This interview took place in Miss Gish's Manhattan apartment on August 1, 1978. She was 84 years old. The interview was arranged by Lillian Vallish Foote, who was named after Miss Gish, and suggested by her husband, Horton; I had met the Footes at that summer's Faulkner conference in Mississippi, and we remained friends. I told Miss Gish that I would be playing this tape for my film history students and that they were her audience. It is significant that Miss Gish did not receive credit as producer or co-producer on La Bohème, The Scarlet Letter, *or* The Wind, *but she never brought that up in the interview, and I forgot to ask about it.*

LILLIAN GISH: Is it on now?
BRUCE KAWIN: It's on. Could you start with the films you produced at MGM?
GISH: Well, Irving [Thalberg]... When I was signed by MGM, I didn't want the contract they gave me. It was for a lot of money, a million dollars for six pictures, and I wanted $500 a week and a *percentage* of my film, just enough to live on out there—Mother...—and they wouldn't give it to me. Because I had made films for inspiration and I had a percentage, a gross percentage, not a net; you never see a net percentage. And I knew what films made, but they wouldn't do that. But that was Nick Schenck; he was the one that signed me. And at that time they were having a battle, East and West, Mr. Mayer out there... They didn't have a story for me, of any kind, and I was on a weekly salary. Well, this bothered my conscience. I can't take money for something and not work for it; I've never done that. And so I went to Irving, because he had met us at the station, *all* of them had met us, Mr. Mayer, everybody. And I said, "I always carry a lot of scripts with me. If you haven't got a story, do you mind if I go through my scripts and bring an idea to you?" "Oh," he said, "I'd be delighted." So, I had a friend named Madame

de Grésac, who was Victor Maurel's wife; he was the great baritone of the last century; he worked with Verdi on all his operas, and Francis Robinson, who knows the history of ballet as I know the history of silent film, said that there was no one in this century like him, that he was such an idol, and I was his last pupil. I studied phonetics with him, and voice. And Madame was a playwright; she had written *The Marriage of Kitty* in 1893 for Réjane in France and Mary Tempest in England. And I had a script of *La Bohème*, which as you know was a novel in 1846 or '48, and then I think it was a very successful novel, play, and around the beginning of the century, just before the beginning of the century, two men made it into an opera. And I said, "Would you let me do that story?" and he read it and said "Yes," and he said, "Now who do you want to make it, to direct it, act it?" And I looked at their films—I'd been away from there seven years, so I didn't know who the people were out there—and I saw two reels of an unfinished film called *The Big Parade*, and I said, "I like that director, I like that leading man, that leading lady, and that tall man (Karl Dane)," and he gave them all to me. And I said, "I'd like Madame de Grésac, a Frenchwoman, to write the scenario with my help, because she doesn't know about pictures." And she did, the two of us did the story, and King Vidor was very sympathetic. Up until that time I'd never made a film that I didn't *rehearse*. You know you rehearse a play three weeks. Well, we rehearsed *The Birth of a Nation* for *months*. Everybody rehearsed it—not the parts you were to play, but whoever was free came in and rehearsed. They were all sworn to secrecy, because if the word got out what we were doing, other people—Ince and other people like that—would do it ahead of us. So he said, "Yes, I've never rehearsed," but all the people came on the set and, you know, we had chairs and tables and started rehearsing, and I opened an imaginary door and did everything out of—just as I was used to. And the others were just *embarrassed* when they got up. They were so self-conscious, they'd never done that, they didn't know *how* to do it. And then we got on the set and they had *music*. And well, that upset me because—I like music, I like to listen to it, but I can't *work* and concentrate while music is playing. We *never* had music. We just rehearsed and did it. Well, anyway, I had to give in; there was only one

Kawin:	of me, and there were a lot of people working in *Bohème*, so I had to do without rehearsals and I had to have music for their sake. And Irving put it all in my hands. He didn't interfere with me in any way.
Kawin:	Well, that showed good sense.
Gish:	And then, he didn't have a story, again. We finished it, and Mr. Mayer, who hadn't said anything about it, came to me when it was finished and he said, "Miss Gish, I don't care if it doesn't make a cent, I'm proud to have my name on that film." So it pleased them, so they let me—I said, "Mr. Mayer, I've got another story I'd like to do, that I wanted to do for a long time but I couldn't find the man to play the lead. And it's called *The Scarlet Letter*." "Oh," he said, "I know that," he said, "we've tried to do that, and I know the man that could play it. He's a Swedish actor." And I said, "Well, *why* can't I do it?" He said, "It's not allowed." I said, "But it's taught in *schools*, it's a classic, it's a Hawthorne story, and *I'm an American*, why can't I do it?" He said, "Because of the churches and the women's clubs." And I said, "Mr. Mayer, if I get them to lift the ban, would you let me do it?" And he said, "Certainly." And I said, "May I—have you got a film with this actor in it?" And they ran *Gösta Berling* for me, and there the man—I said, "Why, he *is* Dimmesdale! Would you bring him over?" Yes, he'd bring him over. Well, I wrote to the women's clubs, the churches that objected, and they wrote back and said, "Miss Gish, if it's in your hands, we'll lift the ban. But they could take that story and do things with the minister that would—we wouldn't approve of. But if you'll be responsible for it, you can do it." So I took it to Mr. Mayer, and they had to put it in my hands again.
Kawin:	Mm-hm.
Gish:	And Irving was just wonderful about it. He never interfered, gave me anything and everything I wanted. I'd heard that Mr. Walthall hadn't worked in a long time, and I wondered about that, and I asked if he could play the husband that has been away for seven years and comes back. And they said Yes, if they could find him, and they found him, and he was getting $1,000 a week so I thought, well, that must be all right. But he hadn't worked in years, and that's—he worked three weeks, I think, got [*laughs*] $3,000. And he was so little he had to stand, not on boards but on a *box* to play with me

by that time. [*Pause*] I'd grown so much taller since *The Birth*. Anyway, we made it, and they were pleased again. We had about another week's work [to be] done on it. My sister was in England, working for Herbert Wilcox, and Mother had a stroke over there. Mother was trying to be with her and with me, and she was going back and forth. And I got the wire, of course there were no planes, it was '26. And that company worked three days and three nights, and I got on the train in my costume. And other people went with me to Pasadena, and I took it off, and they got off there. But they were so dear and so sympathetic. And I got to London as fast as I could, and I was gone a long—three weeks, four weeks—I had to get back. And Mother didn't gain consciousness; she was very ill. And finally I was with her by her bedside, and I said, "Mother, if you want it, I have to go back because of the contract you know I have, and Dorothy has to stay here because of hers. Now do you want to stay here with Dorothy, or do you want me to take Dr. Rowan and a nurse and go back with me? If you want that, squeeze my hand once, and if you want to stay here with Dorothy, where you'll be beautifully looked after," because everybody in England had sent help, and she squeezed it once. And then I asked her again, I said, "Now, Mother, are you sure? Squeeze it again if you want to go with me, one time, if you want to stay with Dorothy, twice." And she squeezed it a second time. And I said, "That means you—we have to leave by ambulance and get out to the coast that way, do you *mind* that, Mother?" Well, that's what she wanted. So I had to take Dr. Rowan and an Irish nurse; I had my secretary with me. James Rennie came over to Dorothy immediately. He was her husband, the only husband she ever had. I never married. And neither one of us had—naturally, I didn't—she didn't have any children. We got Mother to Southampton by ambulance and the nurse got seasick the first night we were out, so she was no good. Dr. Rowan took eight hours with Mother, I took eight hours, and Phyllis Moir, my secretary, took eight, so Mother was never alone. And we had to stay in New York for three weeks because it was June or July; then we had to take a private car and put it on the back of a fast freight train to get her out as quickly as we could. We had to get her cook and staff and that. Oh, it was a terrific thing—Dr. Rowan, with us, crossing

	the desert we had to put big tubs of ice and have fans playing on it to keep her... And we got out there and everybody was down to meet us: Mr. Mayer, Irving, everyone. And Dr. Rowan found a doctor out there for us. And *they* made the next two movies, because I was too busy then. They made, one was *Annie Laurie*, I've forgotten the name of the other. And then Mother got better, and I made *The Wind*. I found that. I found this book by Dorothy Scarborough, about Texas, and I read it, and it was constant motion—moving indoors, outdoors. And I thought, this is the perfect film because it moves all the time. This would have been, this *was*, my sixth unhappy-ending film. Well, *one* film with an unhappy ending was supposed to finish you in pictures; you couldn't—
KAWIN:	But you had *Broken Blossoms*—
GISH:	Oh, *Broken Blossoms* and many others too. *The White Sister, Romola, The Scarlet Letter, Bohème*—this was my sixth. So they objected—I think maybe Mr. Mayer didn't like that much, but Irving let me do it. Irving, by this time, he'd let me do *any*thing I wanted to. Because he's... The other two pictures, I just went to the studio like an actress and did what I was told; I had nothing to do with either the story or anything about it. Anyway, it was '28 when we made *The Wind*, and I think it was released in '29, and you know that was the end of silent films. And eight weeks after we'd finished it, they called me back and changed it. They had a happy ending on it.
KAWIN:	How did it end in the first place?
GISH:	Well, I go out and disappear into the sand. Anyway, we changed it.
KAWIN:	Was that Irving Thalberg's decision?
GISH:	I think it was something we used to call "ex-abiders." Exhibitors. [*Laughs*] We always said they were a race apart. Ex-abiders.
	[*After a break, we talked about Griffith.*]
GISH:	It's strange, you know, he told me all about being this... descended from the Welsh Griffiths kings of Wales, and about two years ago I had an eight-page letter from a lady in New England, giving me all the history. She wrote it in longhand, about the kings of Wales. I didn't know they were twelfth and thirteenth century. And she had to do with that strain and she *knew* that Griffith had. And he certainly acted it and

looked it. Because he was always...he never asked anyone, including his workmen, to do a job that he wouldn't do, and very often he'd take up a pick and shovel and do what they do. [*Her assistant notifies her that she has only five minutes before she has to get ready to leave for a taping.*] Oh, you don't mean to tell me I have to go, dear. All right. So, and then his mother's people were Oglesbys and Carters. I told the president that when I was there at the White House in November, and I told it from the stage. They didn't get it on television because [*laughs*] George Cukor was there, and he was between me and the camera, and they couldn't see me. Anyway, I thought it might interest him and please him.

KAWIN: Same Carter?

GISH: Well I don't know, but you always think, you know. The Gishes, we're—one came here in 1733. There are 4,000 of us now. They're Pennsylvania Dutch. And Mother's people came in 1632, and I don't know how many there are, but we stem from England, Scotland, kind of thing.

KAWIN: Can you tell me about the smile in *Broken Blossoms*?

GISH: *Broken Blossoms*? That—the business of the... Well, that came in a rehearsal. I didn't think of it, I just did it. And I was just recovering from Spanish Influenza and I was—when I'd come near Griffith, I had to put a mask on. He was afraid of germs. But when he saw that, he jumped up and ran up to me; he said, "Where'd you get that gesture? I never saw that gesture before! We'll use it all through!" And I said, "I don't know, it just came." And he forgot all about the germs and everything [*laughs*] and used it all through. But that was from rehearsal, you see, you had to get your character. It had nothing to do with you. I always saw myself as a painter. Other people paint on canvas with water, oil, water colors; I painted with what I had, my body and my face. And I never connected myself or anything that had to do with me with the characters I played. They were always out of my imagination.

KAWIN: Would you rehearse the entire film in sequence, or—

GISH: Oh, we—I had to pick my rushes; I had to be in the projection room every night. Everybody did. Well no, not everybody, but...that's how I learned what was wrong. When I worked with other directors I had to put a mirror on the camera because I found I overdid when I didn't... Because it was

Figure 12.1. *Broken Blossoms*: The smile.
© 1919 D. W. Griffith.

	impersonal what I was doing, and yet it had to be the person I was playing, but it wasn't me, and that still is, I can still look and it isn't me, and I just wonder why people mistake *me* for that *shadow* they've been looking at, because that hasn't really anything to do with…my life: first of course the fact that I was put in the theater at the age of five and worked and learned to act and tried to hold an audience. But the only acting lesson I ever had was to speak *loud and clear* or they'd get another little girl. And I still hope I speak *loud and clear* [*laughs*].
KAWIN:	What's your favorite of your movies?
GISH:	Oh, none of them. You never realize fully, from beginning to end, any film. In the theater you're happier because you can't see yourself. People come back and tell you you're good often enough, you begin to believe it.
KAWIN:	You are good.
GISH:	[*Laughs*] Well, I hope so. Anyway, I'm lucky that I know [*draws herself up*]…coming in under the auspices of such a great man as the father of film…and watch him work. No wonder he left things to me because think of having to design every

set in *Intolerance*, every costume, even the false eyelashes that were used for the first time. That's a genius man, isn't it? And write the story of all of it and then put it together. There never has been a man like that. This is *forty—two—centuries* of history in one man's mind. I'm glad you appreciate him. You know we got a stamp for him. And now, gradually they are realizing who is responsible for film. And we have good and bad film, but you have good and bad of everything, including people. And you bring about the good film and marry it to music and let it speak to the world again, please.

13

HOWARD HAWKS

This interview took place in Mr. Hawks's home in Palm Springs, California, on May 24, 1976. He was 79 years old. Mr. Hawks was very generous with his time—we talked for four hours—and a few weeks after the interview he was good enough to send me the two Faulkner scripts he had mentioned. One of them turned out to be War Birds, *on which Faulkner had been working at MGM, with a new title,* A Ghost Story. *(It can be found in my book* Faulkner's MGM Screenplays.*) The other one, the vampire story, was* Dreadful Hollow—*not an original as Hawks remembered but Faulkner's adaptation of the novel of the same title by Irina Karlova. It still has not been produced. To prompt Hawks's memory, I brought screenplays for the films that he and Faulkner had worked on together, beginning with* Turn About *(from Faulkner's story "Turnabout," which was first published as "Turn About"; it was released as* Today We Live*) and including* The Road to Glory, To Have and Have Not, *and* The Big Sleep. *He touched on many things besides Faulkner, including the contributions of a chorus girl he called "Stuttering Sam" to the screenplay of* To Have and Have Not, *his own contributions to* The Bridge on the River Kwai, *the influence of* His Girl Friday *on* Citizen Kane, *and his use of "opposites" in* I Was a Male War Bride. *Just part of what's wonderful here is the way he talks in scenes. I dedicated my book* Faulkner and Film *to Hawks, and my friend Jack Anderson made him a copy bound in saddle leather, but he didn't live to receive it. Please note that ellipses indicate pauses; no words have been taken out.*

BRUCE KAWIN: Mr. Hawks, I'm writing a book on Faulkner's career in film. I'd like to ask you some questions about your work with him from 1932 to 1954, and about the way you work with writers in general. I want to know what you look for in a script, how you change a script, and how much of the writing you do yourself.

HOWARD HAWKS: Well, I've got two original manuscripts of Faulkner's—that have never been published.

KAWIN: Really, what are they?

HAWKS: Stories that he wrote—one of them a horror story, I mean a vampire story, and the other one—he'd just been to see *Secrets*, a Norma Shearer picture, and he said he didn't like it. And I said, "You make me mad, for goodness sake. A ghost story is really a *good story* and this is beautifully told." So he went off and he wrote a ghost story. He'd [the boy] got old enough to know that the man who taught him to shoot—took him fishing—took him hunting…it was a German who shot his father, killed him, and that the woman who lived with his mother was a German sweetheart of that fellow… So the ghosts of the past are coming up, you know, and it's a very interesting story.

KAWIN: Have you thought of making it?

HAWKS: No, I'll let somebody else make it.

KAWIN: When did he write them?

HAWKS: I don't know…

KAWIN: In the '30s?

HAWKS: Oh, it could have been later than that. Bill died about five years ago, didn't he?

KAWIN: More like thirteen.

HAWKS: Thirteen years ago?

KAWIN: Yeah.

HAWKS: It's hard to believe. [*Looking over Faulkner's second draft of* Today We Live, *which opens with several scenes of Claude, Ronnie, and Ann as children*] This we did not use because we—I picked up some children. The mother taught them English accents, and it sounded terrible, so I never used it.

KAWIN: You never even shot the whole children sequence at the beginning of the film?

HAWKS: I never used the children sequence at all.

KAWIN: It was a fairly long film as it was, wasn't it? *Today We Live*—almost two hours.

HAWKS: Yeah, if they had—two-hour pictures then. "Turn About" was the original story and…he'd written the script in practically no time at all. I can remember Irving Thalberg…I said, "Close your door and start looking this over." He said, "Are you going to muddy it up by changing it?" and I said, "No, I'm not going to muddy it up at all. I just want you to read it and see what a guy who doesn't know how to write scenarios, what he wrote." The next thing, he came to me and said, "By the way, are you about getting ready to start?" And I said, "Yeah, I'll get Gary Cooper. I've got two kids—one called Bob Young and the other Franchot Tone. And we're all ready to go." And he said, "Well, you've got Joan Crawford, too"—she was the

	biggest star at that time. And I said, "You've got the wrong person," and he said, "Nope, we can't miss her—we haven't got a picture for Joan—we can't miss one, so you're stuck with it." Back to Bill, and I said, "Bill, we've got to put a girl in here," and he said, "Okay," and we made a picture and it wasn't a bad one at all.
KAWIN:	Uh-huh. So the whole business with Ann was written in *after* the screenplay was first finished?
HAWKS:	Oh, yes, there was no girl in it.
KAWIN:	And he did most of the writing on that first script? 'Cause what's in the MGM vault is signed by both of you.
HAWKS:	Well, I don't know whether I signed it because I wrote it…or because I bought the story. It was a *Saturday Evening Post* story called "Turn About."
KAWIN:	I've got it here…
HAWKS:	You've got the script on *Turn About*?
KAWIN:	Yeah.
HAWKS:	Well, then, what the hell am I telling you—you can tell how good it is.
KAWIN:	Well, I know how good it is but I don't know who did what—or what happened when, or why the changes got made—which I'd like to know.
HAWKS:	Hmm?
KAWIN:	For instance, I was curious why the girl was thrown in.
HAWKS:	Well, that was the story. They lose a million dollars if they don't have a [girl in the] thing, so Bill wrote the script. As a matter of fact, I bought the story, and I wired him and asked him if he'd like to come do the script. He wired back that he'd like to and that he'd arrive on a certain day. He came in. I said, "My name's Hawks," and he said, "I saw it on a check." He lit a pipe and I said, "Well, I'd like to have you do your story, 'Turn About.'" And he didn't say a damn word and I began to get mad, you know. So I talked for 45 minutes about what I wanted to do, and said, "That's it." He got up. I said, "Where are you going?" "Going in to write. I'm going to write it." So I said, "When will I see you again?" He said, "About five days." I said, "Mr. Faulkner, it shouldn't take you five days to get started…[and then] to come back and talk to me," and he said, "No, I can *write* it in five days." And I said, "Well, now, look, really, I *found* you because I read a book a long time ago"—this was about 1932—"that you'd written," and all the intelligentsia around New York were staying around Ben Hecht and Charles MacArthur's house…I can't remember all the names…
KAWIN:	That's all right.

HAWKS: And I said, "Have you fellows ever read William Faulkner?" They said, "No." I said I'd read a story that he wrote and I thought that he was one of the best writers of the present age.

KAWIN: What was it that you had read? *Sanctuary*, or...

HAWKS: *Soldiers' Pay*.

KAWIN: *Soldiers' Pay*? That's his first novel.

HAWKS: Yeah. So all of a sudden I made Bill famous. And he was clerk in Macy's basement, selling books. And as you know, authors didn't make any money in those days—until paperbacks came in *nobody* made any money—Hemingway, Faulkner, or anybody. So, Bill said it would take him five days to do the script. And I said, "Okay, would you like a drink?" He said, "Yes." Well, we woke up in a motel in Culver City the next morning. [*Laughter*] He was fishing cigarette stubs out of a mint julep glass. And in five days he came in with the script. And we became good friends—we liked to fish, we liked to hunt. When he needed money, he always used to call me and say, "Do you have anything for me to do?" and if I didn't, I'd make up something, you know. I don't know...the story's been told, I think before, but it's...

KAWIN: What, the dove hunt with Gable?[1]

HAWKS: Yeah.

KAWIN: I've heard it.

HAWKS: You heard that...

KAWIN: Was it ducks or doves?

HAWKS: Doves.

KAWIN: Doves. I've heard it both ways. That's a good story.

HAWKS: It's a *very* good story—because I don't know whether Faulkner'd ever seen Gable in a movie... I'm quite sure that Gable had never read Faulkner's books.

KAWIN: Was *Turn About* the first screenplay that he wrote?

HAWKS: Yeah.

KAWIN: Had you contracted with MGM for the picture or did they contract with you?

---

1 Hawks often said that he took Gable and Faulkner dove hunting in the Imperial Valley. According to MGM executive and historian Samuel Marx, who told me this in a closed office a few years later, the "dove hunts" were wild weekends in rented bungalows. In any case, Hawks and Faulkner were talking about literature while on a "dove hunt," and Gable asked Faulkner who were the best contemporary writers. Faulkner answered, "Ernest Hemingway, Willa Cather, John Dos Passos, Thomas Mann, and William Faulkner." Gable did a double-take and asked, "Do you write, Mr. Faulkner?" Faulkner replied, "Yes, Mr. Gable, what do you do?"

HAWKS: Oh, I'd contracted. I bought the story, and contracted with them to make the picture...so that they had a perfect right to stick a girl in it, you know. I could have fought it, you know, but...

KAWIN: How did he decide to stay on? You know he was at MGM for the next two years.

HAWKS: I doubt if he was on two years. He went back in the meantime...

KAWIN: Well, they have scripts that are dated that he wrote in 1932 straight through '33—there's one every couple of months.

HAWKS: Is that right?

KAWIN: Yeah—there're about 12 of them. You were saying that you showed the script of *Turn About* to Thalberg to show him what a guy who couldn't write a screenplay wrote like. And I wondered if that meant that it was unusually good or if it was unusually poor?

HAWKS: Unusually good.

KAWIN: It was good?

HAWKS: Oh, Thalberg was a very brilliant man—he understood it. Of course good writing—it's pretty easy to understand and like. For instance, I worked during summer vacations as a prop man—and one day the part director was in Arizona and McGuire came from Fairbanks and said he wanted a modern setting—nobody knew what the hell it was. But I did...and I drew it out, and he said, "Who did this, this is great." I met Doug and he said, "You look like you play tennis or play golf," and I said, "Well, I was junior champion in the United States playing tennis and a 4-handicap in playing golf," so we became friends. He was courting Mary Pickford and he said to Mary, "Why don't you give Howard this job?" and she did, and I did a couple of things for them and one day this director got drunk and so Mary said, "Can you do it?" and I said, "Sure." So I started my directing. And...that was over at Paramount, and I started to study going into pictures instead of being an engineer—I had my engineering degree. And there was a little red-faced, rosy-cheeked Jewish boy who used to come over to my house and talk about... stories. So one day Jesse Lasky, the head of Famous Players–Lasky, called me up and said he'd like to see me. He said, "Do you think that if I put you in charge you can make 40 pictures in a year," and I said, "If I can get in to see you and if I have plenty of money—if I don't have to go through a lot of things—why, it's not a hard job."

KAWIN: You were producing 40 pictures a year—or directing?

HAWKS: Producing. So I bought two Zane Greys and two Joseph Conrads... You know, I'd read everything, and I knew when the stuff was good or not—and nobody had *done* that in pictures. So I bought

KAWIN: about 32 out of the 40 needed, and the other eight, why, we took some ideas and gave them to good screenwriters and we made 40 pictures and they made more money than any time in the history of Paramount.

KAWIN: When was that?

HAWKS: Oh, about 1924. So then I said, "Now look, I want to direct. This is too much work preparing 40 pictures for someone else," and they said, "Oh no, we can always get someone to direct, but we need someone to handle scripts," so I said, "Okay, I quit." And Irving Thalberg heard about it and said, "Howard, come down here." And Irving and I were good friends. I said, "Irving, I want to direct." "Okay," he said, "you can direct, but come down and help us out for one year." And at the end of the time again *they* didn't want me to direct—they wanted me to do stories. So I quit. And I went out and played golf. I ran into Sol Wurtzel who was the head of Fox—it wasn't Twentieth Century Fox, it was William Fox. He said, "What are you doing?" "Playing golf." He said, "No, I mean what are you working on?" I said, "Playing golf." He said, "Aren't you working for Metro anymore?" and I said, "No." He said, "Well, you started to work for Fox this morning." I said, "Now look, Sol. I am *not* going to do that kind of work. I will buy stories if I can get a job directing." "Well," he said, "you've got a job directing—you can direct." "What about the stories?" I said. "Write your own." And the first one I did was a very somber, tragic thing, like any kid would do who gets a chance to do dramatic stuff. After we finished this first one, Wurtzel, who was a smart, nice man, said, "Howard, you've shown me you can direct. The critics loved it and that's fine, but for *God's* sake make entertainment. And I wrote a story that night called *Fig Leaves* and it got its cost back in one theater...and I've been doing that, making entertainment ever since. And I've never taken sides, I don't give a *god damn* about politics. I'm just going to make the pictures.

KAWIN: You do all right.

[*Laughter*]

HAWKS: Yeah, the things that I've done wrong have been from trying to help friends. They want me to do a story and I say I don't know how to tell that story...I don't know how to tell it. They say, "Well, Howard, we're stuck, now I want you to do this." I've never been able to work with Sam Goldwyn... I made one good picture over there, two good pictures.

KAWIN: Which were they?

HAWKS: *Ball of Fire* and an Edna Ferber story, *Come and Get It.*
KAWIN: I like *Ball of Fire* very much.
HAWKS: That's the only one I ever made that Sam Goldwyn let me alone on. And then he wanted to re*make* the thing. With…at my suggestion… Danny Kaye…but they wanted to do it over and make it about music.
KAWIN: Uh-huh.
HAWKS: Oh, isn't *that* the great idea! And they worked about two months on it and called me up and said, "Howard, they told me it wouldn't work if they did it in 1922." You know, if they're searching for new music and they go out and discover "Alexander's Ragtime Band," that's silly. They had to make it modern. Well, he just made himself a pest. And finally he followed me down to Palm Springs. "There must be some way that you'll do the picture," and I said, "Yeah, $25,000 a week and I'll do the picture." So we made a deal. Oh, he made life miserable for me. So, I never saw the picture—*A Song is Born*. I never saw it, I didn't see the rushes. One of the things I said to him, I said, "Virginia Mayo is out." But Virginia Mayo was under contract. Not only that, but he wanted her to play it how Barbara Stanwyck played it. And there's *no* relationship to Barbara Stanwyck, who was just fantastic. But it's just a question of picking the story. I believe the director is a storyteller, but if I don't *like* the story, if I don't *believe* in it, I can't do any good. I *never* wanted to make a big picture, I always wanted to make something and have it turn out to be good. When I came back from Europe, Jack Warner said, "What do you want to do?" and I said, "A Western." "Oh, Hawks, you don't want to do a Western." So I said, "Okay, I'll just go someplace else with it," and he said, "No, no, you do it your way"—and it made a *lot* of money. *Rio Bravo*. That was a damn good film.
KAWIN: Can you say what it was that you liked about Faulkner's work?
HAWKS: Well, look, I thought he was a great writer. I met him. We liked each other *personally*. And that's about all. I used to kid Hemingway, "Okay, I'll get Faulkner to do it, he can write better than you anyway." That used to get him so mad. You know, *we* were friends. I tried to get Ernest to work for pictures. "No," he said, "I'm good at what I'm doing…I don't want to buck hours." "You don't have to buck hours, we'll meet just the way we're doing now"—we were fishing—"you don't even have to write *down* the story, I'll dictate it."
KAWIN: Uh-huh.
HAWKS: I said, "Ernest, you're a damn fool. You need money, you know. You can't do all the things you'd like to do. If I make three dollars

in a picture, you get one of them." I said, "I can make a picture out of your worst story." He said, "What's my worst story?" and I said, "That goddamned bunch of junk called *To Have and To Have Not*." He said, "You can't make anything out of that." I said, "Yes I can." So for about ten days we talked. There was the character Harry Morgan and his wife. I said, "All you have to do is make a story about how they met. Because you've got the *character* of Harry Morgan. I think I can give you the wife." So we talked about it for a while and he sold it for $10,000 and I bought it for $80,000 and I sold it to Warner Brothers for a half interest in the picture.

KAWIN: How did he feel about your having Faulkner work on the script?

HAWKS: Oh, I used to kid him, you know. When I told him how much that picture made, and I said, "You got $10,000," he wouldn't talk to me for six months. What I used to do—I had great writers all through my career, and I think it's because I had enormously good writers that I did so well.

KAWIN: Didn't you do a lot of your own writing too?

HAWKS: *Re*writing, I did. I switched dialogue to my kind of dialogue. Jules Furthman, Dudley Nichols, Leigh Brackett, [Charles] Brackett and Wilder, Hemingway, Faulkner—you can't get much better.

KAWIN: No, you don't.

HAWKS: Just the same—practically every comedy I made was made with Cary Grant. Practically every Western—as a matter of fact, *every* Western—

KAWIN: John Wayne?

HAWKS: John Wayne.

KAWIN: Do you think of any of your other films as Westerns, besides *Rio Bravo*, *El Dorado*, *Red River* and *Rio Lobo*?

HAWKS: Yes, I think you'd call *Hatari* a Western. *Rio Lobo* was *not* a good picture. I had Wayne; CBS ran out of money, the money that their parent company had allotted them. And my story was built for two *men*—and I don't feel that Wayne—there's something wrong in every story that he does where he hasn't got a really good man with him. I put Montgomery Clift in *Red River*, Martin in *Rio Bravo*, and Mitchum in *El Dorado*, so when we came to *Rio Lobo* it was a story for two men. I didn't feel I could tell the story that I had, so I threw the story away and wrote a good one. But I don't think the picture was any good, I didn't like it. It had some good stuff in it—that stuff about stopping the train was great, and some of the other stuff, but…Duke needs some man to work with. It just blows him right off the screen when he hasn't got anybody.

KAWIN: Yeah, I think about the only woman he can really act with is Maureen O'Hara—in *The Quiet Man*, for instance.

HAWKS: Well, she's good, and he's bucking against a girl who's good. *The Quiet Man*'s one of the best pictures I've ever seen. And he was awfully good in *She Wore a Yellow Ribbon*. Ford, when he saw *Red River*, he said, "I never thought the big son of a bitch could act!" *Red River* came out, Ford's picture came out, somebody else did *Sands of Iwo Jima*, and all of a sudden Wayne was the biggest thing in pictures.

KAWIN: Sure. And there's *The Searchers* too.

HAWKS: Yeah, but you see, you get to be big by being in good pictures, and Metro was very very successful because they didn't give their stars *any* choice of the stories they were put into, that Thalberg thought they should be in, and he saw to it that the stories fitted. The average star today—I told Wayne—I said, "If they say that 'Big Bob Tennyson was 6'4" and he had a cock a foot long and everyone wanted it,'" I said, "you read that much and you say, 'That story's for me!'" I said, "You never liked a story that I made, did you?" And he hadn't! He couldn't see it. Cary Grant never liked a story that I had for him.

KAWIN: Not even *His Girl Friday*?

HAWKS: No.

KAWIN: Let me get back—

HAWKS: I think I know who good writers are. And I know who bad writers are. Carl Foreman I thought was a *hell* of a good writer. You know his work?

KAWIN: Yeah, sure.

HAWKS: Well, I was thinking about doing *The Bridge on the River Kwai*, you remember? I was skiing, and—

KAWIN: I wish you *had* made that.

HAWKS: All my friends said, "Can't you get rid of that *goddamned* producer?" What was his name?—Sam Spiegel. So I said, "Okay, I'll take it down to London with Sam and get him off your hands." And I met Foreman, and we worked out the story of that thing—and then I told Carl, "Carl, I'm not going to make this story because I *can't* put up with Spiegel. He goes off and talks about things during the day and then he comes in just about the time, you know, to drink, and wants to know what we'd done on everything we did—I'm not going to go through with it." I hadn't been used to that. I could have made it, but it's made out of—from my ideas.

KAWIN: I never knew that.

HAWKS: No, I didn't get any credit for it. I didn't want credit for it.

KAWIN: On the subject of credit—one of the things that Faulkner said was that you had gotten him a lot of screen credit that he didn't deserve and supported him through the industry, and taught him all he knew about film. I wanted to know a couple of things: like, in the first place, what he *did* know about film when he came here, and in the second place, what screen credits he got for the films he didn't do.

HAWKS: Faulkner's a great writer.

KAWIN: Yes.

HAWKS: We did that first picture together. So that neither one of us had any qualms about speaking to the other, saying, "This is no good" or "That's no good," or—

KAWIN: Yeah.

HAWKS: We understood each other, you know, and we became friends. He came over and worked on *The Land of the Pharaohs* with Harry Kurnitz, who was a *hell* of a good playwright. We had a *very* good time working on that.

KAWIN: I enjoyed that film.

HAWKS: But...the mechanical part of the picture was great and the other stuff wasn't good.

KAWIN: How do you mean?

HAWKS: Well, Jack Hawkins. You had nothing to *root* for—it was my mistake. The way I made it, they were all louses or heavies. The girl was a bitch—what's his name—Chaplin—young Chaplin—was no good. Hawkins—everybody was lousy.

KAWIN: Except the fellow who built the pyramids and his son.

HAWKS: Well, I know, but that isn't enough—you didn't have any rooting interest in the story.

KAWIN: I felt that you could get excited about Joan Collins' getting smashed; there was a payoff in that.

HAWKS: Well, she was—there was a payoff, but I don't think...I started on the story because I thought the public would be interested in the fact the Pharaoh lived in fairly ordinary circumstances and for his death built one of those great huge things—for after life, you know, the way they believed. I thought Faulkner would be good on that—but—*something* went wrong. I didn't like it much.

KAWIN: Did you work from an original story?

HAWKS: We made up the story. A lot of the men who were living in Egypt—digging up things, cutting historical stuff—thought that our method of using sand hydraulics to seal[2] a pyramid was as feasible as

---

[2] He may have said "conceal."

anything that they got hold of—and that the ramp we used to take the stones up—those really were mine and Faulkner's ideas. We didn't have too much time to get it ready, and…Jack Warner offered me $2 million for my share, and I was going to take it right then and there, but my agent said, "No, no, no, don't, don't, don't you take it." He said, "This is a great picture." I said, "No it's not, it's a lousy picture." I didn't take it. Oh, it made a little money but not enough to go through all that work for. But: I could call Faulkner up—for instance—I made a picture called *Air Force*, and in the end of the picture we needed a death scene for the captain of the thing, you know, this crew—and I said, "Bill, I need some help," and he said, "Can I see what you've made already?" and I said "Sure." We ran it the next morning and he had a great scene. The scene was the captain was dying and he prepared for take-off and all—and the crew answered him. He died—taking off. Well, that's Faulkner's. I just shot it, *exactly* the way he did it. And then other times, I can't remember all of them, you know—

KAWIN: Can you remember just offhand some other pictures on which he did one or two scenes' work?

HAWKS: Yes, he did some work on *To Have and To Have Not*.

KAWIN: I understand he did a great deal of work on that.

HAWKS: Well, not too much.

KAWIN: Didn't he and Furthman put it together?

HAWKS: Furthman was pretty good, and then there was a girl that was pretty good. A former chorus girl. I went down to Texas when they had the Centennial down there—whatever it was. Billy Rose was running it. He called me up and said, "Howard, you got to come down and help me out." We wrote *Jumbo* for him and everything in two days or something like that. So I had an airplane and I flew down there. Billy said, "We'll make a tour and I'll explain and then you can give me some ideas." I'd given him some ideas for his theater in New York, and told him to put a girl in a fishbowl downstairs in another bar. I told him to get a good piano player, and he said, "Well, you find one," and I went down to Harlem and picked out Art Tatum and brought him—the first time he'd ever been downtown. Well, he wanted some help on this thing. We were having a beer and sitting up at a table watching a rehearsal and I said, "Look, I'm getting awful sick of you and would like to meet some girl." "Just pick one out and I'll introduce you to her." They had a proscenium arch—a great huge thing—and out came a girl with the loveliest figure and everything like that. I said, "That's the one." She came to the table and she was 6'2"—she was exactly my size, and she st-st-st-stut-stut-stut-stuttered. I called her "Stuttering Sam." I had more fun with her, and she wanted to go to New York so I phoned Billy Rose and said, "I want you to give this girl a job. She's a perfectly good showgirl." She got to New York and tried to call him—but she stuttered so much the secretary hung up on her. She tried twice—finally, she told me, she went out and picked up a sailor and they went out to see the—oh, they went to the big museums and those places in New York and they had a beer and she went back home again. So I called Billy and said, "Goddamn it, Billy, you have somebody down at the train to meet that girl, and tell them that she stutters," and he did and she became a famous showgirl in New York. She could write letters but she cou-cou-couldn't talk. So I hired her to come out and do some dialogue and she did some *beautiful* dialogue—utterly untrained as far as pictures are concerned—and I'd have had her around still but she married a guy with about $20 million, and is very happy.

KAWIN: What was her name?
HAWKS: Stuttering Sam.
[*Laughter*]
KAWIN: So she did dialogue on *To Have and Have Not* then?
HAWKS: Yes, she did dialogue on that and then I'd let her read *The Big Sleep* and she'd give me an idea for something there. On *The Big Sleep* I told Leigh Brackett and Bill Faulkner, I said, "This guy who wrote this thing—"
KAWIN: Chandler.
HAWKS: Yeah—"is better than either of you people about this kind of stuff." He and Dashiell Hammett were so far superior to anybody that there's no comparison. "So I want you to be very very careful about trying to add or change dialogue." So they did it in eight days.
KAWIN: So I hear.
HAWKS: Yeah. And they just hooked some stuff together good and they did contribute some stuff into it—you have to—but they also left a great deal of Chandler in the thing. You see that—Bill recognized good writing—what the hell—
KAWIN: Sure, why change it if it's good?
HAWKS: He said, "Howard wouldn't want me to change it if it's good," and he told me so—so he said to Leigh Brackett—and that's why in the picture there are some things that are unexplained. You don't know who killed who or anything.
KAWIN: I know, like who killed the chauffeur. That's the big one.

HAWKS: Yeah.
KAWIN: Well, but the thing is I just read the script a little while ago and then saw the film, and there's a lot of stuff in the script that didn't make it onto the screen. I wondered whether the problem was that the film was going to be too long or if you were deliberately cutting out the scenes in which they explain the story. They're in the script.
HAWKS: They are in the script?
KAWIN: They're in the script but they're not on the screen.
HAWKS: Well, I cut them out. I probably didn't think that they were worth doing. I told Bogey, "If you think that the scene isn't any good, I want you to tell me. If I think you're no good, I'm going to tell you." For instance, the scene of Bogey coming into the book store—do you happen to remember?
KAWIN: Yeah.
HAWKS: He did it and said, "How was that?" and I said, "Well, pretty goddamned dull." So he said, "Why?" and I said, "It doesn't promise anything for inside. There's nothing that I can do. You go in there—too straight—too everything." So he said, "Try it again." And he did the hat and he went in and of course we made up the scene inside to fit it—you know—and he did too. And out of it came two good pieces of entertainment. And then we went over to another book store and by then we are, you know, making up scenes. I got Dorothy Malone—it was the first scene she'd *ever* done.
KAWIN: She was beautiful.
HAWKS: Yes, she was so lovely. She was so scared when she was taking that drink, so nervous that when I stopped working at noon I told the prop man to pour a piece of lead that would fit into the bottom of a paper cup so that she would have something to hold onto to take the drink, otherwise sh-sh-she was just like this [*making his hand shake*].
[*Laughter*]
KAWIN: I noticed there was a lot of joking play back and forth between Bogart and Bacall that was not in the script. Every once in a while the scene, as written, will stop and they'll go on and do a little song and dance, like the time that she scratches her leg.
HAWKS: Uh-huh.
KAWIN: Almost that whole scene isn't in the script, and I wondered if they worked that out or if you worked it out with them.
HAWKS: Oh, I probably worked it out. I wrote a couple of scenes about horse racing.
KAWIN: Yes.

HAWKS: Well, I'll tell you—they were falling in love in the first picture and it was so hard to get their attention that they weren't working well, and I just cut the goddamned scenes out.
KAWIN: Uh-huh.
HAWKS: And then Jack Warner said, "Howard, that picture needs more scenes between those two people. Will you do 'em?"
KAWIN: You mean *The Big Sleep*?
HAWKS: No.
KAWIN: Or *To Have and Have Not*?
HAWKS: Which has the horse racing scene?
KAWIN: *The Big Sleep*. They talked about horse racing.
HAWKS: *The Big Sleep*. So I wrote the story. I had some horses running out at Santa Anita and I couldn't go out—I had to finish these goddamned scenes—you know, make 'em—so I made them about horses, jockeys, and people coming from behind.
KAWIN: I heard a story that the ending of *The Big Sleep* was made up by the censors; is that a true story?
HAWKS: Yeah, mmm-hmm.
KAWIN: How did that go?
HAWKS: Well, they said the scene that I had was very censorable.
KAWIN: As they first had it, Bogart is responsible—well, Marlowe is responsible—for killing Carmen Sternwood. He opens the door, she walks out, and she gets shot.
HAWKS: Well, I had it in a Western too.
KAWIN: I know, in *El Dorado*.
HAWKS: Well, the boys were very nice to me. I think I'd just finished *Male War Bride* and they said, "Howard, you've got to cut stuff out of that picture." It's about a guy trying to get in bed with a girl and it took him till he got into New York harbor to make it. "Well," I said, "I don't want to talk about it now. Let's talk about it tomorrow." They called me the next day and said, "We enjoyed it so much, everything's fine." So we were on very good terms, and when they told me that the ending of *The Big Sleep* couldn't go by their rules, I said, "You bastards make it so tough." I said, "That's a good ending—*give me* an ending." And they gave me the ending.
KAWIN: What did they give you?
HAWKS: Well, the idea that he got there first and was waiting and he sent the guy out the door and [the guy] got shot. It was better than the ending that I had.
KAWIN: And who wrote it then?

HAWKS: I did, I think—yeah. It was easy. Wasn't anything much to talk about—there was just action.

KAWIN: Well, see, that's the point. Bogart's staring at Mars and he explains the whole crime in something like a minute—it's as fast as *His Girl Friday*—he just rattles it off.

HAWKS: Umm-hmm.

KAWIN: And it's one reason most people can't follow the plot—the explanation's played so fast. But it works nicely.

HAWKS: Well, I wrote quite a number of stories, and I could write dialogue. It never bothered me what anybody wrote as long as you don't lose interest in what the scene was—how it goes. How it told the story. I'd change it around. I never had a writer get mad at me until we made *El Dorado*. *El Dorado* had a different title—the book he wrote would be a perfect Greek tragedy where Wayne would have come back with TB and all kinds of stuff. And we had a beautiful script, and I said to Leigh Brackett, "Leigh, this is going to be one of the worst pictures that I've ever made. It hasn't anything in it except about losers—and I *hate losers*. We're going to have to start right from scratch—throw everything away and start over with the picture." "Got any idea what it's going to be about?" And I said, "Well, I've got an idea." We had our little black book and we took Ricky Nelson, who was a good kid and a good shot, but in our little black book I wrote down, "Ricky the kid can't shoot anything." We took that...

KAWIN: You mean *Rio Bravo*?

HAWKS: No, *El Dorado*.

KAWIN: You took the Ricky Nelson character [and] made him into James Caan?

HAWKS: There aren't many things you can do when you've got—if you're doing stuff in *town* in a Western. There are two kinds of Westerns—one that deals with the beginning of the West, like *Red River*, and the others are the ones where law and order was needed and you had a bad sheriff or a good sheriff—you just make up stories.

KAWIN: Sure.

HAWKS: And Jimmy Caan played a guy that couldn't shoot, so that gave us four or five scenes. And then other scenes came from the fact that I told them I didn't think—you remember that film where Gary Cooper played a sheriff?

KAWIN: *High Noon*?

HAWKS: *High Noon*. I said, "That's a lousy story." They said, "Why do you think that?" Well, he is supposed to be *sheriff* and he ran around like a chicken with his head off asking everybody to help him and finally his Quaker *wife* saved him—and my idea of a sheriff is if he's in trouble and someone comes up and says, "What can I do to help?" he'd say, "How good are you? Well, I, look, you know, you'd like to help but you're not good enough—I'd just have to take care of you. Just one more person to take care of." And then there was another picture where the sheriff had a prisoner and he was getting nervous because the guy kept saying, "Wait until my friends catch up with you." I said that wasn't a sheriff—that was ridiculous—because a good sheriff would say, "Brother, you better hope they don't ever catch up, 'cause you're going to be the first one that's killed." So we used that, and…

KAWIN: So why did your writer get mad at you?

HAWKS: [*Laughs*] Oh, the writer got mad at me for changing his story. And I said, "Well, if you're mad then I'll take your name off it." He said, "No, no, I don't want my name taken off it." And I said, "Well, then, don't call me again about it. I'll write you a letter about how good the picture did," and I wrote him a letter and I said, "I've already gotten $1.8 million out of it. I don't think I did you any wrong at all. You can have the goddamned story back again—for nothing." The only scene we used was the scene where Wayne shot the boy in the stomach and brought him back to the father and said, "Here's your son—you left a kid out there doing a man's job."

KAWIN: That was a good scene.

HAWKS: After that it began to get amusing—the story with Jimmy Caan coming in, saying, "Look, I'm not your son and you don't have to take care of me." Jimmy was very funny doing that.

KAWIN: Or when he shot the sign down.

HAWKS: Yeah, and also the idea that he was going to go out and would have run right into the two men, you know, and gotten shot. That was a nice relationship. And I've got another modern Western I may do—and I've got another one that's got to do with the opening up of the West—it's more historical. I don't know which one I'll do. Depends on who's available that I can put in it. I'm going to miss Wayne like hell.

KAWIN: You can't work with him?

HAWKS: He's too old. What am I going to do?

KAWIN: Tell a story about an old man.

HAWKS: Oh, I've got half a story, but to be perfectly honest, Wayne's last pictures haven't done anything. He needs boosting up and gets an awful lot of money, and in today's market I don't think it's

	worthwhile. I told him so. He was down here—he spent a couple of days down here and said, "Howard, do another one." He has reached the stage now where I think probably we could do another one. In other words, he's not trying to be a young man any more. I didn't like the one he got the Academy Award for—
KAWIN:	*True Grit*.
HAWKS:	And the one that he did called *Rooster Cogburn* with Katie Hepburn was a complete bust. And they're good—both of them. I don't think today's audience is interested. He's doing one now with a damned fine cast—he's a man who's got cancer. He's almost doing his own story. But if I could find a story I'd love to make one with Wayne. I told him, I said, "I'm never going to pay you a million dollars, but I'll split with you on the thing." Let's see, you wanted to know about Faulkner, and here I am talking about other things.
KAWIN:	That's okay. Now, when he first came to Hollywood, what did he tell you about film, what did he know about film? Had he *watched* films?
HAWKS:	No, he didn't know about films at all. He came really out of curiosity—and to get some money.
KAWIN:	Yeah.
HAWKS:	And we became friends. I helped him when he was in trouble. I have a marvelous letter from him. He said, "I'm sitting on the porch in a very comfortable rocking chair. Alongside of me is a jug of very good whiskey. I know the guy that makes it. There's a little drizzle, and I just heard a noise that I've never heard around here before—the toilet flushing. Your money bought a new toilet." Marvelous letter, really—great sense of humor. If I was around, he wouldn't drink.
KAWIN:	He did drink too much though?
HAWKS:	No doubt about it. One time about four or five in the morning a couple of cops pushed open the door and dragged in a bloody guy. He had a Legion of Honor in the buttonhole and they wanted me to take care of him. He got the idea he'd like to go up to Montmartre where he'd been before, and he got drunk, fell in the gutter, and busted his—you know, had blood all over; and I had to take care of him. I was very fortunate—I knew a good doctor and he[3] knew a good red-headed nurse and boy they rode it. He wasn't a constant drunk but he did get—something would send him off on—and he would just drink himself blind.

---

3 He may have said "she."

KAWIN: He did it here as well as in the South then?

HAWKS: He never did it with me—you know, when we were working. After he'd worked and finished, though… There is a pretty good picture that I made about the war, you know—

KAWIN: *Road to Glory*?

HAWKS: *Road to Glory*, yeah. And he said, "Am I all finished, Howard?" And I said, "Yes," so he got drunk and walked into the back door of Zanuck's office and told Zanuck what he thought of him in no uncertain terms.

KAWIN: What did he do on *Road to Glory*? Did you guys work that out from scratch together?

HAWKS: We had a French picture called *Wooden Crosses* that was very good. It was the story of a company that moved in and then heard that the Germans were mining underneath. I had some very fine film from that, and an idea. After the war my brother and I ran into a fellow with a ring of cops around him. He was saying in a very quiet voice what a bunch of bastards they were. And I said to the cops, "This guy was in the war, do you particularly want to arrest him?" "No, but we've got to get rid of him. Will you take care of him?" I said, "Yeah." Both my brother and I were DKE. We were staying in the Deke House in New York and we took him in there. My brother said, "Gee, that guy certainly started something." This figure rose out of bed and said, "Did I only start it and not finish it?" He was a boy that had edited a Princeton paper—brilliant boy—had been in all the offensives at Verdun and everything. That's where we got our idea for the story. I told Bill Faulkner about it, you know. We wrote a pretty good war story—it was an old man and his son. Because this kid would tell me as he sobered up—after he got sober, he got very apologetic, 'cause my brother would knock him out and lay him into bed until he got up in the morning. And Bill had some ideas and I had some ideas and we just put the thing together—and he wrote it—some great scenes in that one. Old Lionel Barrymore was in it—good actor—so was the famous Russian director, Gregory Ratoff. He was married to a famous Russian actress and was a friend of Zanuck's; he did some pictures over at Twentieth Century Fox. He was the one when they brought in some helmets—steel helmets when they first issued them—and he said, "We're sitting over a mine and they give us this," and he turned it upside down and sat on it. [*Laughter*] The audiences died. You know—he was in it and Freddie March was in it—you know—we had trouble getting a girl.

KAWIN: Uh-huh.
HAWKS: I made a test of Ann Sheridan. Somehow Ann's Southern accent didn't go very well as a French girl. But I told Jack Warner that I had made a test of a girl who was a cinch to be a star, so he signed Ann. And she became a star. I made a test of a little girl, and I didn't think she had a chance at all from the test I made. She had just gotten in making a test—and she'd gotten by and she wasn't selected by the casting director or anything, but they all thought she was so good that I put her in the picture. I had a great cameraman on that, Gregg Toland. June Lang was the girl. I had a *really* good script from Faulkner. Script to me doesn't mean anything. I wrote so many of 'em and read so many of 'em. You don't have to say "long shot," "close-up"—I never read 'em.
KAWIN: So you just had your people write the dialogue and break it up into master scenes, and that was it?
HAWKS: Yeah, sure.
KAWIN: Did Faulkner and Toland meet each other?
HAWKS: Oh, yeah, sure.
KAWIN: Did they hit it off at all?
HAWKS: Bill was a hard person to hit it off with. I mean—he just didn't talk or say anything unless he had something particular to say. He came out and wrote a script for me on *The Left Hand of God*.
KAWIN: Which wasn't used?
HAWKS: Yes, they made a picture of it.
KAWIN: Yeah. Dmytryk made it. Alfred Hayes got the script credit for it.
HAWKS: Bill started to work on it and I had a priest over for dinner and had a few drinks and we started talking about it. "Howard," he said, "I have to tell you that you shouldn't make that picture." I said, "Okay." I'm not a Catholic or anything, but I didn't want to make a picture that would turn the whole Catholic people against it, so I sold it to Zanuck. And he made it. And it wasn't any good.
KAWIN: I remember it wasn't very good, but I was struck by the fact that it was another one of these downed pilot stories. I wondered if you or Faulkner got in on it from the aviation angle. Can you talk about that part of your friendship?
HAWKS: The only thing that I had anything to do with that was I got mad at him one day and I said, "Stop writing about these goddamned hillbillies that you know down there." "Who should I write about?" And I said, "Well, you ought to know about people *flying*."
KAWIN: Mm hmm.

HAWKS: "Oh yeah," he said, "I know—two men and a girl—the girl and one of the men were wing-walkers and [*laughs*] the other was the pilot. She was pregnant and she didn't know which one." I said, "That's a good story. Write it." So he wrote *Pylon*, through the eyes of a drunken reporter—who was Bill himself.

KAWIN: Sure.

HAWKS: I didn't want to make it into a movie or anything. I didn't tell him that. One of the best movies I ever saw was written around a circus where the three guys were on trapeze. It wasn't the *Trapeze* film Burt Lancaster made—it was the one the Germans made.

KAWIN: Oh, *Variety*.

HAWKS: Um hmm. But sometimes I'd cook up something that I'd want—you know—I knew Faulkner needed some money. He bought an airplane. His brother killed himself in it.

KAWIN: Wasn't that before he came to Hollywood, or very early?

HAWKS: It was early, yeah. I'll tell you when it was—it was just before we made the war picture, *The Road to Glory*. It was just before he came on and did the script of *Road to Glory*—because he came on. He told me after it was over and he got drunk and walked into Zanuck's office and everything, he said, "I don't think I've done my best work. There's no mortician in the town and my brother was my mother's—was the apple of my mother's eye and I had to paint his face up and make him look presentable." He came from that to working on *Road to Glory*, and he wanted to get drunk but he didn't. Of course, then, he was swayed quite a bit by a girl—I don't know whether you know about that.

KAWIN: No.

HAWKS: Jule Styne, the guy—head of the Music Corporation—his daughter, very bright, brilliant kid, very studious, adored him for his writing and everything. He rather liked the adoration of the young girl. Bill had a car that the upholstery was gone—you sat on the springs or put a blanket on the springs. It would carry fishing tackle, and we'd go up and go fishing and all. He was a good shot. We had a lot of fun on that dove thing. Gable was a good shot, so was Bill, and I was too. I'd start through a field, you know, and we could get damn near everything we shot at.

KAWIN: I'm curious about why you didn't make any films from Faulkner's novels. You just made the one short story, "Turn About."

HAWKS: I think it would have been difficult for me to have told the story of any of Faulkner's novels. The one that I think that I could have told, but it was so goddamned censorable—

KAWIN: You mean *Sanctuary*?

HAWKS: Yes—I liked that. Making movies is a job and I preferred to make things that I thought I could do an awfully good job on, for the simple reason that you can fall to the bottom or stay up on top.

KAWIN: In *The Road to Glory*, *Today We Live*, and several other films, you tell the story of two men and a girl and one of the men is blind. I want to know where that came from. There is also that blind artist in *Land of the Pharaohs*, and the theme shows up in several of your other films. I think it first shows up in *Today We Live* and I want to know whether that was mainly your idea or Faulkner's, since it shows up consistently in the films you made together.

HAWKS: I think I must have decided to do that—it's always to me been a very very dramatic thing. The audiences seem to think so too.

KAWIN: Yes, it does work.

HAWKS: You see, when somebody says you copy yourself a lot, I just say well, any story that Hemingway writes he's certainly copying himself. Anything Bill Faulkner writes—anything that Picasso paints or anything like that, I don't say I'm as good as those, but I say I have a perfect right to copy my own stuff. I found it's good. Hell, you can't tell—I have used scenes two or three times when they fit into the story. There are *not—many—stories*. I counted one time just for fun and found there are about 30 stories. And even they copy each other—those stories. So I've found that ones that are in a different thing, they seem to go very very well. For instance, a man said to me, I mean wrote about me one time and he said that he had always believed in my stuff because it had always been believable until I made *Only Angels Have Wings*, and then "Hawks carried his imagination too goddamned far." I wrote him a letter and I said I had about 10,000 flying hours and I knew flyers. There's not one single piece or thing that I made up in that picture—everything is *absolutely* true.

KAWIN: Even those women who come in and interfere with the male world?

HAWKS: Well, I was flying with a bush pilot looking for duck down in Mexico, and I had an idea for a Mexican story, and I had dinner with a group that were very interesting. One guy had been in a fire in an airplane. He had no expression on his face—it was all semi-scar tissue—just a marvelous pair of eyes. And they were giving a dinner for one of the boys that had met a little girl who had been in a tab[4]

---

4 He may have said "tap."

	show and stopped on a steamer in a port on a Grace Line boat and got tight with this flyer and fucked with him and stayed there and married him. So that's the whole story, for instance, of that.
KAWIN:	Sure.
HAWKS:	And I told him, I said, there was something I couldn't use because at the dinner this fellow with the face with no expression got up and said to his friend, "This is your anniversary dinner we are giving you and a year ago tonight you got married. You got into bed about two minutes after three—you left the bed for about three or four minutes, then went back to bed about three times during the night." And the girl said, "You son of a bitch, you were peeking." And he said, "No," and he brought out a graph that was in an electrical thing made by the Germans to time an engine: when it bounced for take-off or anything it would make a mark. When it got into the air it made another kind of mark. And he took that thing and hung it over the bed and the girl was just tickled and she said, "When I'm 60 years old, I'll look at this." She put it right up on her mantelpiece! Now I didn't use that. But the Richard Barthelmess character, I saw him jump out of an airplane and I was driving along and I saw this big plane—smoke started coming out of it and everything. They were doing it for a movie. There were a couple of cloud layers so I couldn't see much. I saw a parachute blossom. I knew there were two people in the plane because one of them had to be throwing out the soot and the other one had to be flying. I waited for the other guy to come through and he never came through and I got over to the orange grove that it fell in and the one guy who landed, he was all right, the other guy was dead in the back, so he'd walked out and left him. And that fellow didn't have any friends after that. He spent the rest of his life—he got killed in an airplane under a parachute that somebody gave him that didn't open. He hit[5] in the street and I had to fly around 15 or 20 minutes to get my legs back in working order before landing because they were shaking so much, you know. Everything—the bird coming through the windshield, I saw the airplane that it came through—it dented the thing behind the co-pilot. The take-off from the little place was a place we'd found up in Idaho. We landed so short—I'd borrowed Amelia Earhart's plane that day—and it crashed when it landed. We were perfectly all right. We took down the motor, but there was no way of getting that outfit to that plateau. So I said, "That was true," I said, "I could go

---

5 He may have said "lit."

	on all night long—the death was true—the business of the girl who thought that these guys were callous in not paying any attention, that was true. I saw all that." So the critic said, "Well, I'm face to face with the fact a great deal of your stuff must come from the truth," and I said, "It does." The death of that guy—I saw it. He said, "I feel kind of funny," and I said, "Your neck's broke." And he said, "I saw a picture Hawks made where Pancho Villa wanted Johnny to make up his mind what his last words were going to be."
KAWIN:	Wallace Beery, right?
HAWKS:	Yeah. And the reporter found him in a butcher shop with his head on a side of beef—and made up the thing where he said, "Forgive me, my Mexico. I have done you wrong because I loved you," or something like that. I just finished that. I mean the boy who died, he said he'd just seen that picture and he didn't know what he was going to say. His best friend said, "You want us to get out of here?" and he said, "I wish you would," and they walked away and let him die. I added to it about the rain, you know, and stuff. I dressed it up a little bit. But it's perfectly true, and I did it again in *Rio Lobo*. It's a hell of a good way to die. So, all of this adds up to I don't give a god damn if people say you've used it before.
KAWIN:	Of course not.
HAWKS:	People find a similarity in the girls too. Well, if you like a certain kind of girl and that's the only kind of a girl that you like, what would *you* write about? I said, "That's the kind of girl that I like." And so naturally I used it. And, of course, with Faulkner several times I said, "Bill, you know I've done this scene before. Tell me how you would do it." And we'd find another way of doing it. Same scene, but a different way of doing it.
KAWIN:	What sort of things did he think of? What kind of changes did he make?
HAWKS:	Oh, I don't know, some of them are so minor.
KAWIN:	Let me pose something to you and you can tell me if I am wrong or not. When I read *The Sound and the Fury*, okay, or *As I Lay Dying*, or whatever, one of the things that really strikes me is that he cuts suddenly from one scene to another, that the novels are being cinematic and that he will go from, say, Benjy crawling under a fence when he's 30, to Benjy getting out the other side of the fence when he's eight.
HAWKS:	Uh-huh.
KAWIN:	Then he'll go back again and so on. That's always struck me as the kind of thing you find in films like *Hiroshima mon amour*—it's that same

kind of cutting. And in *The Wild Palms* he talks about Eisenstein. So it's always seemed to me that he *must* have known something about film construction. He might have had that in the back of his head when he was writing those novels even before he started to write for films. Did he ever talk to you about any of that?

HAWKS: Well, when we first met, he asked me how I'd go to work on a film. I said, "The first thing that I want is a story. The next thing that I want is character." "Well," he said, "I like the way you tell a story." I said, "Okay, I jump to anything that I think is interesting. There are only a few plots, so I have to dress the thing up." I talked to an author the other day about a Western story. He wrote a story about a man and a great friend who had caught a bunch of wild horses and broken them, and he'd gone into town and he'd come back and his friend was killed and the horses were gone. Well, he walked into town and he saw the brand, his own, and he killed a very important man. They chased him all the way through. It was really a short story—now it's short, but it allows me a chance to put in all kinds of things and still get a good solid story. The average story that you write, or a story like *Rich Man, Poor Man*, is a hell of a lot better told in 12 episodes than it would be, you know, in two hours. When I was in Europe skiing—I didn't make any pictures for two or three years—the first thing that I saw when I came back was television, and how they had teasers, you know what I mean, to get you interested. So I said, "I'm going to do some of that," and I did it in *Rio Bravo*. There are no words spoken.

KAWIN: Yes, I remember that.

HAWKS: It's a hell of a good opening. And I did that before I went into the main titles of the thing, just like the television.

KAWIN: And now everybody's doing that.

HAWKS: Oh, sure, but nobody saw it in a movie until I did that thing. And it planted things very well. And then people said to me, "Why did Dean Martin kick John Wayne?" and I said, "Well, I don't know whether you've ever been good friends with somebody, but if one of my good friends sneered at me the way Wayne sneered at Dean Martin, *I'd* hit the son of a bitch." And they said, "Okay, okay, you've explained it." [*Laughs*] But the audiences like that kind of stuff.

KAWIN: So you're telling Faulkner that this is the kind of story you want him to do?

HAWKS: Yeah. And he *liked* it. I imagine it affected him somewhat. When I started in using this round-the-corner telling of things, Noel

Coward says, "I've been wanting to talk to you. What do you *call* that dialogue that you use?" "Well," I said, "Hemingway calls it oblique and I call it three-cushion. Where you bounce the ball against one cushion, it goes to another cushion, comes back over here and gets right back to where it is." "Well," he said, "I just want to tell you that I think that you write the best dialogue of any guy that I know of," and I said, "That coming from you—you don't even mind the fact that I've stolen from you?" He said, "Not a bit." And Ford and I used to have an awful lot of fun when he came down here to die. I played golf, and they'd say to him, "Howard Hawks is out there," and he'd say, "Tell him to come in," and he'd start laughing and I'd say, "What the hell are you laughing about?" "I was just remembering some of the things I'd stolen from you," he said. So I had a lot of fun remembering the things that I'd stolen and both of us were pleased that the other guy would steal from him. And Faulkner said, "I have no qualms at all about stealing from you. I think it's good stuff."

KAWIN: I figured *Pylon* came from you.

HAWKS: *Pylon* did come from me. And I think it was probably one of the least valuable of his novels. A little too modern—a little too—he was able to express himself better in some of the other things that he did.

KAWIN: And he never decided to experiment, then, with writing a film that would be constructed in the way his novels were?

HAWKS: He never—he worked at Warner Brothers to get some money. He went home, he came back and went to work again for $300 a week when they were paying a good writer a thousand or $1,500 or more.

KAWIN: Furthman would get that, wouldn't he?

HAWKS: Yes, he was very well paid. Probably because Furthman could only work with Vic Fleming and myself. Everybody hated him so, but we sort of liked him because everybody hated him. And one day in the Metro commissary Fleming picked him up and carried him out of doors and dumped him on the grass and said, "Don't come back and come near me."

KAWIN: What was it about him that was so obnoxious?

HAWKS: Everybody hated him. Nobody liked him. Oh, I don't know, he was just kind of obnoxious—he was—he had a strange life. He was married to a beautiful girl. They had a baby—turned out to be a moron—great *big* moron—didn't recognize anybody. Uhh-uhh-uhh, you know, and it would yell and everything. They had to move from a beautiful home in Bel Air and he went down and bought some property outside of Culver City. It turned out to be the most valuable manufacturing property there was. So he had a couple of million dollars' worth of property. And he was *very* [*laughs*]—if he didn't think anybody had any talent, Christ Almighty, he was a bad person to work for. He wrote for Joe von Sternberg.

KAWIN: What did he think of Faulkner? Did they get on?

HAWKS: Oh, yeah, sure, *they* got on okay. But the average writer, he—In *To Have and To Have Not* he wrote a story where Lauren Bacall had her purse stolen. He wrote a good scene about it and brought it in—very pleased with himself. "What do you think?" I said, "Well, Jules, there's a thing I always get a hard-on about—I get a complete erection for a little girl who's had her purse stolen." "You big son of a *bitch*," he said, and he stalked out and he came back the next day and wrote a scene where she stole a purse.

KAWIN: Yeah, a wallet.

HAWKS: It was eight times as good. And I used to treat him that way, you know, to get him to work, because he did such damned fine work. Good work—because of opposites. When I finish a script I deliberately go over it to see how it would work if it was done the opposite way. That's why the gunman in *Rio Bravo* is a kid who's awfully good, and the one in *El Dorado* couldn't shoot at all. It makes it a little more logical, you know what I mean? Everything works out good if you do it the opposite way. For instance, Cary Grant in *I Was a Male War Bride*—we'd looked forward to doing this scene when the sergeant had to ask Cary the questions that were made for a French girl who's going to marry a G.I. And we rehearsed it and he looked at me and I was looking at him and I said, "Cary, why did we ever think this was funny?" "Goddamned if I know." And I said, "There has to be some way—wait a minute, Cary—you shouldn't be the one embarrassed. You're a man of the world. You should enjoy the poor bastard who has to ask all these questions." And I said, "Okay, you two are stupid sons of bitches—you rewrite the scene," and they went off and rewrote the scene and came back in 15 minutes, and did the dialogue. A complete flop-over. The sergeant was embarrassed and Cary would say, "Go on, there are some good ones coming." And very often you can—I like the way *El Dorado* started with Wayne shooting the boy in the stomach. And the boy killing himself because it hurt so much. I thought that that was very real. And then the fact that he'd throw a dead boy over a horse, bring him in and say, "Here's your boy."

KAWIN: That's a very fine story.
HAWKS: That's a good *situation*, you know. And then his getting wounded by a girl brought the girl into the story. Made him feel that he owed the MacDonalds something. He killed their son, you know, and everything. That's my idea of the way people work.
KAWIN: I missed your point about Furthman.
HAWKS: Well, Faulkner and I were the same about doing opposites. I worked with Faulkner well, and if he did something that was corny, I could check him up and he'd take it. He'd get mad for a moment then go off and write it. Then he wrote good. And he didn't get mad when I changed stuff on him at all. Matter of fact, none of the writers that I worked with did. I'd just tell them, "Look, there's two ways of doing this thing. I don't happen to know how to do it but one way, so it'll come out the same thing." And, you know, it'll shape up.
KAWIN: Did you know that Furthman did a screenplay of a Faulkner story in 1932?
HAWKS: No, what did he do?
KAWIN: The story called "Honor." It's very similar to *Pylon*.
HAWKS: Oh yeah, did they ever make it?
KAWIN: No, they've still got it in the vault.
HAWKS: I've got it here, too.
KAWIN: Oh, you do?
HAWKS: Yeah. I was looking at it the other day and I thought I didn't think it's been made.
KAWIN: That might be worth making. Certainly a lot of talent went into it.
HAWKS: Well, it would be very easy for me to dictate a story *from* it that would work with it, you know, because it doesn't take me very long if I know a story to change it so that you would never recognize it.
KAWIN: I wanted to ask you something else about aviation. So many of the things that Faulkner wrote that weren't produced are about aviation one way or the other. There would be two old friends and one of them will be a pilot or both of them will be pilots. You used that in *Today We Live* and I also found it in a treatment he wrote earlier called *Absolution*, and quite a few other places. And there was a Latin American kingdom story he made up that looks so much like *For Whom the Bell Tolls*, except it's about pilots.
HAWKS: Well, in the ghost story that he wrote, aviation played a part. Faulkner was very interested in aviation.
KAWIN: Was there a reason he specifically did so much of that in film?
HAWKS: He liked to play—I mean he liked to fly—I don't think he ever fought in one. There are very few people who fought in the first

war in airplanes. I had about an hour, about an hour and a half in an airplane before I went into the ground school—into flying, you know. We were down in Texas and there were at least 2,000 cadets down there and seven airplanes, and they didn't have enough instructors or anything. An instructor took me out and did the usual speech about showing me a wrapped-up wrench. He sat in the back seat and if you grabbed the stick, why you get hit over the head. And after I made about four good landings—after the second time I went out they made me an instructor—after an hour and three quarters! And I was just as good as anybody else—this was the beginning of flying. Faulkner was in some kind of a French thing. I don't think that he flew in combat. Willy Wellman flew.

KAWIN: Do you think Faulkner just happened to write about flying because he thought it was a good subject for pictures or was he assigned aviation pictures because he was a pilot?

HAWKS: I don't know. Faulkner knew aviation—people knew he wrote for Hawks on aviation, so it was one of those things. And they didn't understand a lot of—oh, you know—his other kind of stuff.

KAWIN: So, you have these two unpublished works? The vampire and the ghost stories?

HAWKS: Yeah, but I can't show them to you now. I'm having them Xeroxed.

KAWIN: Can you send them to me when you get them back?

HAWKS: Oh, sure. A guy at *Playboy* heard about them and offered me quite a bit of money for them, to publish them. And then I could sell them to pictures or anything like that, you know.

KAWIN: Yeah.

HAWKS: I don't know—I'll probably show them to an agent. Matter of fact, my daughter is a literary agent.

KAWIN: Your brother was an agent too, wasn't he?

HAWKS: Yeah, and I hate agents. [*Laughter*] My brother came out. He was the youngest man ever put in charge of an E. F. Hutton office. And I wrote him a letter saying, "You're a goddamned sick man. You should come out here and be an agent. They make more money, and can be stupid in order to do it." He had a great big agency in a year—made $100,000 or something like that. Then he wanted to produce, and I said, "What?" And he said, "Well, I haven't got a story." And I said, "Then you won't be any good as a producer because anybody who wants to really produce is going to have two or three stories that he wants to do." And, sure enough, the first picture he could have had Ronnie Colman, who was

	the biggest—oh—they made a lousy picture. The only good one they made that they made a lot of money on was called *The Tall Man*. And I said, "Why don't you make *Red River* up in the snow?" So that picture made quite a lot of money. If somebody tells you they want to be a producer, they better have some stories that they want to do. If somebody tells you they want to direct, they better have something they want to do, too. And my youngest boy is 20—he's got a story that he wants to make about that guy that was in the race down in Mexico and got lost. Well, Dick Schickel wrote about it in the *New Yorker*, so I wrote Dick and asked if I could get it. He said, "Howard, Ray Stark just gave me some money to go to work on it." And I said, "Dick, do you know anything about motorcycle racing? Well, when you decide not to make it, let me know." [*Laughter*] And they decided not to make it, but my kid has been lost on the desert, and has ridden in dozens of desert races. And he's good mechanically, so he can figure out the mounts and how to get cars out there. As a matter of fact, he's going up next week to get a race car I put together out of a Blazer. I think that's a picture of it over there.
KAWIN:	Oh.
HAWKS:	And that race—the first one we ever made—he was way ahead of his class at the halfway point. Parnelli Jones came in and said, "I was chasing that goddamned kid of yours," he said, "I couldn't catch him." [*Laughs*] He had some mechanical trouble on the way but he still came in third place. So, what I mean is, you do stuff out of what you know how to do. And my brother didn't have any idea—
KAWIN:	He was Faulkner's Hollywood agent, wasn't he?
HAWKS:	Oh, I would tell him people to sign, you know. He was a good agent. But I guess it got boring to him, you know—so he took to producing-directing. Sort of wanted to do what I was doing—you know, I had produced and directed most of the things I had made, especially in the 1940s. I don't know how you tell a good director—I know that Peter Bogdanovich was going to be damned good for a while if he held it—you never can tell. My daughter went around with Bill Friedkin in New York. Once he asked me what I thought of his last picture—*The Boys in the Band*.
KAWIN:	Yes, I know that story, and you told him that it was no good and that he ought to make a chase picture, which turned out to be *The French Connection*.
HAWKS:	Well, if you make a good picture, you can always find somebody that's gonna hire you. If you make a bad one, I don't care how artistic it is, you're not going to get anybody to hire you.

KAWIN: I want to ask you a question about *Land of the Pharaohs*. The woman in that film, Joan Collins, is *such* a heavy that she seems different from the heroines of your films but reminds me of some of Faulkner's female villains. What's the story on her?

HAWKS: Well, let's say that we started out and made up a story and said that the girl would double-cross the Pharaoh and everything. Immediately I start to make somebody the heavy: in reactions, in making scenes, in double-crossing, everything. And I really carried it too far—*everybody*—you didn't like *anybody*.

KAWIN: So was this all your doing? What were Faulkner and that playwright doing all this time?

HAWKS: Oh, we talked about it later, you know. When I work with a writer we talk it over in the morning; they go off and write it in the afternoon; then we talk it over. There's no sense in going through a lot of extra writing. And I haven't found anybody, you know—when they're writing a thing like *The Big Sleep* that's written by a great man—they're just going to make a *scenario* out of it—and I can change afterwards or do anything I want to, you know. But I mean when you're writing on an original story—

KAWIN: Yeah. On the subject, do you know what Faulkner thought of women?

HAWKS: Well, I saw him with this one girl that I told you about before. The girl he married turned into a *drunk*, so I don't think that helped him in his ideas of women.

KAWIN: I guess not.

HAWKS: A complete drunk. But he was perfectly normal in his admiration of them. And perfectly normal in *not* liking a lot of them. [*Laughter*] Who was it—oh yes—Loretta Young started to discuss things with him about *The Left Hand of God*, and boy, did he put her in her place in no time.

KAWIN: How?

HAWKS: I don't remember exactly, but it was a marvelous answer. I think it was, "Miss, if everybody thought the way you do, every picture would be a sort of a do-gooder and it would be a lousy business." You know what I mean. He didn't have to choose or anything because he was doing a story that was a pretty good story. I was the one that didn't want to do it. Because of what that priest had said to me. You see, if you can't make it the way it's written, if you have to slide over things, you know what I mean—you haven't got a good scene. Now *Male War Bride* was one example of that. I told Zanuck that I thought it was a good story when he told me about it. He got a

	script out and wanted me to read the script. We sat on opposite sides of his swimming pool which was over here about two blocks away. Joe Schenck came in. I said hello to him. "What you fellows doing?" I said, "We're reading a script." And Joe was there when I went over and told him I thought it was a lousy script and how I thought it ought to be done. Joe spoke up and said, "Howard, if you're going to do it—" and I said, "No, I don't want to." "Well," he said, "don't you think you can make a good picture out of it?" "Yes, but I don't particularly want to do it." "Well," he said, "I've done you some favors, haven't I?" I said, "Yes, you have," and he said, "Okay, you do me this favor and do this picture!" I said, "Okay, Joe, you write the contract yourself." Well [*laughs*], Cary Grant got yellow jaundice, and I got $10,000 a week while I was waiting. [*Laughter*]
KAWIN:	Pretty soft.
HAWKS:	Joe Schenck wrote the script,[6] and I can't complain about how much I got paid for that picture. Anyway—
KAWIN:	Let me ask you—out of the number of books written about you, is there any one that you think is most true?
HAWKS:	I thought Robin Wood had about as good—there's an Iranian translation of Robin Wood's here if you want to read it.
KAWIN:	That's all right.
HAWKS:	They've asked me to come over there—they want to run about 20–25 pictures that I made. And they want me to make a picture or a couple of pictures backed by Iranian oil money. Which I would like—but I told them that I had a story where one sequence ought to be in Iran because it was about men who hunt for oil. And they wanted to pay my way over there to talk about it—but I said, "Look, if you really want to make a picture with me, I've got to meet on my own grounds," because I've got to have people that can tell them what it means. I said, "Life's too short for me to go into all that." Some Germans came over—they've got tax money that they want to invest. They wanted a *budget*. Well, a budget takes time—it takes two weeks to make it. You have to pay a lot for it, you know. I said, "If you want a budget, it will cost you $1,000." And they got the budget, and were very happy and pleased about it. They've got the tax money over there.
KAWIN:	Do you have a picture to make with them?
HAWKS:	Yeah—two or three of them. They'd like to make them all. But, I feel that if—I hate working with amateurs. I have to work too

---

6 He meant "the contract."

KAWIN: hard—do too many things. I have to follow it through, you know—after cutting. I have to engage the musicians, even the advertising.

KAWIN: Hmm.

HAWKS: They advertised *Hatari* like a bunch of school boys on a—

KAWIN: I remember that.

HAWKS: You remember that?

KAWIN: Yes. I *particularly* remember the advertising.

HAWKS: I went back to New York and I said, "Now you've got to change that advertising." They said, "Oh my God, Howard, we're all tied up here." I liked the man I talked to, so I said, "You let me do the stuff in Europe and I won't say anything about it." Well, I'm sorry that I didn't [do all of it] because the picture deserved a whole lot better than it got over here. But it made most of its money in Europe. But you have to do those things and you have to keep track of the financial things and you're so goddamned busy. My lawyer and I were partners for a while. I asked him in so he'd do the things that—but he hadn't studied to be a lawyer yet—but he had all the money that he needed in the world and he didn't have to say yes to anybody, so I thought he'd make a good partner. And he took *whole loads* off my shoulders. His father was the greatest advertising man in the country. Albert Lasker—you may have heard of him. When he finally stopped, he gave his entire thing to the Mormons—the furniture even. Turned it all over to them. So the first thing Ed Lasker did was to tell me his father was this brilliant advertising—he said, "I'd like to take the picture of yours called *The Thing* and do the advertising for it."

KAWIN: Yes, I remember the advertising for *The Thing*. It was *first* class.

HAWKS: But if I do something with the Germans, I have to work too hard. I have to work *after* the picture's finished! Now where were we?

KAWIN: You and Faulkner.

HAWKS: Well, let me answer you this way. I don't think Faulkner knew anything about films when he came.

KAWIN: Did he go to films while he was here?

HAWKS: I don't think he went to films. But he learned afterwards and he learned from me what I was trying to do, and that made his writing for films easier, you know.

KAWIN: Yes.

HAWKS: I was very pleased that he had respect for my—he liked it very much. And I told him why I couldn't—why I didn't want to make some of his novels, like the novel that he wrote about God protecting the pregnant woman.

KAWIN: *Light in August?*

HAWKS: I can't remember titles. Anyway, she traveled all around and was protected while she was looking for the father.
KAWIN: Yeah, that's *Light in August*. Why didn't you want to make that?
HAWKS: That's not my stuff. I don't know how they could have done that. I choose stories that I think I can tell and very often people won't think anything of them until they see them made.
KAWIN: The one novel he was really upset about—the one he really wanted to sell to the movies was *Absalom, Absalom!* He wrote a treatment of it but apparently it was so poor that his friends urged him to withdraw it.
HAWKS: He had a purely native gift of writing—not a studied gift or anything like that. He just lived in a little town all by himself and wrote—some of the stuff he wrote was awfully good. I think that when he wrote *Sanctuary* he did it for the money. He wrote the dirtiest book he could think of to do and he said, "I got paid for it. The publisher took all the money and I never made a penny out of it. That taught me that I shouldn't do that kind of thing."
KAWIN: So he decided to write for money under contract?
HAWKS: Well, he got a crook who ran off with all the money, so there was nothing left to get. So he wrote about his own—he knew those people. I only know that he worked on some things for me, you know, that he liked. And he worked on a lot of things he didn't like. Not for me, though.
KAWIN: Do you remember any he especially didn't like?
HAWKS: Oh, a lot of those bad pictures that Warner Brothers had. As long as it wasn't costing them anything, you know, they could get a scenario for under $2,000, so they could take a chance and throw it away, and that's it. But as I say, very often—I made five pictures with Cary Grant and he didn't like the idea for any of them. Then we'd go to the preview and we'd meet afterwards and Cary would get on his knees and come crawling over and say, "I apologize, I apologize."
KAWIN: That must have been something to see.
HAWKS: Well, it's just—you know—Wayne's never liked any of the Western scripts. And when Wayne made *The Alamo* I said, "That girl is excellent," and I rewrote the part of the girl...it was a very interesting girl but Wayne said, "I don't know how to do that stuff, Howard, you—you can do it, but I have to stick to the corn"—and God knows he did! Jack Ford and I told him he should cut 50 minutes out of *The Alamo*. He took it off to preview it and he came back and said, "The audience told me you were wrong."

"Where did you take it to?" "Oh, a big town in Minneapolis," or something like that. "How many previews do they have there?" "This was the first one." I said, "You think an audience like that is going to tell you anything about it?" And he put the picture out at hard tickets, you know. We were just about to make *Hatari*. "Well," I said, "I've got a friend who's one of the great salesmen in the country and he'll sell your picture." I asked him, he said he'd like to look at it. And he said to me, "It's *not* a reserved seat picture—it needs 50 minutes or an hour taken out of it." And I told Duke. It cost him $50,000 to $60,000 to change the music. We took the 50 minutes out and he got his money back. He didn't make a fortune but he got his money back and he was goddamned lucky he did because he started putting it in down in Arizona and everything he touched turned to gold. Now he's quite a rich man. Jack Ford and I did the cutting in no time at all. We'd seen the picture before. Because I have no respect for my own work—I cut things out *all* the time.

KAWIN: How much do you usually cut out when a picture's finished? In *The Big Sleep*, for instance, it looked to me as if you had shot the entire script and then drastically cut out scenes to make it less than two hours. You leave out a sign that indicates Eddie Mars's casino is over the Nevada line, but you show Bogart and Bacall driving back from the casino across the Mojave Desert as if you had originally meant to indicate that they would have been driving as far as Nevada.

HAWKS: Well, I figure most of that out *before*hand. Usually I run a picture two days after I've finished with that picture. Just as long as it takes to get the film. Then I run it and I say, "Take this out, take that out." It only takes a few days.

KAWIN: Can you summarize what you got from Faulkner and what he got from you?

HAWKS: Well, I got help whenever I wanted it from Faulkner. And I never knew him to miss. Just when I thought that I was going wrong, you know, I'd have a scene where I didn't know what the hell to do, I got a good answer from him. I got help in writing, and we were damned good friends, and we had fun together, you know. Just like the help that I got from Hemingway. He said, "You can't make a movie out of that." So we sat there fishing for ten days and talked about it. When I came home, it was nothing to do the script. And I enjoyed Bill—that's the whole thing. And, as I told you, I think, I was one of the first people to appreciate him. He was working in Macy's basement where they didn't pay him too much.

KAWIN: My father started out packing books in the May Company—I know how much they pay.

HAWKS: Is that a fact? Bill's automobile was an old open Ford with the springs showing but it chugged around—it got around all right. He didn't have toilets in his town. And he enjoyed being out here for the very simple reason that his wife was a dipsomaniac. And also he was a very very shy man. Very shy. After he became more or less famous he had no trouble standing up for himself, you know, or taking care of himself or making an answer. He lost all fear of that. But I'm sure I was the first one to buy a story from him. And the first one that wanted to work with him. We became friends.

KAWIN: That's why I came to *you*.

HAWKS: [*Laughs*] I think there've been some other things about Faulkner where people haven't come to me and they have made a ridiculous story. The state of Mississippi had a script about him. You know, they were very proud that he lived there and they want to make a tribute to him. It will be a semi-documentary. I wrote them back, and I said, "You haven't written about *Faulkner*. You've just written about some idealized character." I said, "He was a *drunk*," you know. After I got to know him—when he got drunk I wouldn't have anything to do with him. I'd get a doctor or nurse and wait until he got sober again. I'd had experience with drunks before. One of the most brilliant men I ever worked with was a drunk. The work at Paramount was too goddamned much. He would choose the most inopportune times to get drunk. He didn't drink usually, and those are the guys you have to watch out for. I saved his life for a long time, but he was just a falling down gutter drunk.

KAWIN: So you thought this Mississippi documentary was idealized?

HAWKS: Well, they didn't write that he drank. You know, they made him out of an author. They didn't know why he wrote, they didn't know anything about him.

KAWIN: Did you know why he wrote?

HAWKS: Yes, he liked to write and he found that he got started—I told you the experiences of these men—they could make any writer—those men in New York: Charles Walcott, a whole bunch of those fellows—some Irish guys, a guy that ran the *New Yorker*. They could make somebody by just starting to talk about him, and before they'd realized it and gotten around to it, I read the *Saturday Evening Post* story and bought it. I just sent him a check for it and told him I wanted to make it, and Thalberg would let me do anything, but I didn't like working at Metro a bit. Well, like the thing of putting

KAWIN:	a girl into that story *Turn About*. They only did it because Thalberg was away. Sometimes you get stuck—and I didn't like the man—I didn't like Louis B. Mayer at all. When I worked on—
KAWIN:	Who was it exactly who put Crawford into that film?
HAWKS:	Oh, a couple of the producers, you know. The men who planned the sales said, "We've got to have a picture with Joan Crawford. Howard can do it." So I got stuck with doing it.
KAWIN:	When you planned the picture first, then, what did you do? What were your first plans for the film if you didn't have the Joan Crawford character in it?
HAWKS:	Didn't do anything different, except there weren't any of the Joan Crawford scenes.
KAWIN:	You still had Ronnie going blind, and so forth?
HAWKS:	Still the same story—every bit of it with the two boys. But what gummed up the story was when they told me Crawford was going to be in it. I used to go around with her when she first came out here. We're still very good friends. And they said, "By the way, Joan's down in the commissary waiting to talk to you." And I went down there and Joan said, "Is it true that there's no girl in your story?" Tears started to fall into her coffee cup and I said, "Now, look, I don't think you can get out of this. I don't think I can get out of this. We both have contracts. You can make it absolutely miserable unless you accept this well. And if you start taking it miserably, those are the kind of scenes you're gonna make. I mean to tell you now that I don't give a god damn what we do." Well, she promised me she would pin a flower in my lapel and give me a kiss each day before we started work, and she was just great. But she read the dialogue that the boys had—which was Faulkner's dialogue—and she wanted dialogue like that. And that subtracted from them being, you know, so emotional. And also the clothes that she wore—Jesus Christ!
KAWIN:	There's a scene that you cut out of *The Big Sleep* that I want to ask you about. In the novel you remember the scene where Marlowe's been out with Vivian and there's Carmen naked in the bed and he throws her out. But while he's arguing with her he plays with a chessboard that's on the table and then he says to himself, "This is no game for knights." When that scene was done over for the script, he didn't play with the knight, and of course Carmen is dressed for the sake of the censors, and she starts to bite her thumb. He tells her to stop biting her thumb and she shows him that it is not her thumb—that in fact she is sucking on the white queen. He gets angry

and knocks it out of her hand. So that switches the emphasis from chivalric behavior, what's expected of a knight or a hero or a good detective, to the issue of Carmen's promiscuity—her unmaidenly behavior—from male honor to female dishonor.

HAWKS: Well, she was my idea of a nymphomaniac. And I thought I cast her very well.

KAWIN: Oh, yes.

HAWKS: Those big eyes. Looks like a little virgin. And, of course, she ends up the heavy. I probably just didn't like that scene very much. I don't remember whether we substituted or what.

KAWIN: Well, in what you left, he's playing with Carmen and you make it clear that it's a seduction scene but he just throws her out. She bangs on the door and he goes back, I think, to working on the code book. It's a short scene. The interesting thing is that at the end of this scene, in the novel, Marlowe tears the bed apart in a rage because she's been in it. And in the screenplay this scene ends with his taking the white queen and smashing it in the fireplace with fire dogs, and it goes to fade-out. The script kept his rage. You know, it's the one place in the whole story where he breaks.

HAWKS: Hm hmm.

KAWIN: And in the film he never breaks. You lose that sense that somewhere in the course of his involvement with this crazy family, he starts to crack. In fact, I thought you made a poor decision.

HAWKS: I don't think I liked it. I was dealing with a situation whereby, for instance, the—I met the New York critics after I made that picture and I got up to talk to about 30 of them. I said, "I've just made a picture that I don't think you'll like." "Why won't we like it?" "Well," I said, "if you're going down the street in an automobile and you put out your hand to make a left turn and then you turn left, you come to a stop sign and you stop, and you put your hand for a right turn or you [*makes a right-turn signal with his left hand*]—if the picture had all the things right in it and makes exactly the right moves and it's all very clear, you know what to write about. But you're *not* going to know what to write about this goddamned picture!" I got the best reviews I've ever gotten. [*Laughter*] It's just like Dick Schickel, the guy who made *The Men Who Made the Movies*. He called me up the other day and said, "I just want to tell you that your episode has about three or four times the demand of the others." I said, "That's very nice." He said, "I just want to apologize." I said, "Why, Dick?" and he said, "I completely left out your comedies." "Well," I said, "that's just par for a good critic. You don't know what makes a thing funny."

KAWIN: Yeah.

HAWKS: "So you don't write about it. I don't know what makes the thing funny. I make it 'cause it's funny to me." And he started to laugh. I said, "Do you know *one* critic who has a real sense of humor, who knows why a thing is funny?" and he said, "No." So I said, "Well, then, don't apologize for it, you're just being a critic." He said, "Can I do a story on this?" [*Laughter*] I don't know whether you know that *Twentieth Century* and *Bringing Up Baby*, some of those things *didn't* get started well at all.

KAWIN: No…

HAWKS: Audiences didn't know why we were making them.

KAWIN: *Twentieth Century*!?

HAWKS: Yeah.

KAWIN: If I ever saw a *natural*, that was one.

HAWKS: Yeah, but it picked up—afterwards—but when it opened it was different, you see. Carole Lombard was brand new to pictures. I made it in three weeks.

KAWIN: No kidding?

HAWKS: Yeah.

KAWIN: It plays like you made it in two hours, it goes so fast.

HAWKS: Well, Lombard was a second cousin of mine. We were born in the same little town. She got me in the woodshed one Halloween night and locked me in. When Carole came out here I was the first person she came to. And I was making a movie at the time and she hung around the house a lot and she was absolutely marvelous—so completely—she said *anything* that came into her mind. A complete extrovert and just the opposite from what you'd think. She had some money—she didn't have to have a job. She dressed better than any starlet. Paramount gave her a contract. She could wear clothes so well, she was sort of a clotheshorse—she had five lines. I thought if I could get her to act the way she did when she was around the house—I don't know if you know about the story—I took her for a walk after the first rehearsal and I said, "Carole, you've done a lot of work, you know your lines perfectly. What do you get paid for in this picture? How much do you earn?" "$5,000." I said, "What do you get paid for?" "Well, *acting*." I said, "Supposing I tell you that you've earned the $5,000, you don't owe a nickel." She stared at me and I said, "What would you do if a man said such and such thing to you?" She said, "I'd kick him right in the balls." I said, "Barrymore says that, why don't you kick him? What [would] you do if a man says such and such?" and she waved her hand—you know—in a typical Lombard gesture.

KAWIN: Yeah.
HAWKS: "We're going back in there and we're making a take. And if you don't kick him right where you said you're going to, and if you don't wave your arm or something, you can do any goddamned thing, but if you don't stop *acting*, I'm going to fire you and get somebody else!" And she said, "You're serious?" and I said, "Yeah." So we went back and I said to Barrymore, "We're going to try a take." He said, "We're not ready," and I said, "Who's running it?" and he said, "You are." I said, "Okay, we're gonna do a take." She made a kick at him, he jumped back, protecting himself, started pointing at her and she ended the scene—it is about a 12-page scene—on her couch kicking at him like this [*kicks in the air*].
KAWIN: Right!
HAWKS: He was talking and finally he went off and made an exit and I said, "Cut, print it," and he came back in and he said, "That was magnificent. Have you been kidding me all this time?" and she broke into tears and ran off the stage. And he said, "Howard, what the Christ is going on around here?" So I told him what I'd done and everything. And he said, "Well, she's going to be a star—she's a cinch." And we made the picture in three weeks.
KAWIN: But the story you're telling is the story of the picture!
HAWKS: Hmm hmm. But, the critics didn't know what to do about those early comedies. Now they get good reviews, but very often in my pictures I guess that I've diverted—gone away from the usual stuff and put in some stuff that helped. For instance, *Scarface*—

At this point the recorder malfunctioned. The last half hour of the interview was lost. During that time Hawks spoke of his respect for Faulkner and of how much it gratified him that Faulkner respected him. I asked him whether he had ever introduced Hemingway and Faulkner to each other, and he said that he hadn't. He thought it was funny that Hemingway was always asking him about Faulkner and Faulkner about Hemingway, especially on their hunting and fishing trips. We also talked about Furthman's retarded child and how it was likely that Furthman warmed up to Faulkner because of the sympathetic portrait Faulkner drew of the idiot Benjy in The Sound and the Fury. *Hawks also emphasized that Faulkner had enjoyed working on pictures until his experience at Warner Bros. He told me that a good picture was one with four or five good scenes in it. We talked some about* Citizen Kane, *and he said that Welles had asked him to look at the picture. Hawks had said, "Well, this is your first picture, isn't it?" Welles had said, "Yes," and Hawks had said, "Well, why don't you make a few more and then we'll talk about it." Then he saw it and realized how good it was, and they had a talk, during which Welles admitted that he had had*

His Girl Friday on his mind while he was directing the newspaper sequences and that he had used Hawks's three-cushion dialogue throughout. Hawks also spoke about the French directors and critics who see so much in his work; he enjoyed talking to them but thought they were reading in a lot of meanings he didn't intend. Then I got his autograph and he went back to work, picking a script for his next picture.

Part V

LITERATURE AND NARRATION

14

THE MONTAGE ELEMENT IN FAULKNER'S FICTION

This paper was presented at the Faulkner and Yoknapatawpha conference at the University of Mississippi in the summer of 1978 and published in 1979 in the volume Faulkner, Modernism, and Film: Faulkner and Yoknapatawpha, 1978, *which was edited by the organizers of that extraordinary conference, Evans Harrington and Ann J. Abadie. Many of the points made here were made more briefly in my book* Faulkner and Film. *I had been told that Hugh Kenner would be in the audience and wrote this with him in mind.*

It should be noted that later scholarship discredited much of what both Pound and Eisenstein had to say about Asian writing systems (for example, one is rarely conscious of montage when reading an ideogram, although it is still reasonable to say that an ideogram has a montage structure); nevertheless, it remains interesting that the two men said much the same thing. La Pointe-Courte, *while decisively influenced by* The Wild Palms, *as Varda confirmed when I spoke with her at the Telluride Film Festival and on other occasions, has two cross-cut but not "parallel" plots, was co-edited by Resnais, and is "generally considered" a forerunner of the New Wave, not its first film. When writing about Faulkner's use of opposites, I should have brought in what Hawks said about opposites in the interview in this volume. Finally, Beckett's* Film *is overrated here as a reading of Keaton, and when I was talking a few years later with director Schneider, he emphasized that Keaton hated making it. The rest stands.*

The relations between literature and film are notoriously difficult to sort out. Writing goes back more than 4,000 years, film less than 85; some of the greatest literature of the twentieth century is regularly characterized as elitist and noncommercial, just as film is dismissed as populist and commercial; a book tends to be written by one person in solitude, and a feature film to be made by approximately 100 people under factory conditions; a word [may unite] a sound and a concept, while an image [may unite] reflected light and an object. On the other hand, it is readily apparent that these media have often told similar stories and engaged in similar meditations; there is not that much difference between *U.S.A.* and *The Man with a Movie Camera*, between *Absalom, Absalom!* and *Citizen Kane*, between *Mutiny on the Bounty* and *Red River*, between *McTeague* and *Greed*, between "Song of Myself" and *Dog Star Man*, or even between *Gone With the Wind* and *Gone With the Wind*. Gertrude Stein insisted, in "Portraits and Repetition," that she was "doing what the cinema was doing," even though she admitted she rarely went to movies and at the time of her major experiments might not have seen *any* films. Pound and Eisenstein, working independently of each other, each recognized their central aesthetic principles in the same source, the structure of the ideogram, and the montage principle at work in *The Cantos* is certainly comparable to that in Eisenstein's great film *October*. Dos Passos admitted taking inspiration from Eisenstein, and Eisenstein and Ruttmann were the two directors Joyce considered capable of filming *Ulysses*. And although it is often observed that D. W. Griffith took most of his inspiration from Belasco and Dickens rather than from, say, Picasso and Hegel, it is still evident that his *Intolerance*, with its four plots butted together, is a major influence on Russian theories of montage and one of the most accessible prototypes of modernist film. The closer one comes to the present, the more difficult it becomes to discuss the achievements of the most significant films without some appeal to their parallels in modern literature, not just in the extreme example of Alain Robbe-Grillet, but also in the cases of Godard, Resnais, Antonioni, Kubrick, Losey, Fassbinder, Bergman, and Welles. By the same token, it is profligate to consider *Gravity's Rainbow* apart from the work of Fritz Lang, Robert Wiene, and Mack Sennett, not to mention *King Kong* and *The Wizard of Oz*—but one could go further and assert that the two metaphysics central to that novel are those of psychic contact and of film itself. Joyce's interest in silent comedy is reflected in Beckett's *Waiting for Godot*, and Beckett's own reading of what has to be called the metaphysic of Buster Keaton is, as Beckett and Schneider's *Film* incarnates it, a profoundly accurate one, and a good measure of the distance between the contemporary situation, where literature and film can be said to have caught up with each other and to enjoy each other's company, and the twenties, when the author of "The Waste Land" (a montage if ever there was one) could dismiss cinema as a "cheap" and pointless art, and the author of *À la recherche du temps perdu* could wax eloquent on the magic lantern but denigrate both photography and film, considering them incapable of metaphor at the very time his compatriot, Abel Gance, was finishing *La Roue* (which, with *Intolerance*, was one of the two films most carefully studied during the next three years by the Soviets). And at the center of this vortex spins the complex and brilliant career of William Faulkner, whom I have called the most cinematic of novelists and who considered much of his Hollywood career a terrible waste of time.

One of the most interesting things about the early twentieth century is that the arts of literature, painting, and film went through the modernist crisis at approximately the same time, despite the fact that film was a fledgling art and the others were well into their maturity. Whether they did so in response to each other (influence), or independently, in response to the state of Western culture (parallel development), is extremely difficult to establish. André Bazin has eloquently suggested that novelists have been influenced not by the specific films made in their times but by the *idea* of cinema: "If we maintain that the cinema influences the novel then we must suppose that it is a question of a potential image, existing exclusively behind the magnifying glass of the critic and seen only from where he sits. We would then be talking about the influence of a nonexistent cinema, an ideal cinema, a cinema that the novelist would produce if he were a filmmaker; of an imaginary art that we are still awaiting."[1] It is my contention that this ideal cinema is reflected in the greatest novels and stories of Faulkner but only pops up occasionally in the films he helped to write—that Faulkner at his best was thinking not in terms of movies but in tropes that are most convincingly explicated in cinematic terms. This is to employ the term "cinematic" in an idealized fashion, to say that it appeals to an archetype of kinetic and visual presentation. It is also to be sensitive to the pervasive nature of modernist aesthetics in the crucial works of this century, an aesthetic whose fundamental expression is found in what Eisenstein called the montage trope. The fact that Faulkner the novelist, when he *was* a filmmaker, did not produce "pure cinema" is attributable to a number of factors, ranging from the economics of the film industry and Faulkner's own need for Hollywood money, to the aesthetic convictions of his mentor, Howard Hawks, and Faulkner's own apparent lack of conviction that film was a major art. We can suggest that Faulkner missed the point of some of his own best work, but we can also observe that the montage archetype was pervasive in the culture even apart from the forms it took in various films.

The central anxiety of modernism—that the old, harmonious world lay busted into fragments—was central to its triumph. That triumph consisted in acknowledging fragmentation and then butting the fragments up against each other; this juxtaposition itself did not so much provide the longed-for connective tissue as it pointed beyond itself to a conceptual space in which the fragments might cohere. For instance: we live in a fallen world where archetypal heroes are hard to come by. Joyce gives us Leopold Bloom, who is both parody and the real thing. The reader of *Ulysses* constructs the ultimate Bloom, a "hero" in the modern world, out of two terms—the given Bloom and the implicit Odysseus—whose relationship is purely dialectical. Thesis Bloom evokes antithesis Odysseus; this collision

---

[1] André Bazin, "In Defense of Mixed Cinema," *What Is Cinema?*, 2 vols (Berkeley: University of California Press, 1967), I: 63.

dominates the reader's experience and leads him to generate a synthesis. We could call that synthesis "modern hero" or "Bloom as Odysseus," but it is more proper to call it *Ulysses*. Pound generates an epic history out of fragments of letters, poems, etc., not by trying to include in his poem the continuity they suggest but by letting their juxtaposition speak for itself, so that the "live tradition" truly hovers in "the air" above the poem. This dialectical, fallen space made Eliot nervous and Pound excited; Eliot's nostalgia for the ultimate connection must have had a great deal to do with his conversion, but it was especially significant for its charging "The Waste Land" with the latent instruction, Transcend this fragmentation. Picasso and Braque fragmented vision into multiple but simultaneous perspectives, past which one had to appeal for a sense not of the object that might have preceded the Cubist painting (the "What *is* that, anyway?" syndrome) but of the object perceived in time and in multiplied space. The basic metaphysic of Proust's *À la recherche du temps perdu* is that Self A, in the present, collides with Self B, from the past; in the instant that they become simultaneous, two things happen: time is abolished, and the timeless Self C becomes manifest yet remains ineffable, unnamable. This is Hegelian dialectics at its most profound and straightforward level: thesis collides with antithesis and generates synthesis. The fact that Proust could not see this same device at work in film is not the point; the point is that it is (in ideal terms) the same device, as becomes clear when one confronts the films and theoretical writings of Eisenstein.

Here are Pound and Eisenstein, each writing somewhat after the fact, on the nature of the ideogram, which is a montage signifier; all they had gone on to do was to add the element of time (the line of words, the ribbon of frames). First Pound, in 1934:

> But when the Chinaman wanted to make a picture of something more complicated, or of a general idea, how did he go about it?
>
> He is to define red. How can he do it in a picture that isn't painted in red paint?
>
> He puts (or his ancestors put) together the abbreviated pictures of
>
> ROSE   CHERRY
>
> IRON RUST   FLAMINGO[2]

---

2 Ezra Pound, *ABC of Reading* (New York: New Directions, 1960), 21–2.

Now Eisenstein, in 1929:

> The point is that the...combination of two hieroglyphs of the simplest series is to be regarded not as their sum, but as their product, i.e., as a value of another dimension, another degree; each, separately, corresponds to an *object*, to a fact, but their combination corresponds to a *concept*. From separate hieroglyphs has been fused—the ideogram. By the combination of two "depictables" is achieved the representation of something that is graphically undepictable.
>
> For example: the picture for water and the picture of an eye signifies "to weep"; the picture of an ear near the drawing of a door = "to listen";
>
> a dog + a mouth = "to bark";
> a mouth + a child = "to scream";
> a mouth + a bird = "to sing";
> a knife + a heart = "sorrow," and so on.
>
> But this is—montage![3]

Montage is the French term for editing or cutting; its sense is that shot A is "mounted" next to shot B, etc. I am using it here in the sense Eisenstein does, concentrating on the special case of "dialectical montage," which means simply that shot A collides with shot B to generate C, a concept in the mind of the viewer. This trope is useful because it is probably impossible to photograph an idea (literature has the edge here), but it is also useful when one is trying to deal with a fragmented world and can't simply name, even with words, the integrating force. And if you accept the Hindu notion that the universe is One and that language—because it splits the truth up into individual words—is hopelessly false, montage is even more useful, even urgent, since it continually calls attention to the need to transcend fragmentation; nor is film, which fragments the world into shots—and angles of view—exempt from the problem. In my book *Telling It Again and Again* (Cornell, 1972) I attempted to show that this problem is relevant whether or not one is a mystic (let alone a modernist) and that the two most interesting tropes for confronting it are montage and repetition, the latter because it is a minimal syntax that charms the mind into a perception of the One. Without going headlong into that argument here I would like to point out

---

3 Sergei Eisenstein, "The Cinematographic Principle and the Ideogram," *Film Form* (New York: Harcourt Brace and World, 1949), 29–30. Abel Gance made a similar observation about the hieroglyph; see Walter Benjamin, "The Work of Art in the Age of Mechanical Reproduction," *Illuminations* (New York: Schocken, 1969), 227.

that repetition and montage are the two central linguistic and structural devices in Faulkner's fiction, as they are also central to the metaphysics of Proust. To one side of this pair are Pound and Joyce, who were interested more in montage than in repetition, and to the other side are Beckett and Gertrude Stein, to whom repetition was simply basic. I suggest that these six are the most exciting and significant writers of the century, and that this is the way their achievements interrelate.

I hope I have made it clear by now that if I say Faulkner uses montage I mean not that he got the idea from films and not that he thought in terms of films, but that he was doing something that the cinema also did. (His most likely source was Joyce, though he was in fact aware of both Griffith and Eisenstein, each of whom is more relevant to this aspect of film aesthetics than is Hawks.) Let us go on, then, to examine the varieties of montage in his work.

These varieties of montage take five basic and sometimes overlapping forms: the oxymoron, dynamic unresolution, parallel plotting, rapid shifts in time and space, and multiple narration. There is a related aspect of his work, which is the role of photographic imagery, and that may be the best place to start. In the first section of his story "All the Dead Pilots," Faulkner discusses "the snapshots hurriedly made" of the World War I pilots with whom his story is concerned. He suggests that the eye of the writer or of history itself can behave like a flash camera, and also that the snapshot as a form is like an illuminated moment, an incredible concentration of force on the instant:

> In the pictures, the snapshots hurriedly made, a little faded, a little dog-eared with the thirteen years, they swagger a little. Lean, hard, in their brass-and-leather martial harness, posed standing beside or leaning upon the esoteric shapes of wire and wood and canvas in which they flew without parachutes, they too have an esoteric look; a look not exactly human, like that of some dim and threatful apotheosis of the race seen for an instant in the glare of a thunderclap and then forever gone.

Faulkner goes on to say that he will take such moments—revelations that are like photographs, the Kodak as epiphany—and arrange them in what one has to call a montage, though he calls it a composite series: "That's why this story is composite: a series of brief glares in which, instantaneous and without depth or perspective, there stood into sight the portent and the threat of what the race could bear and become, in an instant between dark and dark."[4] He is making of his insight a principle of composition. The basic difference between this method and that of *The Sound and the Fury* is that in the latter he mounts

---

4 *Collected Stories* (New York: Random House, 1950), 511–12.

together fragmented scenes without having to consider them "without depth or perspective"[5]—that he moves, in other words, from the series of vignettes to the more complex collision of scenes.

Walter Slatoff has shown in *Quest for Failure* that the basic quality of Faulkner's imagination is its ability to suspend oppositions—that his novels build not to resolutions but to the tension of unresolution. If you don't understand this, you run the risk of missing the points of his novels by trying to make everything fit, as in those inane oversimplifications of *As I Lay Dying*, for instance, that convert it into some kind of good-humored epic of survival, and ignore all that business about language, madness, ruin, and failure, along with what I feel must be called the metaphysical implications of the montage structure of its narrative. To take a simpler example, however, it is important to notice that the last phrase of *The Sound and the Fury*—"each in its ordered place"—has a dialectical relationship with the title and drift of the novel, rendering this sense of order as ironic as possible. The order achieved at the end is created by Jason and through violence; it is artificial, even if the order becomes that of "post and tree" under the serene gaze of the idiot Benjy. The novel's title, of course, implies that the "tale told by an idiot" will be full of sound and fury and might signify nothing, but one must remember that Faulkner is alluding to what Macbeth says when he sees the ruin of his enterprise and just before "the time is [set] free" by his death. (Part of Shakespeare's point is that insane and unnatural control stops time.) One of the characteristics of Faulkner's novel is that time is approached as an organic chaos that could be called "free," at least in that part of the tale that *is* told by the idiot. (Quentin, who is aware of time, has other problems, including a nostalgia for timelessness; the freed time he envisions is that of the Christ who is [...] no longer "worn away by a minute clicking of little wheels," but it is also the freedom *in* time characteristic of Benjy and achieved by Quentin whenever he forgets about his watch.) The innocence of Benjy's perceptions is certainly preferable to the rigidity of Jason's. In fact the whole novel is structured between the poles of freedom and control, which represent two kinds of order, the former natural and the latter cultural. Each of the Compson brothers wants to control Caddy, who wants to be free; it is interesting to note that Caddy's being damned and doomed is the result not of her being evil but of her attempt to function as a sexual being, whereas precisely the opposite is true of the more profoundly irresponsible Temple Drake. Caddy's problem is that she is surrounded by controlling forces

---

5 Photography, for Faulkner, was as "flat" as Popeye's stamped-tin face; epiphanic or not, it was characteristically and phenomenologically modern, whereas fiction could achieve a sense of depth from which Faulkner felt less alienated. Even without raising the question of his ignorance of film history, then, it should not be surprising that he did not compare his novels to movies in spite of their structural complementarity.

who will destroy her but whom she loves. The rage to create an artificial order is what drives both the Compson family and Thomas Sutpen, and in both cases it is poor Quentin, the heir of Stephen Dedalus, who is left to puzzle out the cultural shambles but who would really rather live in some paradise before the fall into time and history. Such polar oppositions abound in Faulkner's work, but the simplest way to organize them, in terms of *The Sound and the Fury*, is to say first that the novel begins in apparent disorder and ends in apparent order, and second that the novel begins in an innocence of perception that reveals truth and ends in a sophisticated, third-person perspective that misses a great deal. The sound and fury of the idiot's tale signify most, and it can hardly be an accident that the structure of Benjy's monologue is mirrored in the structure of the novel whose four parts are out of chronological sequence. To strive for order in the manner of the Compson brothers is to achieve the order of death; thus the novel comes to a very dubious sense of rest at its close. [...] Similarly, the ending of *Absalom, Absalom!* occurs at a moment of absolute tension; Shreve's attempt to wrap it all up into a flip kind of order ("So it takes two niggers to get rid of one Sutpen") is hardly a resolution, and Quentin's frantic "*I dont hate it!*"—i.e., "I don't want to admit that I hate it"—is the simultaneous X and not-X of unresolution.

If Faulkner thinks in terms of opposites and throws these opposites together, it should be no surprise that one of his central devices is dialectical montage. In a work like *The Wild Palms* he lets these polar perspectives alternate, in the equivalent of a trope that Eisenstein called parallel montage; at the ends of *The Sound and the Fury* and *Absalom, Absalom!* he compresses the opposites into simultaneity—which is not at all to say that he unites them in one term. In this context, there *is* no such term. The oxymoron (a rhetorical device characterized by the juxtaposition of incongruous or contradictory terms) allows him to carry on dialectical montage within the sentence, and is often his way of evoking—through a state of contradiction—that kind of synthesis-term whose equivalent Eisenstein called "graphically undepictable." Here is a representative excerpt from the second page of *Absalom, Absalom!*:

> Out of quiet thunderclap he would abrupt (man-horse-demon) upon a scene peaceful and decorous as a schoolprize water color, faint sulphur-reek still in hair clothes and beard, with grouped behind him his band of wild niggers like beasts half tamed to walk upright like men, in attitudes wild and reposed, and manacled among them the French architect with his air grim, haggard, and tatter-ran. Immobile, bearded and hand palm-lifted the horseman sat; behind him the wild blacks and the captive architect huddled quietly, carrying in bloodless paradox the shovels and picks and axes of peaceful conquest. Then in the long unamaze Quentin seemed to

watch them overrun suddenly the hundred square miles of tranquil and astonished earth and drag house and formal gardens violently out of the soundless Nothing and clap them down like cards upon a table beneath the up-palm immobile and pontific, creating the Sutpen's Hundred, the *Be Sutpen's Hundred* like the oldtime *Be Light*. Then hearing would reconcile and he would seem to listen to two separate Quentins now.[6]

It is not impossible to imagine a "quiet thunderclap," an attitude "wild and reposed," a shovel in the role of a rifle, a "peaceful conquest," an earth that could be at once "tranquil and astonished," a silent but violent construction project (even if the silence is that of Quentin's mind's eye), and so on. It is not impossible, but the effort involves dialectics, creates a conceptual space in which an event or pose can best be described in terms of the poles it transcends and conjoins. This series of oxymorons leads directly and naturally into the description of Quentin's being split into two selves, and it is of course appropriate to find "the two separate Quentins now talking to one another in the long silence of notpeople, in notlanguage." The oxymoron, in other words, operates within the sentence in the same way that dynamic unresolution structures the novels, and both of these are montage tropes.

Many of Faulkner's doubling gestures that appear simply to be repetitive turn out also to be polar—the two trials at the end of *Sanctuary*, for instance, in each of which the jury is out for the same eight minutes. Each jury finds the innocent defendant to be guilty. But the first jury—Lee Goodwin's—achieves injustice, while the second—Popeye's—achieves legal injustice but poetic justice. It is a process I like to call "repetition in reverse," as if the trials were, in part, mirror images of each other; in any case, the point is that this is the very edge of the interrelation between repetition and montage, where both are going on and are doing so with the same terms. Two plus two is four (repetition), two times two is four (montage). We still get to "four," but feel different along the way. Something very like this parallel-trial device goes on in the larger structures of the novel, where the innocent Benbow and the innocent Temple are each made to confront the absolute death of innocence, the absolute absence of sanctuary—i.e., of a safe and honorable space to which to retreat from evil and horror (in Temple's case, the corncrib and the class system; in Horace's, the court and the ideal of womanhood). Horace and Temple are—in several crucial respects but not in their entirety—opposites maintained in parallel, like Hamlet and Laertes, or Hamlet and Stephen Dedalus. The device is called parallel montage, and it reaches its most complex and beautiful expression in *The Wild Palms*.

---

6 *Absalom, Absalom!* (New York: Random House, 1936), 8–9.

Montage in Faulkner's work is not something added after the fact, not the product of rearrangement, but integral to each fragment. Faulkner did not write the novella "Old Man" and then the novella "Wild Palms" but wrote them in alternation, chapter by chapter, letting each suggest the other. Faulkner used the terms "antithesis" and "counterpoint" to describe the ways these stories gave each other "emphasis."[7] As usual, he appears to have been "doing what the cinema was doing" but thinking in other terms—in this case, dialectics and music. Nevertheless, one finds in this novel a direct reference to Eisenstein and another to Joan Crawford (who had starred in *Today We Live*). These two references suggest the poles of Faulkner's attitude toward film:

> "I thought—" Wilbourne began. But he did not say it. They went on; the last glare of the snow faded and now they entered a scene like something out of an Eisenstein Dante. The gallery became a small amphitheatre, branching off in smaller galleries like the spread fingers from a palm, lighted by an incredible extravagance of electricity as though for a festival—an extravagance of dirty bulbs which had, though in inverse ratio, that same air of sham and moribundity which the big, almost barren building labeled *Commissary* in tremendous new letters had—in the light from which still more of the grimed, giant-seeming men in sheep coats and with eyes which had not slept much lately worked with picks and shovels with that same frenzy of the man running behind the loaded tram, with shouts and ejaculations in that tongue which Wilbourne could not understand almost exactly like a college baseball team cheering one another on, while from the smaller galleries which they had not penetrated yet and where still more electric bulbs glared in the dust-laden and icy air came either echoes or the cries of still other men, meaningless and weird, filling the heavy air like blind erratic birds.[8]

In this first passage, "Eisenstein" may simply be a stand-in term for "Russian," but since the novel itself is so deliberately an act of montage, and since the harshly lit and chaotic mine is described in a manner that echoes the early Eisenstein's *mise-en-scène*, I consider it safe to assume that Faulkner did not drop the name lightly. (Eisenstein never met Faulkner, though he did meet Joyce. The closest Eisenstein and Faulkner came to meeting, however, makes a story in itself. Each of them worked on the script of *Sutter's Gold*—Eisenstein in 1930 and Faulkner in 1934—when each was, from Hollywood's point of view, an aesthetic outsider; neither of their scripts was used, though Eisenstein's has been published and

---

7 Malcolm Cowley, *The Faulkner–Cowley File* (New York: Viking, 1968), 164.
8 *The Wild Palms* (New York: Random House, 1939), 186–7.

Faulkner's has a number of connections with *Absalom, Absalom!*, which followed shortly.) It is certainly significant that Faulkner teams Eisenstein's name with that of Dante, [here the author of the *Inferno*,] though he uses [Eisenstein] only as an adjective; the sense of the reference, in any case, is to a serious artist.

The reference to Hollywood, on the other hand, is both hostile and generalized:

> They rode two nights and a day in day coaches and left the snow behind and found buses now, cheaper now, her head tilted back against the machine-made doily, her face in profile against the dark fleeing snow-free countryside and the little lost towns, the neon, the lunch rooms with broad strong Western girls got up out of Hollywood magazines (Hollywood which is no longer in Hollywood but is stippled by a billion feet of burning colored gas across the face of the American earth) to resemble Joan Crawford, asleep or he could not tell.[9]

Although there appears to be no animosity toward the figure of Joan Crawford, there is a great deal of it toward the cultural imperialism of Hollywood. The "silver dream" of film, as it is described in the story "Dry September," is escapist and dangerous; in *Pylon* his metaphor for film distribution is that of contagion, and its echo of the *Wild Palms* passage is close enough to bear quoting here:

> ...and looking out through the falling snow she saw a kind of cenotaph, penurious and without majesty or dignity, of forlorn and victorious desolation—a bungalow, a tight flimsy mass of stoops and porte-cochères and flat gables and bays not five years old and built in that colored mud-and-chickenwire tradition which California moving picture films have scattered across North America as if the celluloid carried germs.[10]

For Faulkner, then, the film industry was in the disease business, but Eisenstein was an artist, and one with whose work he appears to have been familiar. It is possible, then, that Faulkner recognized a difference between the terms "Hollywood" and "film," although many of his biographers, critics, and colleagues seem to have missed that particular boat.

The Wild Palms, in any case, tells two parallel but opposite stories, in alternation. "Old Man" is the story of a tall convict whose youthful misfortune was to believe what he read in cheap fiction about the easy rewards of banditry;

---

9   Ibid., 209.
10 *Pylon* (New York: Signet, 1968), 215.

he is, in other words, very much like Don Quixote—even to the extent that he curses, when he has been imprisoned, not the lawmen who caught him but the authors of the pulps who misled him. The convict is accidentally freed from prison during a flood, and spends most of the rest of the story trying to get back to jail; in the meantime, however, he helps a woman give birth and discovers the rewards of working for a living. He rises to the challenge of freedom and autonomy, but when he is recaptured he does not put up any significant resistance, even when his sentence is drastically increased. His last line is "Women[,] shit," [which means, in part,] that if it had not been for the pregnant flood victim who needed rescuing, the convict might never have really had to deal with life.

Harry Wilbourne's last line, however, as he sits in jail at the end of "Wild Palms," is *"between grief and nothing I will take grief."* Grief is his memory of his beloved Charlotte, who would cease to exist—along with what is left of their love—if he were, by committing suicide, to cease being able to remember her. Harry is dragged away from his safe life as a medical student by Charlotte, a romantic overreacher who hooks him on the ideal of absolute and realized love—a hook on which he proves to be even more caught than she. The freedom to love completely, however, is almost impossible in society, and even their escape to the wilderness confronts them with both the cultural and the existential limits of their quest. (They are like some Don Quixote who could see what was really going on.) Where the convict helps a woman deliver a child, Harry—who has medical training but is too emotionally involved to do the job correctly and in time—botches Charlotte's abortion and thereby causes her death. At the end, then, Harry and the convict are both in jail. Each has been yanked into freedom by a woman, each has some nostalgia for the safe life before the crisis, and each has been trapped by society's insensitive enforcers. But the convict had found freedom through a kind of passivity (his characteristic pose is to lie on his back and bleed), while Harry had pursued his freedom like a grail. Both the convict and Harry begin in safety, go through a period of activity and growth, and end in a state of arrest—but their perspectives are precisely opposite. It is a definitive example of parallel montage, giving rise to a complex vision of the demands of freedom and the nature of endurance that neither story, on its own, presents.

The term "montage" is more regularly associated, however, not with this elegant device of continuing antithetical counterpoint, but with the more apparently chaotic series of pell-mell collisions achieved through "rapid cutting." The most famous examples of rapid cutting—which was perfected by Abel Gance but had such an influence on the Soviets that it came to be known as "Russian cutting" before the term "montage" subsumed it—are Gance's *La Roue* and *Napoléon*, and Eisenstein's [*Battleship*] *Potemkin* and *October*.

Many of the shots in these films are only two frames—about an eighth of a second—in length. The sense of collision here is more kinetic than intellectual (the dialectical processes are still at work, but the shots go by so rapidly that one tends to miss some of the conceptual overtones, unless one can examine the film on an editing bench). One way to conceptualize the difference in rhythm between parallel montage and rapid cutting is to compare *Intolerance* with the Odessa Steps sequence in *Potemkin*, the alternating narrators of *Bleak House* with those of *As I Lay Dying*, or *The Wild Palms* with *The Sound and the Fury*.

The Sound and the Fury is structured by oppositions and characterized by collisions. The cinematic feel of this novel is the result of two challenges Faulkner set himself in the Benjy section but which show up, in simpler terms, in the other three chapters. Because Benjy is an idiot and does not have words for most of the things he encounters, his experience is highly sensual; his dominant sense is the visual. It is clear from how it looks that the opening scene is of golfing, for example, and that Benjy does not know the word (or have the full thought) for that. Benjy's chapter is a sequence of primarily visual scenes, with sound and scent and touch playing important but secondary roles; it is a series of views, transcribed by a writer.

The second challenge was to dramatize psychological time. While most of us can think about our experience through a combination of memory and verbal labeling, Benjy's associative process actually hurtles him from one event to another in a sequence of (re)livings. The reader understands that many of these are memories and that the links among scenes (dialectically generated) are the nearest Benjy comes to thinking: this looks like that, this feels like that. Benjy cannot rise to generalization, cannot interrelate concepts, cannot distinguish past from present—but he can *feel* the difference between scene A, where Caddy is around, and scene B, where she is not, and start to bellow. The reader achieves complex insights from the montage inside Benjy's head; one *watches* Benjy's mental experience and understands the rudiments of human thought (Benjy has subjectivity but not consciousness; "consciousness" is used here in the sense suggested by Ervin Laszlo: "awareness of subjectivity"). Benjy is going through a series of Proustian shifts—nonverbal association as time travel—but cannot step back and watch himself or understand what these shifts mean. This is the closest Proust and Faulkner get to each other, so this is as good a time as any to quote Robbe-Grillet, who considers them two of the basic influences on modern fiction and film:

> The cinema knows only one grammatical mode: the present tense of the indicative. In any case, film and novel today meet in the construction of moments, of intervals, and of sequences which no longer have anything

to do with those of clocks or calendars. Let us try to specify their role a little.

It has very often been repeated in recent years that time was the chief "character" of the contemporary novel. Since Proust, since Faulkner, the flashback, the break in chronology seem in effect at the basis of the very organization of the narrative, of its architecture. The same is obviously true of the cinema: every modern cinematographic work is a reflection on human memory, its uncertainties, its persistence, its dramas, etc.

All of which is said a little too quickly.[11]

Like film, Benjy's mind has only one tense. (This is, by the way, the key to Gertrude Stein's basic insight about the continuous present in film, literature, repetition, and consciousness.) For Benjy the contents of a memory are present events. It works the same way in film: it is only through context that one understands a given scene as "not happening right now"—the point being, of course, that it *is* happening right now and only now, and that any other chronology is metatextual. The order of Benjy's scenes *is* his mental experience. By being true to his conception of an idiot's visual, kinetic stream of consciousness, Faulkner developed a narrative mode that really cannot be called anything but cinematic, since it presents the story in a series of visions, both of the mind's eye and of the physical eye, with all narrative time being present and all transitions *de facto*, instantaneous, cuts. A cut is an instantaneous shift in time and space; one is at X, and now one is at Y. Without saying more about it, let me simply quote one of Benjy's transitions and ask you to think of this as a three-shot sequence:

> We went along the fence and came to the garden fence, where our shadows were. My shadow was higher than Luster's on the fence. We came to the broken place and went through it.
>
> "Wait a minute." Luster said. "You snagged on that nail again. Cant you never crawl through here without snagging on that nail."
>
> *Caddy uncaught me and we crawled through. Uncle Maury said to not let anybody see us, so we better stoop over, Caddy said. Stoop over, Benjy. Like this, see. We stooped over and crossed the garden, where the flowers rasped and rattled against us. The ground was hard. We climbed the fence, where the pigs were grunting and snuffing. I expect they're sorry because one of them got killed today, Caddy said. The ground was hard, churned and knotted.*

---

11 Alain Robbe-Grillet, "Time and Description," *For a New Novel* (New York: Grove, 1965), 151–2.

Keep your hands in your pockets, Caddy said. Or they'll get froze. You dont want your hands froze on Christmas, do you.

"It's too cold out there." Versh said. "You dont want to go out doors."

"What is it now." Mother said.[12]

The tense used throughout Benjy's section is the past. This does *not* signify that Benjy knows the difference between now and then, but instead asserts the equivalence of all time, and does so in a tense with which the reader can deal easily (tense is used with greater complexity in *As I Lay Dying*). In any case, the logic of the cuts is clear: Benjy gets caught on the fence while he is with Luster, and flashes to his getting caught on that fence when he was with Caddy. He lives in that other scene, then, as Caddy gets him uncaught; it is Christmas and the ground is frozen. Caddy tells him to keep his hands in his pockets because it's cold, and he cuts to another scene in which Versh had told him something similar. The reader feels the collision and understands the link. Scene follows scene in a chaos that is only apparent and in a syntax that is thoroughly cinematic, not just because it is comparable to dialectical montage and not just because it reminds one of Resnais as much as of Eisenstein, and regardless of whether Faulkner was thinking in terms of film, but primarily because it is told in one tense, with straight cuts, and with minimal appeal to the act of naming things. Benjy thinks like a modernist film, and Faulkner discovered a means of dramatizing that process so that the reader could, in his mind's eye, *see* Benjy's thinking. One could film *The Sound and the Fury* with hardly a change—even Quentin's section, which cuts less frequently but in the same manner as Benjy's (since Faulkner is saying something universal about thought) but is easier to follow, since Quentin knows the names for more things and can conceptualize time. Jason is more rigid, more locked away from fluid phenomena into a wall of preconceptions, but even he has his share of flashbacks. The final section is conventionally chronological and third person. No matter how eloquent the narrative in that last chapter, then, one is alienated from its capping the novel's increasing sense of order, as if a complex and tasty solution had precipitated itself into a beaker of water and a couple of little rocks. The more conventional the narrative becomes, the more it moves from "ideal cinema" to nineteenth-century narrative, the more its order seems imposed and artificial, cut off and closed, not just to the film-oriented critic but to anyone who has been paying attention to Jason (whom Faulkner must have been in a very bitter and ironic mood to have characterized as "sane").

---

12 *The Sound and the Fury* (New York: Random House, 1929 facsimile [n.d.]), 3.

In *Absalom, Absalom!*, however, as in much of *As I Lay Dying*, the primary orientation of the narrative is toward language and not toward the visual. The montage here—which builds on that of the four parts of *The Sound and the Fury*—is of narrative points of view, and the conceptual interactions are extraordinary. Even so, one of the first and most arresting things that happens in *Absalom* is that the tensions of language embattled against itself (in dialectics, in oxymorons, in Rosa's voice, in Quentin's character, and so on) result in the *vanishing* of language and the appearance of the figure of Sutpen as an image in Quentin's mind's eye, an inner theater [that is] as silent as the films of his period.

Sutpen is the embodiment of the concept that arises from the collision of attempts to describe him. Sutpen is not *in* the novel, just as Charles Foster Kane is not *in* Welles's film. To be more precise: Kane appears in the narrative present of *Citizen Kane* only in fragments (a close-up of his mouth, a hand, a shadow) and then only at the moment of his death; all the rest of the time one sees only the images of Kane that his friends and associates and the news media have of him, images that reflect each narrator's bias. With the camera—even more than the reporter, Thompson, who is less than a Quentin figure—the viewer explores the pieces of the puzzle and assembles them into a concept of the hero's nature; the dialectic of points of view impels one to generate a synthesis, Kane, who does not and probably cannot appear whole in the film.

To paraphrase Beckett in *Watt*, the ineffable is what one can't eff. Not just a demon, a madman, a patriarch, an Agamemnon, a David, a Shakespeare, a victim of colonization, and an imperialist, Sutpen is primarily an occasion for meditation—and a particularly fine one in that he eludes exhaustive description; what he does is to exhaust description. He does this not because he is some kind of transcendent figure but because the method of description itself generates the sense of its own failure. That failure generates further attempts, and the rhetoric and pace of the work become an eloquent frenzy; nailing this henhouse together in a hurricane, Faulkner achieves something that is metaphysically startling: the henhouse *as* hurricane. What is at stake here is not the nature and history of Sutpen but the indomitability and impotence of language.

When description A fails, and description B fails, one can hope that their juxtaposition will point toward C, the thing itself (by which I mean not Sutpen the man but Sutpen the force or concept). *Absalom* is montage's last stand, the trope chosen because montage is an important and perhaps necessary means of dealing not just with the "graphically undepictable" but with its linguistic equivalent, the inconceivable. The problem of the ineffable is one that seems not to have troubled Joyce, even though Stephen does think about it ("Ineluctable modality of the visible," etc.); in this context, Joyce's limitation as an artist is that he had a word for everything, that given infinite time he appears to have felt that he could carve almost anything out of the not-yet-said. The problem is central, however, to Proust and Faulkner as well as to Beckett (whose ties with Joyce are, I feel, much overstated; the place to locate Beckett is between Proust and Stein). The ineffable *per se* does not play a crucial thematic role in *Absalom* or *Kane*—it is more a case of by direction finding indirection out—but the dialectical process does, the problem of accurate description is paramount, and the generated concept of the hero exists (or takes place) outside each work. Where this all comes together is, of course, in the montage narrative of *As I Lay Dying*, a novel centrally concerned with the limits of language and of consciousness, whose "I" is either that of the novel or that of a woman who "speaks" long after she has begun to decompose, and whose major narrator (Darl)—at the moment he begins to make contact with the narrative force that arises out of the montage of individual narrators, to which Addie is ineffably connected and for which she is perhaps responsible—suffers a split into two voices, for one of which he is "I" and for the other "Darl."

Rather than attempt to explicate *As I Lay Dying*, however—since that would take at least as much time as I have already taken[13]—I would simply like to suggest that Hegel had a profound intuition when he proposed dialectics as a means by which the ineffable could realize itself, that Eisenstein incorporated this aspect of dialectics into his own theories when he suggested that a synthesis could be "graphically undepictable," and that Faulkner often used montage not just for psychological realism, for rhythm, and for conceptual complexity, but also as a means of turning language against itself so that such unnamables as the power behind Sutpen's power and the language of Addie's silence could, in Wittgenstein's highly appropriate phrase, "make themselves manifest."

The connection between *Kane* and *Absalom* raises one final point. It is difficult, as I've said, to prove Faulkner was influenced by the cinema; on the other hand, it is clear that cinema has been influenced by Faulkner—not Faulkner the screenwriter, but Faulkner the novelist. *Absalom* came out three years before Herman J. Mankiewicz wrote the script for *Kane*, and there is no way to know for certain whether that novel was an influence on that film, especially since Mankiewicz's widow has said he was definitely influenced by *The Great Gatsby*; so one may have a case here of Mankiewicz's and Faulkner's each discovering the same way of complicating the collision between the antihero and his observers that Fitzgerald explored. *Kane* itself, however, was a profound influence on the next generation's sense of narrative complexity,

---

13 [The argument was published later, in Bruce F. Kawin, *The Mind of the Novel: Reflexive Fiction and the Ineffable* (Princeton: Princeton University Press, 1982), 258–72. Reprint available from Dalkey Archive Press.]

effectively readying such directors as Resnais and Fellini to deal with material of Faulknerian intricacy. The catalyst was the translation into French of *The Wild Palms*, which preceded the New Wave by less than five years. Agnès Varda was inspired by that newly translated novel to write and direct a film with two parallel plots, *La Pointe-Courte*, which is generally considered the first New Wave film and which was edited by her friend Resnais. Resnais led Duras and Robbe-Grillet—novelists who were, to say the least, familiar with Faulkner's work—into scripting *Hiroshima mon amour* and *Last Year at Marienbad*, respectively, and made possible—though not entirely legitimate—Robbe-Grillet's characterization of "every modern cinematographic work" as a dramatization of mental time. For Robbe-Grillet the crucial Faulkner novel is presumably *The Sound and the Fury*, but it is *The Wild Palms* that keeps showing up, even in so recent a work as Wenders's *Kings of the Road*. Godard has adapted *The Wild Palms* three times, in *Breathless, Pierrot le fou,* and the great diptych, *Made in [U.S.A]* and *2 or 3 Things I Know About Her*. One of the last projects of the transcendent genius Carl Dreyer was to have been an adaptation of *Light in August*. The point, of course, is not that Faulkner's stories are being turned into movies, but that his *methods* are deliberately being used in films and that Faulkner has indirectly kept the art of film in touch with its own modernist heritage as well as enriched the psychological and metaphysical applications of the montage trope. So the "ideal cinema" Faulkner practiced found its way at last into the movie theaters, regardless of whether it started there in the first place, and can now be seen to have had as profound an influence on film as it has had on the history of modern literature.

15

HORTON FOOTE

Every year the Telluride Film Festival pays special tribute to three people who have made vital contributions to the cinema. In 1997, one of the people honored was Horton Foote, who had been chosen for his work as a screenwriter. My job was to write the note for the festival program and the handout for the tribute, but thanks to a revised printer's deadline, I had to do them in one day. It was the day my father, Morris Kawin, died suddenly in a hospital a thousand miles away, and these pieces, which were very hard to write, are in his memory. They are also dedicated to my good friend Horton, who died in 2009 at the age of 92, still working.

Festival Program Note

People die for no good reason. Horton Foote doesn't know why, either. But he knows what to do: endure the pain that cannot go away—literally, live with it. Horton Foote's latest film, *Alone* (1997), was written after the death of his wife, Lillian Vallish Foote; its star, Hume Cronyn, also lost his wife, Jessica Tandy. But this film is no dirge—it's an attempt to heal with art, to find a place where a writer and an actor and an audience can come together in a place of grief and find the continuing love that keeps us going.

He knows the words for the biggest things are simple: "I seen the river" (*Old Man*, 1960).

For Horton Foote, there are no empty lives. The old woman—on TV, Lillian Gish; on film, Geraldine Page—makes *The Trip to Bountiful* (TV and stage, 1953; movie, 1985). Bountiful may be overgrown and abandoned, but it restores her strength and dignity. The woman and child who drop into the life of the solitary hero of *Tomorrow* (TV, 1960; movie, 1972) and are almost as suddenly snatched away *are* his family. If Foote is, as he has been called, "the Chekhov of the small town," one could say that his characters never "go to Moscow," but it doesn't matter and may be the best thing. (If they do go, it's to Houston, where they can't find work.)

Terrible things happen in Foote's work, but there is an answer to it. We see the answer in the personal moral strength of the lawyer in *To Kill a Mockingbird* (1962). We see it in an ordinary phone call in *Alone*. It comes down to the courage to love.

O'Neill and Williams let others make movies out of their plays. Foote writes his own filmscripts—and has won Oscars and WGA Awards for both *Mockingbird* and *Tender Mercies* (1983). He recently won the Pulitzer Prize for his play *The Young Man from Atlanta*. And this season, his script for the new version of *Old Man* was nominated for an Emmy. In the American theater, he is our greatest realist. In the golden age of TV, he was a legend—and now he has returned to TV with *Old Man* (1997) and Showtime's *Lily Dale* (1996) and *Alone*. In the filmmaking world, he spans the gap between the studios and the shoestring independents—from *Baby the Rain Must Fall* (1965) to *1918* (1984). He writes roles a great performer can inhabit—from Lillian Gish, Kim Stanley, Geraldine Page, Gregory Peck, Robert Duvall, and Olga Bellin to his daughter, Hallie Foote. The amazing thing is not that he can write in all these forms with such a feel for the rhythms of each medium, and not that he can adapt a work by Harper Lee or William Faulkner so brilliantly that what he adds to the original appears to have been there already, but that his work—whether adapted or original, for the tube or the screen or the page—is a whole. At Telluride this year we honor that body of work and the gentle man who wrote it.

Tribute Handout

Horton Foote was born in 1916, in the Southeast Texas town of Wharton. When he writes about the place, he calls it Harrison. Faulkner lived in Oxford and called it Jefferson. Each of them wrote overlapping and interconnected works that wove recurring characters, story lines, narrative devices, symbols, and themes into a textual world so intimately observed that its relevance was universal. Each of them returned to rework a situation or relationship in search of a fuller expression: as Faulkner wrote *Absalom, Absalom!* after *The Sound and the Fury* and found the tragedy that had been missing from the melodrama, Foote revisited *Baby the Rain Must Fall* in *Tender Mercies* and found a way for a singer and a mother and child to become a family. Foote has also revisited and reimagined the same works for different media—for instance, when writing *The Trip to Bountiful* as a play, as a teleplay, and as a screenplay. Or when adapting Faulkner's story "Tomorrow" for TV and for the movies. But Faulkner's world and Foote's are very different. There is little sound and fury here, no gothic, and much less violence. There is cruelty, but not cruel humor. And there is no authorial posturing, no overwriting. Silences and simple speeches convey the most here, and Foote's humility and compassion leave him everywhere and nowhere in his works, which are suffused with his care but presented as if without his interference.

In his teens he fell in love with the theater and left Texas to become an actor in New York. He began writing plays in 1939 and had one on Broadway by

1944, the same year he did his first screenwriting at Universal. Uninterested in the formula writing Hollywood wanted from him, Foote returned to the East and the theater. In 1945 he married Lillian Vallish, and soon he was writing and directing and acting and even teaching to keep food on the table. In 1951 he was writing for *The Gabby Hayes Show*. In 1953 he wrote *The Trip to Bountiful*.

What Horton Foote wrote for TV in the 1950s and early '60s ranks with the best of Rose and Chayefsky. Intensely moving and rigorously economical, his teleplays (and their stage versions) revealed his power and vision, his sense of character, his probing moral intelligence, his compassion, his irony, and his urgent heart—without making a big deal out of anything. In addition to *Bountiful* (which starred Lillian Gish, as inspired and gripping as she was in *The Night of the Hunter*), three stand out: *Old Man* (1958), *Tomorrow* (1960), and *Roots in a Parched Ground*, broadcast as *The Night of the Storm* (1961). *Old Man* was based on a short novel by Faulkner—actually, half of the novel *The Wild Palms*, in which chapters of *Wild Palms* alternate in [a parallel montage, perhaps influenced by Eisenstein] with chapters of *Old Man*—and was faithful to everything but Faulkner's ironic, downbeat ending. When Foote had the chance to rewrite *Old Man* for Hallmark's 1996 production, he used the extra hour to show even more of the relationship between the convict and the woman, and pushed the ending where he had always wanted it to go. *Tomorrow* is faithful to Faulkner's story—except for the fact that it is told more efficiently and that 75 percent of the material is 100 percent Foote. The woman who was played so memorably by Kim Stanley on *Playhouse 90* and by Olga Bellin on the screen, the woman who speaks so simply and powerfully, whom we feel that we know so well, and whose growing relationship with her practically silent benefactor is so carefully traced—that woman has, in the original story, less than a paragraph of dialogue.

Roots in a Parched Ground became the first play in his nine-play cycle, *The Orphans' Home* (completed 1977), a fictionalized version of the life of his father, here called Horace Robedaux. A brilliantly understated work that is as moving as anything by Chekhov, *Roots in a Parched Ground* declared the terms of Horton Foote's world. It is a place where a person can be in hell and say "Yes, Ma'am." Where people lose their jobs and towns dry up and desperate decisions have permanent consequences—and where the best in people comes through as the downcast and outcast find and save each other. It is the world of *Tender Mercies* (1983). In his preface to the published version of *Old Man*, *Tomorrow*, and *Roots*, Foote wrote:

> Much of our dramatic writing today concerns itself with despair for man and the life about him. In these three plays we are with the dispossessed,

the broken, the cheated, the deprived; I have tried to show courage and humanity even here.

He returned to screenwriting in 1956 with *Storm Fear*, and stayed to collect a couple of Oscars and WGA awards—for his adaptation of Harper Lee's *To Kill a Mockingbird* (Robert Mulligan, 1962) and for his original *Tender Mercies*. He was also nominated for an Oscar for the movie version of *The Trip to Bountiful* (1985), and when Geraldine Page won for Best Actress in that picture, she waved the statuette above her head and thanked Horton. No discredit to the director here, for Foote has been lucky in his directors—especially Robert Mulligan, Ken Harrison, and Peter Masterson—but the *auteur* here is the author. The only director to have worked against a Foote script and survived was Bruce Beresford, who rushed the pace of *Tender Mercies*, cut out beats that mattered.

After *Mockingbird*, Mulligan and Foote made one more picture together: *Baby the Rain Must Fall* (1965), best described as Foote's answer to Faulkner's *Light in August* (they end with practically the same line, and both feature a "traveling lady"—the name of Foote's original play—and a man scarred and scattered by an abusive childhood). *The Chase* (1966) was adapted by others from his novel. Outside and beyond Hollywood, Foote found directors and co-producers, or they found him, and the result was a crop of well-crafted, uncommercial, terrific independent features. The first of them, Joseph Anthony's *Tomorrow* (1972), has the sharp, stark look and the hidden subjectivity of a photograph by Walker Evans. It must have sold 500 tickets. Then came Beresford's *Tender Mercies*, Ken Harrison's *1918* (1984), Peter Masterson's *Bountiful*, the American Playhouse productions of *Courtship* (Howard Cummings, 1986) and *On Valentine's Day* (Ken Harrison, 1986), Masterson's *Convicts* (1991), Gary Senise's *Of Mice and Men* (1992), and the Showtime productions of *Lily Dale* (Masterson, 1996) and *Alone* (Michael Lindsay-Hogg, 1997). However they were financed, these are movies. Many of them are part of *The Orphans' Home* cycle: *Convicts*, *Lily Dale*, *Courtship*, *On Valentine's Day*, and *1918*.

He's done some other things, from TV adaptations of *The Displaced Person* and *Barn Burning* to a couple of new plays every year for years, and all of this work is tight and strong and gentle, especially when it hurts. He has lines that can kill you and put you back together. If his vision could be summed up, it might be in the lines of William Blake he chose as an epigraph for *Roots in a Parched Ground*:

> T E R R O R in the house does roar,
> But Pity stands before the door.

In a world whose losses hurt only because what life gave first was so precious, Horton Foote has the ticket to Bountiful.

16

AN OUTLINE OF FILM VOICES

> Mindscreen *examined first-person cinema, and this article added second- and third-person cinema to the mix, enhancing what is proposed and, I think, delivered here: a description and organization of voices in the cinematic narrative system. The discussion of interactive cinema needs to be updated in terms of today's and tomorrow's computers, but the category exists. This was published in* Film Quarterly *in 1985.*

In his recent *Film Quarterly* article, "Tense, Mood, and Voice in Film: Notes after Genette," Brian Henderson initiated a stimulating attempt to rethink film narration in terms suggested by his reading of Gerard Genette's *Narrative Discourse*. While I agree with him that the problem of narration—of who says what and how it gets said—is fundamental, and a useful site for interrelating our understandings of literature and film, I remain disturbed by his discussion of point of view and voice-over narration—particularly with his implication that they and subjective camera account for most of what could be called first-person cinematic narration—and with some of his remarks about what can and cannot happen in literature and film. What I should like to do here is to take issue with a few specific points raised in that article, and then go on to present an expansion of my argument in *Mindscreen*[1] concerning film voices.

It is important to remember that discourse, whether in words or in images, can be magical, transformative, even when one is involved in making academically precise distinctions. Noting that Huw, the voice-over narrator of *How Green Was My Valley*, does not seem to age while those around him do, Henderson says, "The duration of the plot and that implied by the performance level are contradictory, something that could not happen in literature." This is, however, one way of describing precisely what happens in the first scene of *Hamlet*, where ten minutes of unbroken action take the story from midnight to dawn. It would be more accurate to say that language has ways to avoid introducing such a level of contradiction and that it can also happily manipulate paradoxical discontinuities should it be called upon to do so.

---

1 Princeton: Princeton University Press, 1978. [Reprint available from Dalkey Archive Press.]

Henderson goes on to argue that when Huw is not heard voice-over or his visual perspective is not adopted by the camera, the film is proceeding "in an objective way." While the voice-over is certainly used in that film to inform the audience at the outset and rather blatantly just who is the narrator, that announcement carries with it the expectation (which the audience comes to trust) that the film as a whole is intended and will continue to reflect a coherent and personalized perspective (Huw's), unless distinct signals are given to the contrary. Narrative discontinuity is not the normative expectation but the complicated exception, or at least that would be the case once the possibility of coherent narrative structure, with its option of creative and coherent—i.e., readable—discontinuity, has been understood by critics and theorists and accepted as a viable option by filmmakers. In *How Green Was My Valley*, *Double Indemnity*, *Dead of Night*, etc., the narrative focus does not blur simply because the voice-over is not there to hold the audience's hand at every moment, as it might in a sentence from which the pronouns had been deleted. In a film like *Lady in the Lake*, the ever-present subjective camera becomes an oppressive reminder, as the ever-present first-person pronouns in the novel of the same name do not; the repeated subjectivity code is oppressive partly because it is not necessary to our understanding.

There is a significant difference between an angle of vision and an experiential or moral perspective. Henderson writes:

> Older Huw is the narrator of *How Green Was My Valley*—it is literally his voice that we hear; but this does not control the question of mood. We almost never see things from young Huw's visual perspective. *How Green* is non-focalized in that no sequence, let alone the whole film, is shot from any one character's perspective. It is variably focalized in that it frequently borrows a character's perspective for one or more shots... Huw's arrival at school is shot in a non-focalized way; he is small and timid in the hallway but no character is looking at him in this way.

The character looking at Huw this way, I would suggest, is the older Huw—the narrator—presenting his impression of how he looked at the time. (The same logic covers his presenting how he says others saw him and the valley.) The fact that the first-person narrator of *Madame Bovary* disappears after the opening schoolroom scene would not lay him open to the charge of being a mere narrative convenience or puppet who has, as Henderson says of vanishing voice-over narrators, an elaborate wind-up but "nothing to pitch." Ishmael often vanishes from *Moby-Dick*, presents information he could not have obtained first-hand, etc., and is at the center of a brilliantly sustained and coherent narrative drive. What we have in *How Green Was My Valley* is the story of his youth as the older Huw tells and remembers it, complete with his ability to concentrate now on himself and now on the people around him. His life, like his tale, is a matter not just of what he saw through his eyes (subjective camera) but also of what he came to know. It is both too particular and too literal to insist that every perspective be anchored by a gaze, of person or of camera, in order to be understood. When Henderson says that "The puppet narrators of cinema...may have integrity as characters but they have no integrity as narrators, no resistance to the demands placed on them," he is forgetting about hundreds of narrative *tours de force*, from *Caligari* to *Marienbad*. Even if there were not examples available of cinematic narrators with integrity and "something to pitch," it would still be suspect for Henderson or anyone else to write as if complex and viable cinematic narrators *could not* exist, because of some inherent limit in film as a narrative system.

Both film and literature are organized expressions, and what they can do or present depends on the characteristics of their respective signifying systems or "languages." Without getting into linguistic arguments about double and triple articulation, or brain-lateralization theories about verbal *vs.* spatial-information processing, it remains evident that film has no discrete pronouns and that words and pictures have different ways of presenting information and of establishing narrative or anti-narrative frames of reference.

Because people often think in words, and of course speak in them, there is a natural association between first-person discourse and first-person experience; it is easy to imagine a speech-act as telling what a speaker wants to tell. But when subjective camera adopts the position of a character's eyes and offers that as an equivalent to first-person discourse, the analogy is forced, for although visual experience is as appropriate to film expression as verbal expression is to writing, the eyes are passive organs of reception, not of expression, and it is not natural to *tell* by *seeing*. We may share Bruno's perspective as he is slugged in the face by Guy, in *Strangers On A Train*, but that is not the same as feeling that, for the length of that shot, Bruno was explicitly telling us about that experience; the former interpretation—that we share his perspective for a while—is the more "natural," one based on a normative construct of the function of the eye. To introduce the concept of telling into the passive system of vision, some encoding is necessary. There must be ways to establish whether deliberate, personalized narration is taking place, whether a given view is objective or subjective, whether whatever subjectivity does appear is authorial, and so on. And in the interest of sustained narrative complexity, there ought to be a more useful and comprehensive master code available than that of "POV and voice-over for subjectivity, everything else for objectivity."

The evidence of film history is that such a master code does exist, and in *Mindscreen* I attempted to sort out its first-person structures. One thing that emerged from that study, and which needs to be emphasized here, is that these codes and subcodes are not inflexible; they are often creatively redefined by filmmakers and need to be understood in the contexts of particular films. In some cases, a firmly and consistently established narrative structure can instruct the audience how to interpret the film; this is the case in *Dead of Night*, *8½*, *Life Upside Down*, *The Wizard of Oz*, and *Rashomon*. In other, more ambiguous cases, it may be necessary to interpret the film as a whole before one can establish, in relation to this larger structure, the likelihood of a given effect's having had a certain narrative intent.

In the case of the subjective-camera slugging in *Strangers On A Train*, for example, the first thing one might look for is any evidence that Bruno acts as the narrator of the film as a whole, and as it turns out, there is no such evidence. From the very start, when the camera divides its attention equally between Guy's and Bruno's shoes as they converge, to the end, when the story continues after Bruno's death, what evidence there is is on the side of an authorial, third-person narrative mode, a camera that is equally outside both characters and that is letting the audience in on an interesting story. Within this structure, the camera toys with letting the audience share—momentarily—the interior perspectives of the central characters. Sometimes we see what they see (subjective camera), and sometimes we see or hear what they think or hallucinate (mindscreen). At times Hitchcock uses the same camera set-up to convey objective and subjective views (the slugging sequence, Bruno's meeting with Babs at the country club, etc.), and what emerges from that apparent muddle is a brilliant game, conveying the unsettling sensation that any point of view can suddenly be appropriated by a subjectivity whose perspective may prove abnormal, and thus advancing the picture's general theme about the darkness that hides within what we might like to think of as a safe and stable social and psychological norm (which is comparable to the objective norm of the third-person shot). The larger point to be gleaned from such an analysis is that in any film, the camera's view is always a *potential* field of view, capable of being appropriated or defined according to the intentions of the filmmaker. As long as he or she insures that the visual field is defined in a manner the audience can follow, the filmmaker is free to experiment with ways of achieving such definition. Although the number of possible film voices is not infinite, there is no necessary limit on the ways those voices may be encoded.

The issue is not one of pronouns, nor of recognizing formulas and graving them in stone (like the current, inaccurate assumption that the subjective-camera shot is necessarily bracketed by objective shots, usually of the looker, and is not otherwise comprehensible). The question is one of *voice*, and it provides a very useful link between the discursive structures of literature and cinema. Words and film share the ability to personalize discourse, to give the impression that someone or some category of voice is telling, presenting, falsifying, arranging—in short, narrating—the text, regardless of what kind of text it is. These practices are found in narrative, nonfiction, animated, and avant-garde films, regardless of period. There is something in the cinematic system, be it ever so visual, that corresponds to voice in both commonplace and complex organizations of spoken and written language, even if the eye cannot speak.

Mindscreen was concerned almost entirely with first-person voices. In recent years, more and more critical attention has been devoted to sorting out the first-person aspects of third-person narration (as in the problem of Hitchcock's personal attitude toward Scotty in *Vertigo*, or Ford's vision of the history of the West), and so to forestall a critical muddle, it seemed important to suggest some distinctions among kinds of third-person narration. What then stood in the way of a comprehensive rhetoric, or at least of a full-fledged cinematic equivalent to the pronominal code, was the concept of second person, since it is hard to imagine anything as impersonal as a film in the act of talking about or directly to the audience. Most second-person prose, however, is just as impersonal as film; what both do is to take a position of addressing or describing a "you" who is absent and largely unknown, and who may or may not be listening carefully or willing to respond (which might be like answering mail addressed to "Occupant"). Leaving personal letters and direct speech aside, second person is primarily an "as if" discourse, and has the same characteristics whether or not it accurately describes its audience, whether it remains unpublished or in the can. Beyond that, there is no reason except the economic to prevent a film's being made for a particular, known, even single audience—like the mindscreen tape that the husband in *Brainstorm* creates for his wife, or those project-oriented films shown to businessmen in certain conferences, or a poetic film one might make only for himself although others may be invited to look at it. There is room for argument about whether second person ought to be set in the context of the pronominal code, as I am doing, or within the larger domain of rhetoric, so that what might be involved would be a shift not from third to second person, but from the declarative to the imperative. Not all the second-person instances outlined below, however, are in the form of commands, and the possibility of interactive modes has little or nothing to do with the imperative. And so for the time being I will persist in this formulation.

A first-person film or shot tells "my" version of what happened, whether or not it happened to "me," whether or not the action or percept is completed and whether or not "I" am aware of sharing this version with anyone. A second-person film or shot tells "you" what to do, involves "you" in the narrative project, or attempts to engage "you" in a version of conversation. A third-person film or shot tells what happened or is happening to ["him," "her," "it," or] "them." The following is a short outline of film voices, arranged in order of increasing complexity within each of these categories, with sound being left for last not because it is most complex but in order to keep the arrangement as simple as possible.

I. **FIRST PERSON**
   A. **Subjective Camera**
   B. **Point of View**
   C. **Mindscreen**
   D. **Self-Consciousness or Reflexivity**
      1. *Authorial Self-Consciousness*
      2. *Systemic Self-Consciousness*
   E. **Sound**
      1. *Voice-Over Narration*
      2. *Subjective Sound*

II. **SECOND PERSON**
   A. **One-Way Address**
      1. *Neutral Monologue*
      2. *Persuasion*
         a. Propaganda
         b. Commercials
         c. Other Coercive Narrative Projects
      3. *Intimate Discourse*
   B. **Interactive Dialogue**
   C. **Sound**

III. **THIRD PERSON**
   A. **Neutral Presentation**
   B. **Perspectival Presentation**
      1. *Single Author*
      2. *Multiple Authors*
      3. *Ideology as Author*
   C. **Sound**

I. FIRST PERSON

A. **Subjective Camera** (share my eyes). This is sometimes called the point-of-view shot (POV). The camera attempts to imitate the exact visual experience of the narrator (*Lady in the Lake*) or viewing subject (Bruno as Guy hits him).

B. **Point of View** (share my perspective, my emphases). Although the mode of presentation is apparently objective, the audience is restricted for part or all of a film to the experience of a single character and learns information much as that character does (*The Big Sleep, La Chienne*), though dramatic irony is always possible (*Vertigo, All That Heaven Allows*).

C. **Mindscreen** (share my mind's eye). The audience sees what a narrator tells or invents or deliberately presents as his own experience (*Rashomon, Annie Hall, Dead of Night*), or what a character who is not in a deliberately narrating posture personally experiences as an imaginary reality, hallucination, thought, vision, or dream (*The Wizard of Oz*, the framing story in *Dead of Night*). When the actress in *Hiroshima mon amour* remembers her German lover, that shot is not simply a flashback (an objective cutting back to an earlier part of the story, showing in an impersonal manner what happened at that time) but a mindscreen that presents her memory of the event. In *Brainstorm*, since it is the brain and not only the eye whose perspective is shared, the "full sensory tapes" are recorded mindscreens, distinguished from normal visual experience not only by the science fiction premise and by a number of subjectivity-establishing shots but also by a change in lens, aspect ratio, and image clarity.

D. **Self-Consciousness or Reflexivity** (share my awareness that this is a discourse or artifice).
   1. *Authorial Self-Consciousness.* The filmmaker (real or as a persona) makes it clear that he is aware of creating a discourse within the context of other discourses, sometimes undermining the audience's suspension of disbelief and taking the stage in the process. One recognizes an authorial level of commentary or interference when the character "Jaws" bites a shark in *The Spy Who Loved Me*, when Hitchcock is excluded from the bus at the start of *North by Northwest*, or when Pudovkin quotes *Intolerance* in *Mother*.
   2. *Systemic Self-Consciousness.* The film itself appears to be aware of the fact that it is a deliberate discourse, or a resonant center of consciousness within the narrative structure appears to be aware of being presented within a deliberate discourse—and this imitative awareness is not passed back to the real or implied author. The system appears to narrate itself, almost as if it had consciousness, so that what the audience sees in this case is the film's mindscreen (*Persona, Tout va bien*). The term also applies to such radical uses of mindscreen as that in *Dead of Night*, where the reflexive mindscreen of the principal narrator appears to be aware of the ways it corresponds to the terms of the horror film, and within which a character who is not the dreamer compares her situation to that in *Through the Looking-Glass*, advancing the (correct) notion that she may simply be a character in the principal narrator's dream. Throughout *Dead of Night*, the parallel between being in an altered state and being in

a movie (i.e., being an element in a discourse) is understood from within the system.

E. **Sound.** In contemporary filmmaking, sound applies integrally to all categories and is able to rely on the pronominal code of spoken language. Not to belabor the obvious, I will leave dialogue spoken by characters out of this, unless that character is also a narrator. The point here is to address those uses of sound that specifically help to define or clarify the narrative structure.

1. *Voice-Over Narration* (listen to my words) [(V-O)]. The narrator speaks to the real or fictive audience but is not shown while speaking. This is often used in conjunction with mindscreen, as in *Rebecca*, and sometimes with authorial self-consciousness, as in *2 or 3 Things I Know About Her*. In some cases the filmmaker will narrate the film voice-over, as Bergman does briefly and more or less anonymously in *Persona*, and sometimes he will make sure that the audience recognizes that his voice is authorial, as Orson Welles does in *The Magnificent Ambersons* (particularly in the closing credits, which he narrates) or as producer Mark Hellinger does at the start of *The Naked City*. *The Cabinet of Dr. Caligari* is an example of the equivalent of voice-over in silent film, where the visuals are interrupted by first-person, past-tense title cards.

2. *Subjective Sound* (share my ears). The audience hears what the character or narrator hears, remembers hearing, or imagines he hears (as Bruno hears "The Band Played On" when he looks at Babs in *Strangers On A Train*). This of course can include silence, as in Gance's *Un Grand amour de Beethoven* (silence as deafness).

II. SECOND PERSON

A. **One-Way Address** (now hear this!). The film addresses the audience directly, as if aware of its presence, but the audience cannot talk back. To the extent that it is called upon to respond, to learn, to change its attitude toward the material being presented, to obey commands, to listen, etc., the audience—or the rhetorical expectation that there will be an audience that will be called upon to react in some or all of these ways—is part of the narrative structure of the film.

1. *Neutral Monologue* (you might find this of interest). Material is presented, almost as in a lecture, to a personalized audience. In first-person voice-over narration, the narrator is primarily concerned with his own experience or tale (*Rebecca*), or helping the system to find personalized expression or to describe itself (*The Naked City*); in second-person neutral monologue, whether or not voice-over is involved, the narrative or rhetorical emphasis is on the act of addressing the audience, not just of speaking or telling

in a vacuum. The presenter can be unemotional about his subject, as in your average instructional documentary, or passionately involved, but he is in either case projecting a definite relationship with his audience. This relationship is not coercive; hence the term "neutral." What distinguishes this from third-person neutral presentation is that in this case the audience feels personally addressed by the film and will not be comfortable adopting an entirely detached attitude (an attitude that might be appropriate when watching a third-person film). What is coercive, even in this neutral case, is the structure of address itself, the rhetoric of the situation. There are various ways of establishing such a relationship with an audience. In some narrative films a character might be addressed in the second person by the voice-over narrator—"You think this is going to be an ordinary day, don't you, Mr. Jones. Well…"—and the audience enters the narrative system by identifying with that character, sharing the position of addressee. Rod Serling's voice-overs for the *Twilight Zone* series often addressed the audience personally and directly: "Picture if you will…"

2. *Persuasion*. In this case, the presenter clearly wants the audience to be won over to a certain attitude or position, and perhaps to act on it.

   a. *Propaganda* (you will believe that this is true).
   b. *Commercials* (you should want this and buy it).

   The distinction between propaganda and commercials (and, indeed, the coercive documentary or narrative film) is largely one of genre rather than voice, but also relates to the commercial and/or political context for which a film is made. It could be argued that in the present political situation, where economics and ideology are so inevitably intertwined, there may be no difference between propaganda and commercials, so that a Calvin Klein ad, an Air Force recruiting ad, the CBS Evening News, a patriotic documentary on the Unknown Soldier, and *Flashdance* might all be conveying essentially the same message in different genres, "selling" the "American way" just as *Triumph of the Will* and *Jud Süss* each promoted Nazi ideology. The difference [that], as an aspect of voice, does separate propaganda from commercials is that of tone: the manner or mood in which the coercive discourse takes place. Even so, it might be appropriate to allow for generic differences within this category, adding the coercive documentary whose interests are not necessarily those of the State (distinguishing it from official propaganda), and the coercive narrative film (e.g., *Jud Süss*), keeping in mind that those voices are different, or have a different rhetorical project, from the "this is how I see it" attitude of first- or third-person perspectival voices. Thus:

   c. *Other Coercive Narrative Projects*.

3. *Intimate Discourse* (you and I should examine this together). In this mode, which Francesco Casetti has called the "I and Thou," the film takes a less authoritarian and more personal tone when addressing the audience; the overall impression is that the film is trying to tell us something and that we have the option of making up our own minds […]. Where the audience is encouraged to change its mind in a certain way in the persuasive mode, the audience of intimate discourse is left free to respond in any way and to arrive at any attitude. Sometimes paired with self-consciousness, intimate discourse includes such friendly or sarcastic "asides" to the audience as those often made by Groucho Marx and W. C. Fields (the saloon/soda-fountain scene in *Never Give a Sucker an Even Break*).

B. **Interactive Dialogue** (let's talk). The film addresses the audience directly, and the audience is able to "talk" back, either by altering the progress of the system (choosing a pathway on an interactive laserdisc), feeding in responses (voting on a program's resolution, giving instructions through a computer), or yelling at the screen (*The Rocky Horror Picture Show* has become interactive in the course of its history). The greater the possibilities for authentically spontaneous response, the less easy it is to call this "a film," but the category nevertheless does exist, even if it wreaks havoc with conventional notions of closure. Some films allow for the possibility of audience response by including pauses (black leader and silence [or intermissions]), creating time for the audience to think or to consider its response or to respond. In *Mr. Sardonicus*, producer William Castle pretended to allow the audience to vote on the fate of the villain; the audience was given glow-in-the-dark thumb cards and instructed (by Castle, on the screen) to hold them up or down while Castle pretended to count them, announced that the vote was against the villain, and then returned to the story to show Sardonicus's unhappy ending.[2] The most thoroughly realized interactive films were the "follow the bouncing ball" singalongs.

C. **Sound** (listen, you). Voice-over narration in the second person: "You'll like our beer," etc. For a silent-film equivalent, consider Eisenstein's titles urging the audience to "Learn the use of arms!" in *October*. Direct address, rather than voice-over, is common in asides.

III. THIRD PERSON

A. **Neutral Presentation** (here it is). This is sometimes called "no one's shot." The camera and projection apparatus re-present, as if with perfect

---

[2] Harold Schechter and David Everitt, *Film Tricks: Special Effects in the Movies* (New York: Dial/Harlin Quist, 1980), 215.

objectivity, what is or was there to be shown. Even in a scientific film, such objectivity is an ideal category, but it has been taken, with some looseness, to be the basic method of "classical cinema." Either there is no foregrounded narrator, or the cinematic apparatus itself functions as an invisible narrator to which the audience is not supposed to pay particular attention. This category includes impersonal flashbacks and flashforwards as well as impersonal presentations of the real or fictive universe in the narrative present (*Footloose, The Ra Expeditions, Watering the Gardener*). The difference between this mode and second-person neutral monologue is in the film's expectation, conception, or degree of awareness of its audience—the terms of address.

B. Perspectival Presentation ("here" it is). There is an implied authorial perspective on what is shown; "authorial" here refers to the real point of origin of the discourse, whether that be a person, a studio, a mechanism, or a culture. This can also refer to a relatively free-floating, noticing, fictitious intelligence, like that of the camera that seeks out Rosebud in the furnace and finds it significant. The camera in *Citizen Kane* can be considered authorial in that it is the point of origin of the discourse, is not unalterably identified with any particular character at this point in the film, and does what Welles wanted it to. At times it appears to know as much about the situation as the author, while remaining as curious about it as the audience. What makes *Kane*'s camera different from the norm—and the norm, in this case, is that the camera is the organ of the author's attention and intentions—is that *Kane*'s appears self-directed, interested for its own reasons in "trespassing," going past closed doors, through a skylight, and eventually into this furnace as if to satisfy its own curiosity. Taken to its logical conclusion, this could be seen as a variant of systemic self-consciousness, and so the camera in *Rules of the Game* might serve as a less problematic example of the camera as a perspectival site.

  1. *Single Author* (this is how I see it). Without taking center stage or undermining the audience's suspension of disbelief, the filmmaker conveys a judgment or attitude toward the material being presented (Ford in *The Man Who Shot Liberty Valance*, Hawks in *Bringing Up Baby*, Coppola in both *Godfather* films [...]). For the literary equivalent, consider *Middlemarch, Oliver Twist*, or *The Bacchae*. Much of the "auteur theory" is devoted to identifying and interpreting this level of authorial commentary or favoritism. What distinguishes this from first-person authorial self-consciousness is that here the audience is not encouraged to think about the author or to suspend disbelief. At the end of *Stromboli*, Rossellini subtly expresses a judgment of the heroine's situation in perspectival third person, but at the end of *Voyage in Italy*, when the shadow of the crane enters the image, he makes sure the audience is aware that the judgment is that of the filmmaker (authorial self-consciousness).

2. *Multiple Authors* (this is how we see it). It is rare for a film to be made and truly controlled by a single person or even to appeal back to a consistent perspective. (Although the converse is common in literature, which is usually written by a single author, there are examples of collaboration between authors—as in Nordhoff and Hall's *Bounty* trilogy—or between an author and one or more editors, as in the case of Thomas Wolfe's novels, or even between author/editors, as in Wordsworth and Coleridge's *Lyrical Ballads*.) This is the reality of the situation critically oversimplified by auteurists, and it suggests that coherence functions at a narratorial or systemic *level* rather than proceeding directly from the intentions of a particular artist, in other words that it is an aspect of having a structure. There are examples of collaboration that affected—if not effected—the value and narrative structures of finished films, such as Welles and Mankiewicz on *Citizen Kane* [or the producer and co-writers and co-directors of *Singin' In The Rain*], and there are examples of creative conflict that were equally significant: Resnais and Robbe-Grillet are said to have disagreed about whether the seducer in *Marienbad* was lying, and the film can be seen to reflect this.
3. *Ideology as Author* (this is how it is). There are levels of control that affect meaning in ways the filmmaker may or may not be aware of and may or may not be able to do anything about. A picture of a bank may carry different implied meanings in capitalist and noncapitalist cultures, and this level of meaning may operate alongside or in contradiction to any other and more deliberately controlled authorial intentions. To be free of an ideology one has accepted as "natural," one might have to become a different person. These ideological interventions or overlayings can be deliberate, as in *Red Planet Mars*, or inadvertent, as in *Gentlemen Prefer Blondes*. The difference here depends on the extent to which the author is aware of subscribing to a particular ideology and either does or does not set out to construct a film that will reflect that ideology; in either case the film does reflect the ideology. Both types are programmatically less coercive than propaganda [although the ideological film can *condition* the audience to accept the picture's norm as valid and in force]; that difference in tone may be the only thing that finally distinguishes the intentionally ideological third-person film (*Gentleman's Agreement*) from a coercive narrative project like *Jud Süss* or the ending of *The Great Dictator*. The inadvertently ideological film is likely to be even less coercive, since the filmmaker may be unaware of holding a position that needs to be argued; indeed, if the ideology is accepted as "natural," there may not be anything that the filmmaker might want the audience to change or rethink. On the subject of inadvertence: in the case of *Gentlemen Prefer*

Blondes there are grounds for arguing that the ideological perspectives of artist and culture were congruent and that Hawks did not set out to make a self-consciously patriarchal statement about capitalism and coupling, complete with a "male" camera. There is a further level of inadvertence, amounting to an ideological imperative and phrased in those terms by Comolli and Narboni: "*Every film is political*, inasmuch as it is determined by the ideology that produces it."[3] This category, which obviously is capable of overlapping with any discursive mode, can usefully be focused on those cases where the artist cannot be said—as it could be said of Hawks—accidentally to have agreed with himself. Where it is most useful is in identifying a film that appears to have no author *except* that of the ideology of the culture that produced the film, i.e., where it doesn't matter who the real author was, because the dominant perspective has been created as if without the author's participation or interference. *Gentlemen Prefer Blondes* is not overwhelmed by the voice of ideology—Hawks's voice never entirely disappears—and the same is true of *October*; thus in these cases it is appropriate to speak of an intentional (Eisenstein) or inadvertent (Hawks) ideological authorial project, with the voice of ideology a variety of co-author or co-speaker, whereas in the case of *Flashdance*, which has no significant authorial voice, the third-person presentation reflects the perspective of contemporary Hollywood on a Horatio Alger binge, and that perspective only. In general, then, the difference among these three voices depends on whose perspective is being advanced: his [or hers] (single author), theirs (multiple authors), or "everybody's" (ideology).

C. **Sound.** Sounds are presented as if with perfect objectivity; the illusion is that the audience hears what is or was there to be heard. [Sound effects, music, and even dialogue can be manipulated to clarify the scene's emotional and narrative content.] If there is a voice-over, it describes or relates the condition or history of him, her, it, or them in an apparently impersonal manner.

Those are the three major conventional modes of film discourse, but there are others, some of which are produced by the interaction or cross-fertilization of various simpler modes. There is, for example, something I have called "secondary first-person narration," which is at work in "Heart of Darkness," where Marlow tells Kurtz's story by telling his own story.[4] The implied message

---

3 Jean-Luc Comolli and Jean Narboni, "Cinema/Ideology/Criticism," in *Movies and Methods*, ed. Bill Nichols (Berkeley: University of California Press, 1976), 24–5.
4 Bruce F. Kawin, *The Mind of the Novel* (Princeton: Princeton University Press, 1982), 33–80. [Reprint available from Dalkey Archive Press.]

is, "I present another's experience through the filter of my own experience," and what this opens up for film is a way to deal with certain highly experimental uses of found footage (*Night and Fog*), particularly when the other's footage is only one aspect of a complex narrative system; it also accounts for one device that was put to silly use in *Eyes of Laura Mars*, and intriguing use in *Brainstorm*, where "I see what another sees." These two approaches to secondary first-person narration overlap in Michelle Citron's *Daughter Rite*, where it becomes important to analyze the "look" implied by the father's home movies. But it is not necessary that found footage play a part in cinematic secondary first-person narration, and this is evident in Sally Potter's *Thriller*, where the central character attempts to sort out her identity and the value structure of her personal and social history with reference to the figure of Mimi in *La Bohème*. A mode this intricate opens the whole question of bracketing and overlap—in other words, the true complexity of discourse and presentation.

It should be noted that all these voices allow for truthfulness, lying, analysis, and irony; that they often overlap; and that they make it possible to see how cinematic narration has the capacity to be as complex or as straightforward as verbal narration. It is that equivalence of range that has allowed film and literature to seek equivalent range as vehicles of human expression.

17

DOROTHY'S DREAM: MINDSCREEN IN *THE WIZARD OF OZ*

This article was written for the book Film Moments, *edited by Tom Brown and James Walters and published in 2010. The editors wanted film scholars to write short pieces about significant and memorable moments in films, preferably only as long as a shot, a scene, or a brief sequence. I had been referring to the dream sequence in* The Wizard of Oz *for years, but a hard look at this 16-second shot made the whole sequence finally clear. I apologize to the reader of this volume for defining mindscreen again in this piece, but the argument demanded it.* The Wizard of Oz *is not just a ready example, but one of my favorite movies.*

In L. Frank Baum's original novel, *The Wonderful Wizard of Oz* (1900), Dorothy actually travels to Oz, when the cyclone picks up her house, and back to Kansas; Aunt Em and Uncle Henry have built a new house by the time she returns. In the Oz movies made by Baum and others from 1910 to 1933, either a cyclone blows Dorothy to Oz or she is already there. MGM's *The Wizard of Oz* (Fleming, 1939) is the first movie to present the trip to Oz as a dream.

It is often said casually that the Kansas sequences are in black and white and the dream is in color. To sort this out, it is profitable to examine the dream sequence as a mindscreen whose offscreen narrator is the dreaming mind of Dorothy (Judy Garland) and to establish just when the dream begins.

A mindscreen presents the audiovisual field of the mind's eye. I coined the term and developed the theory in 1978 and am glad to have the opportunity to provide here a further example of its application.[1] Mindscreen offers the cinema a first-person mode of discourse, presenting matters as a character or some other narrative agency (even the self-conscious narrative system itself) sees them. For example, a flashback—a switch from the narrative present to an objective view of the past—is third person, but a memory—a mindscreen of how the past is remembered, whether or not that memory is distorted—is first person. A POV or point-of-view shot is also first person; so is the voice

---

1 Bruce F. Kawin, *Mindscreen: Bergman, Godard, and First-Person Film* (McLean and London: Dalkey Archive Press, 2006).

of a film that presents itself as a film, as does the extremely reflexive *Persona* (Bergman, 1966). A mindscreen can present an honest tale or a lie, a dream or a fantasy, a memory or a subjective view of the present; it can narrate what it tells in voice-over or let the unseen, unheard narrator remain an implicit aspect of the narrated field. In *The Wizard of Oz* the mindscreen's narrator is unconscious, dreaming what we see, and her dream includes an image of herself as she moves through the dreamed world. Her dream has a point, which is that everyone already has everything that he or she needs—for example, the Scarecrow (Ray Bolger) is already smart before the Wizard (Frank Morgan) gives him a diploma, and Dorothy has always had the ruby slippers though she has not known how to use them. In effect, the dreaming Dorothy is giving herself a lecture on her decision to run away to keep Toto from Miss Gulch (Margaret Hamilton), her need to discover her own power, and her desire to find shelter from the twister at home.

The Kansas sequences at the beginning and end of the movie establish its narrative frame; they were shot in black and white and given a sepia tint and may best be described as monochrome. The opening sequence includes information that will make it clear, in retrospect, that Dorothy dreamed her trip to Oz, that the terms of her experience were the terms of a dream and followed, at least in part, a dreamlike logic as they masked the characters and events of the day. Hunk, the farmhand who will become the Scarecrow, tells Dorothy to use her head to solve her problem with Miss Gulch (he says one would think from the way she'd been acting that she hadn't "any brains at all," and he does suggest a practical solution); he also says her head isn't "made of straw." Zeke (Bert Lahr), who will become the Cowardly Lion, shows fear after a brave act; Hickory (Jack Haley), who will become the Tin Woodman, jokes about a statue's being erected in his honor and holds still to pose for it; and Dorothy calls Miss Gulch a "wicked old witch." All this becomes material for her dream, the key to who the characters really are and to the ways each of them seeks or manipulates power. It should be kept in mind, however, that Dorothy, the dreamer, is the true source of all the power. To take a Gestalt approach, one could say that she divides her power among the characters or projections she confronts as well as her "small and meek" questing self. But the first time we see the movie, we are not meant to know until the end that the trip to Oz is a dream, for we see the house lifted up by the cyclone as if it were really being blown to Oz, where it very solidly lands. On second and later viewings it is clear that by the time the house is swept away, Dorothy is already dreaming.

After Dorothy has run away with Toto, she runs back home to make sure Auntie Em (Clara Blandick) is all right and, as a twister approaches, to seek shelter. (This marks the beginning of the "There's no place like home" theme that will run through and even past the end of her dream—the counter-theme to "somewhere over the rainbow," the lure of the faraway and fantastic.) Unable to get into the storm cellar, she goes into the house. A blown-in window hits her on the head, and she falls onto a bed and passes out. The cut that joins the medium shot of her lying on the bed to the close shot of her multiplied, dreaming face marks the border between objective and subjective narration in this sequence; it is also accompanied by a change in the music, which becomes muted. That shot of her doubled face, a 16-second composite of superimposed moving images, the moment we are here to examine, is complex, for it appears at first to be a transition to a dream but is revealed before its end to include and perhaps constitute the start of that dream. And it is in sepia, as are all the events in the house, whether it is in Kansas or has landed in Oz. The dream sequence is not entirely in color but begins in monochrome. That means that Oz is in color—that color is a property of Oz, not of the dream. That little discovery gives the color a special resonance and makes the monochrome shot that starts the dream worth special attention.

In *Sherlock Jr.* (Keaton, 1924) and *Vampyr* (Dreyer, 1932) a double-exposed image of the dreamer separates from his body, signifying the start of the dream. In *The Wizard of Oz* the dream begins with a close shot of Dorothy's head—eyes closed, on the bed—from which a superimposed second head separates. The two faces, tilting into and away from each other, float above circling bands that represent the cyclone but can also be read as a sign of wooziness as Dorothy sinks or reels deeper into unconsciousness. Circling movements, doubtless inspired by the turning of the cyclone, appear to be the way into and out of Dorothy's dream; at the end Glinda, the Witch of the North (Billie Burke), moves her wand in a circle behind Dorothy's head as contracting concentric circles form in the air, emerald at first but then losing their color, preparing the end of the dream (which ends in sepia, outside Oz, when the house falls to earth once again, presumably in Kansas, giving the dream a nearly circular structure). The circling movements of the cyclone are also reminiscent of the optical effects—wavy lines and so on—sometimes used, particularly in Hollywood, to signify a transition to a memory, tale, or dream. Although the separated faces and the whirling signify that Dorothy is already imagining that she is inside the cyclone, the shot also appears to show her sinking into that unconsciousness. But as the shot continues, dream dominates it and puts its stamp on everything that has come earlier in the shot, marking all of it as a dream. Within the composite, as the cyclone continues to roar and the faces to float, the dream takes shape. What comes is an event we later recognize could not have happened: the one that defines this shot as part of a dream and not just—or no longer—as a transitional device into a dream: superimposed on Dorothy and the cyclonic bands, the turning house is drawn up into the sky (Figure 17.1).

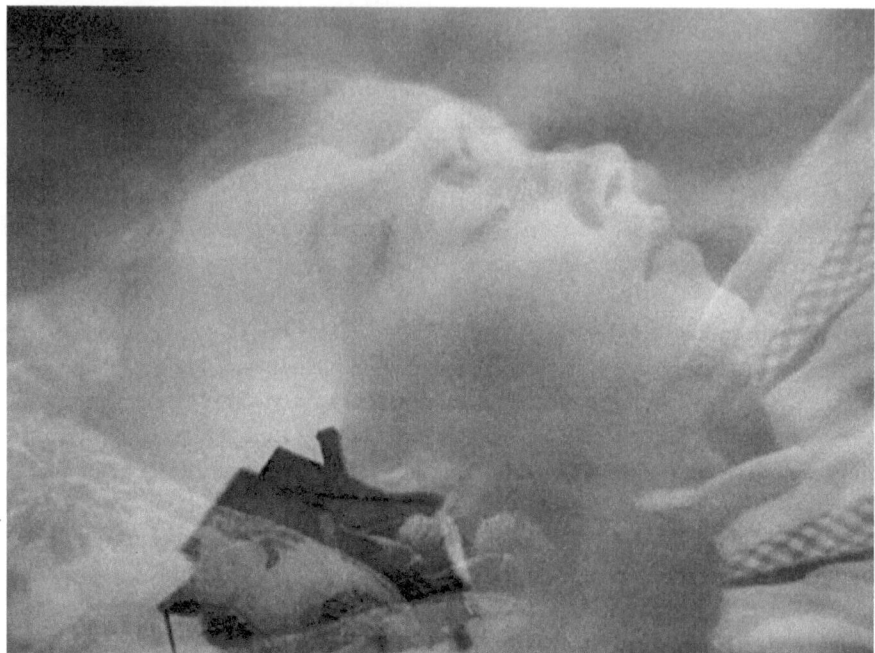

Figure 17.1. The house leaves the ground. From *The Wizard of Oz*.
© 1939, 2009 Turner Entertainment Company. All rights reserved.

Dorothy's face can now be recognized as that of the dreamer in the midst of her dream; the image is and has been not third but first person, the beginning of her experience inside the cyclone after she has passed out. [...] (The audience understands only retrospectively that any of this may be a dream; the first time we watch the movie, we think we are watching her pass out, be swept up with the house, and come to in the middle of the cyclone.) As the composite ends, a blown tree pulls our eye to screen right, and there is a cut to a view out the frame of the busted window (it feels as if the camera had panned to follow the rushing air) as objects are whirled about in the twister, putting the dream in a frame until the audience realizes (sometime during this shot, though not on a first viewing) that the dream includes the entire image, including Dorothy and Toto on the bed.

Once we leave this crucial composite shot, then, we are thoroughly in the narrative realm that we later recognize to be a dream, and Dorothy has a solid physical presence. She sits up on the bed, looks out the window frame, and sees things that are being blown around—most significantly, Miss Gulch on her bicycle, who suddenly turns into the witch Dorothy had called her earlier. But she is not just any witch; she is the Wicked Witch of the West, in costume and with her distinctive laugh. Thus the story of Oz has started, and its dream method has been made clear: Dorothy will turn the characters of her Kansas life into inhabitants of Oz. What Dorothy sees outside the window is plainly impossible and continues to be shown in monochrome. But what is inside the room is as fantastic as what is outside it. We can say that the image of Dorothy has become as much a part of the dream as what she sees outside, or that the entire world of the image, outside the window and inside the room, has taken on a unified reality. (We can also say that the established world of the inner narration includes a projection of its offscreen narrator, the dreaming Dorothy.) In that reality, impossible things happen all the time; the film later gives us the opportunity to attribute the fantastic quality of these events to their having been dreamed. What prepares us for this impossible reality is a shot that can be read as the start of a literal adventure or of a dream, a composite that appears to meld two worlds—of the dreamer and of the dream—as it prepares and yields to a coherent narrative space in which the tale of Oz can be told.

When Dorothy first lands, the house is still in sepia. When she finally opens the door to enter the color world of Oz, the shot is necessarily on color stock, but the interior of the house has been painted in browns to match the sepia, and Dorothy, played momentarily by a second actress, is wearing a brown and white dress until she (Garland) steps outside in a blue and white one. While she remains inside the house, she is in the equivalent of Kansas. The exterior of the house has color, as we can see once Dorothy has stepped outside it into the color-rich world of Oz. At the end, the monochrome of Kansas reasserts itself, together with Uncle Henry (Charley Grapewin) and Auntie Em's explanation that Dorothy, who is on the same bed with the busted window behind her (making it evident that the house never left the ground), got hit on the head and had a dream. Theirs is a realistic, down-to-earth approach and one that correctly points to mindscreen as the narrative mode that made possible the journey Dorothy insists was real. The dream begins in the mode Dorothy has always known, the monochrome of her life, before it turns to color to present Oz. The monochrome is the known world, and color is beyond it, transcendent.

Part VI

GETTING IT RIGHT

18

CREATIVE REMEMBERING AND OTHER PERILS OF FILM STUDY

This article was published by Film Quarterly *in 1978. Coming from a time before video copies of films were commercially available, it is of course badly dated. But it may be amusing for today's readers to see the kinds of difficulties and often crazy solutions one faced at the time. The problem of inaccurate publications has not gone away, however, even though video has made it easier for people to check copies of films for visual details and dialogue. I remain fanatically committed to the importance of simple accuracy in film scholarship, given what is known at the time one writes. For many writers today, that vigilance begins with not taking every date and credit on the IMDb for granted. The comments on Gerald Mast's* A Short History of the Movies *are fateful, because after Gerald died in 1988, I became the person responsible for correcting and updating that book, and edition after edition, the task has proved more difficult and time-consuming than I ever imagined.*

I went to see *The Wild Child* with someone who paid intimate and careful attention to the film; who understood it as completely, as personally, and as intellectually […] as anyone could; and who was yet convinced, not 20 minutes after we left the theater, that the film had been in color. It was how she saw it, what she *had seen*. Without getting into a Gestaltist argument here, or even appealing to Metz's […] notion of the "imaginary signifier," I should like to take up some of the difficulties inherent in writing accurately about a medium that invites an amalgam of subjective and objective response, yet whose texts are often not available for consultation—cannot simply be pulled off the bookshelf—when the moment to write about them is at hand. I should like to offer—from my own experience as a teacher, author, and audience of film criticism—a couple of useful ways of avoiding errors of description.

Last month a student asked me whether I had written anything about film or was just "in the error business." It was at that point I realized just how much class time I had been spending [on] having my students cross out dates and other "hard" information in the texts we were using, and how much they had accordingly come to distrust the books as tools. In fact there is no shortage of good books on film, nor of carefully researched articles. Even reading a good book, however, one is liable to find *some* errors, and in several of the widely circulated textbooks one finds little else. These range from errors in dating and attribution to inaccurate descriptions of what happens in a given film. On page 202 of Sadoul's *Dictionary of Film Makers* (ed. Peter Morris), for instance, Porter's *Life of an American Fireman* is dated 1902 in column A and 1903 in column B—as it is 1902 in Rhode's *History of the Cinema* and 1903 in Mast's *Short History of the Movies* (and in the Museum of Modern Art's film catalogue). Even such a careful, committed study as Rudi Blesh's *Keaton* contains, on page 230, a wonderfully written but simply wrong description of the climax of *Our Hospitality* (compare Robinson's [*Buster*] *Keaton*, 88). On the other hand, Robinson's *Keaton* (96) says that *Sherlock* [*Jr.*] opens with a close-up of Buster, who is revealed two shots later to be sitting near a pile of trash in an auditorium; actually, an auditorium shot occurs before the close-up. So, nobody's perfect, and I don't want to get pedantic here, but I do want to stress that many people depend on these books for descriptions of films they have not been able to see, and have a right to expect accuracy.

Take page 135 of Roud's *Godard* (second edition), which I happened to be using a few days after I had been asked whether I was in the error business and which is, on the whole, a distinguished piece of work. We were showing *Weekend* in class, so it was easy for me to pick out, from this single page, four simple errors of description: the couple does not drive a Dauphine; the traffic-jam track lasts eight minutes, not "a full ten"; the "milkmaid" is Emily Brontë; the rabbit has already been skinned before the mother is killed (and that skinning is never shown). Now it may not be a grave matter that Roud needs a new watch [...], but he uses his description of the way the couple's killing of the mother is presented "in counterpoint to shots of a rabbit being skinned" to make a serious point about the stripping away of "the veneer of civilization," and there simply is no such sequence in the film, even if Roud is right about the general implications of the murder itself. [What happens is that the skinned rabbit has blood poured on it while we hear sounds of the murder and a post-homicidal conversation between husband and wife; presumably it's the mother's blood or a symbol for it, but there is no cross-cutting and no skinning.]

The problem Roud's page manifests could be removed through the application of a rigorous system of notation (more on that later). There are other writers, however, whose work is characterized not by inadvertent carelessness but by real sloppiness—not so much in the matter of description as in that of objective research. I am thinking particularly of two textbooks, Lee Bobker's *Elements of Film* and Gerald Mast's *A Short History of the Movies*, but I don't mean to suggest that Mast's is as poor as Bobker's.

A Short History, when it first came out, struck many of us as a useful expansion of Knight's *The Liveliest Art*; it was, however, marred by a number of errors. When I called this to the attention of the publisher, Bobbs-Merrill solicited corrections from myself and others, and Mast took most of them into account when writing the second edition of his book. This ought to have been a successful instance of the process of informed feedback; the problem is that, even so, the second edition needs to be gone through with a red pencil. [For example,] Prof. Rath in *The Blue Angel* is still Prof. Unrat (178).

Elements of Film (second edition) raises another order of problem. It sells well, is used widely, and is in most respects mediocre. Is there another way to characterize a "textbook" in which a summary of *Jules and Jim* begins by describing "Jules (Henri Serre), an Austrian, and Jim (Oskar Werner), a Frenchman" (193); in which *M* is "Fritz Lang's classic 1917 melodrama" (177); in which *The Servant* is an adaptation "of Pinter's short play *The Servant*" (177) and the victims in *Potemkin* run *up* the Odessa Steps (113)? I spent about a week drawing up a list of errors and quarrels, sent it to the publisher, and received in response a lengthy tape in which Bobker argued that most of the things I had questioned were matters of opinion. Harcourt Brace Jovanovich has still not indicated whether they intend to insert an errata sheet, commission a third edition, or continue to market the text as is; they did, however, let me know that *none* of the book's users had ever complained about its accuracy. What *that* argues is that many of the people who teach film are either incompetent or lazy. It seems extremely unlikely that a national sample of English teachers would assign and endorse a textbook in the history of the novel whose discussion of *Tom Jones* began, for instance, by dating it 1680 and then went on to confuse the names of the major characters.

The best general film text on the market, James Monaco's lucid and rigorous *How to Read a Film* (Oxford), contains the sort of errors that could be corrected between printings: Max Steiner is called Fritz (183), *To Have and Have Not* is dated 1946 (244), *Last Year at Marienbad* shows up in an otherwise excellent chronology as Resnais's big 1959 film (475), etc. But Monaco is a responsible scholar as well as a careful writer, and one can assume that he and Oxford will either circulate an errata sheet or modify the text before the time for a second edition rolls around.

The problem, in its simplest terms, is twofold: some people make avoidable mistakes (with the best intentions, no doubt), and others—from publishers to readers—not only fail to correct these mistakes but actually endorse them. I don't intend to multiply examples, but it seems useful to indicate that serious questions of interpretation and analysis hinge on the issue of accuracy, and that all this can matter to the professional scholar as much as to the beginning student. In the class after *Weekend* we showed *2 or 3 Things I Know About Her*;

I wanted the students to have the text of the metaphysical coffee-cup sequence, so they wouldn't have to spend all their time reading the subtitles, and turned to the screenplay. On page 138 of *Godard: Three Films* I found the kind of minor error that can really mislead: "150 frames" reads "150 pages":

> That was how Juliette, at 3:37 p.m., came to be looking at the turning pages of an object which, in journalistic jargon, is known as "magazine." [Cut] And that was how, about one hundred and fifty pages further on, another young woman, like her in every way, a kindred spirit, a sister, was also gazing at the same object.

The point is not that the pages shown in the second shot occur 150 pages later in the magazine (they don't), but that the film announces the distance along its own length between the start of the first shot and the start of the second. To bury the reference to Baudelaire's "mon semblable, mon frère"—well, I can bring that out in class; but how many people will trust their own memory of "150 frames" when consulting an "official" screenplay, and go on to explore one of Godard's most elegant and accessible reflexive gestures?

At present, then, one cannot automatically trust what one reads in a screenplay, a history, an in-depth study, or even a film encyclopedia. This situation could be ameliorated if writers made a point of re-screening every film they've written about, before their work goes to press, and if readers gave publishers more consistent and rigorous feedback. As it is, there are few film libraries—complete with Steenbeck—to which the scholar can have adequate, regular access. Film scholarship is where it is because one cannot have every film that matters in easy reach, tends to trust his or her memory (especially of a film that has had a strong impact, that matters enough that one wants to write about it), and may in a pinch check "the facts" in a screenplay or [a] study whose author was in this same position. Memory, however, is often creative. What one remembers is what one has seen, felt, thought—not necessarily what was there to be seen; one remembers experience, which is an amalgam. The basic texts in film study are the films;[1] one needs a way to write them down for reference, and must further be willing to see them again, no matter how brilliantly one may have written about them. What follows, then, is a series

---

1 As Raymond Bellour has demonstrated in "The Unattainable Text" (*Screen* 16, no. 3, 19–27), "the word text as applied to film is metaphorical" because a film text cannot be quoted. When we have solved all the problems of access to films, of methods of notation, etc., we will still need to keep up some process of translation between the record of the text and the text itself ("the locus of an unbounded openness"—Bellour, 20).

of elementary procedures the writer may find helpful. In an ideal future they would all be as obvious as they ought to be now, but evidently aren't.

It is, of course, essential to see a film several times before writing anything serious about it. One needs, on first viewing, to be led through the film without knowing where it's going: to be confused, excited, suspended, moved. But one would not write about *Citizen Kane* ten minutes after first finding out what Rosebud was [except to capture first impressions and ideas]. There have to be later viewings, in which one can step back from the film and see its structure, and the ways the shots create that structure. All this is easier on an editing table—or, in the foreseeable future, with videodisc—but if you *have* to do your work in a movie theater, one of the most effective checks on memory is to tape the soundtrack on a cassette recorder. (This is probably illegal, so destroy the tape when you're done with it.) If the screenplay is available, it's important to run through it while playing back the tape, making whatever changes are indicated. To the greatest extent possible, try to turn the printed screenplay (usually pre-production) into a cutting continuity (post-production). It's also possible to make another tape while watching the film again, muttering "cut," "slow dolly-in," etc. (to augment the soundtrack, which should still be clear in the background) or your running insights as you watch the film.

These tapes, however useful, should be supplemented by a written continuity of the visuals. If you can't write by screenlight, you might want to devise a clipboard with a battery-operated light box, or else use a ball-point pen with a built-in flashlight. Keep a running record of the film, sequence by sequence. The second time, try to work in dialogue and commentary. A private, technical shorthand is useful here (T for track shot, or whatever).

Finally, check out your perception of what happened in the film with someone who's seen it recently. At this point you're ready to go home and write it up—to explore every connection, every opening, while remaining in touch with the text. This is also the best time to read other critics on the subject—and to write to their publishers; this kind of grass-roots activity, this checking-out by people who have seen the films recently, can help make the books that *are* available more useful. When your piece is finished, see the film again, to make sure you haven't introduced any errors while following your train of thought. After that, if you still think *The Wild Child* is in color—or ought to have been—you can talk about your experience of having seen it that way, without making your reader wonder why the local theater is showing a black-and-white print. A publisher will market what sells; it is up to us to make sure that what goes into those books is true.

19

LATE SHOW ON THE TELESCREEN: FILM STUDIES AND THE BOTTOM LINE

What can I say about this article except that most of it came true? (I was wrong to be apprehensive about the Library of Congress's National Film Registry, which turned out fine.) It offers a conservative perspective on film and video in 1988, when colorization was rampant and there were no DVDs or HDTVs, let alone 4K digital movies whose frames had the same number of pixels as film frames. Laserdiscs were catching on, but Blu-ray discs were far in the future. Most schools that used video used VHS or laser. It was published in Film Quarterly *the following year. Things had changed a lot since I wrote "Creative Remembering," mainly for the better, but there was a new problem: film studies teachers were on the verge of abandoning celluloid in the classroom.*

At the 1988 joint meeting of the University Film and Video Association and the Society for Cinema Studies (whose official topic was "the relationship of theory to practice"), there were several papers and panels devoted to the relative merits and values of film and video.

The film image was rated superior (be thankful for small favors), but the way this praise was rendered may prove of some interest. It was not that the frame of film—with its dyes, its silver, its tidepool emulsion—stored and yielded an image whose colors and other pictorial values were superior to and of an *entirely different nature* from the pictorial values of electronic imagery—not, in other words, that the film image alone could be the film image—but that the frame of film had the greater number of pixels.

The implication was that the video image could catch up with film if it solved the problem of resolution. Much the same was implied in a paper about the wonders of electronic cinema and high-definition television (HDTV) and the new world in which movies would be broadcast to theaters (that, the speaker said, would be "cinema"), high-definition video copies would be enjoyed at home (that would be "television"), and both of these *screened moving-image programs* would be "movies." Since they would be shot on video, there would be none of the loss of quality typical of the film-to-video transfer. Since home and theater programming would be virtually identical, the field would be unified (probably as "moving-image studies") and the distinction between film and video could become historical rather than so disconcertingly ontological, with films being what were made in the past, or an essentially nineteenth-century mechanical and chemical approach to the storage of information, whereas all good postmodern information is stored, processed, and conveyed electronically. This particular prophet—or in any case this line of thinking—resolved the distinction between cinema and video by abolishing film. And a good number of filmmakers and teachers agreed, saw no problem.

In the context of such nonpictorial values as convenience and cost, video won hands down. It was described as the only cost-effective medium for shooting documentaries. Its role in contemporary post-production, especially in the editing of material originally shot on film, was described and praised; that's here to stay, and it's OK with me, since what starts as film in the camera is released as film by the lab; laserdisc/filmloop editing and computerized color timing are viable advances in the technology of making movies. The video *camera*, however (used entirely in the 1987 theatrical feature *Julia and Julia*, in more and more documentaries, and of course in video art as well as in the taping or broadcasting of movies), creates a different animal, even when its imagery is transferred to film. An electronic image is of course a different animal—like a white horse slashed by the lines of a thousand razors and passed off as a zebra. (Or is it a horse in prison?)

While great energy was expended, conference-wide, in distinguishing "video" from "television," the distinction between "movie" and "program" was abused to the point of redefinition. As far as I'm concerned, a 35mm print of *The Maltese Falcon* is a *movie*, and to see it in a movie theater is a cinematic experience. A 16mm acetate print of *The Maltese Falcon*, being of roughly the same nature as the original (in this case, a nitrate release print), is suitable for classroom study even if inferior in detail and quality, since it is at least a film. *The Maltese Falcon* on TV is a *program*, a broadcast of material that, like Dan Rather, need not ever have been electronic but is transformed into electronic information and decoded by an electronic monitor. What we get here is *video coverage of a movie*, with or without interruptions and in fact whether or not the source is a videocassette or a TV station. And *The Colorized Falcon* is just a particularly bad TV program that bears the same relation to the original as *Star Trek* cartoons do to *Star Trek* episodes: it's a takeoff with no textual authority, like a communion wafer stamped "Nabisco."

My favorite imaginary movie: George Bailey runs through the colorized streets of Potterville until he can't stand it anymore. At last the angel frees him from his dream, and everything is as it should be again, in glorious black and white.

I say that if *They Died with Their Boots On* had been in color, it would have been in Technicolor, not telecolor. I call it *telecolor* because it belongs on a telescreen, the ideal medium for a world or a text upon which values have been imposed so unequivocally that at last they appear to have been desired. That goes for color values too.

So what I never expected to encounter at a film conference was the slightest debate over whether film or video is the proper medium [with] which to teach the history, [aesthetics,] analysis, production, and theory of film. But there it was, and video won. It won for the same reasons it is winning out as a preferred method of documentary overshooting: it's easy to use, and it costs less. I think I heard the sound of film studies' desiring the spectacle of its own destruction, to take a cue from Walter Benjamin and a different war. I think I heard people selling wallpaper for the house of bondage, rationalizing the lowering of pedagogical standards by complaining how underfunded their courses were. Film studies is full of lines—above-the-line, crossing the line, the line producer—so what's another 1,125 or 425 or even, yuck, 330 horizontal ones when we're faced with *the* horizontal line, the one at the bottom?

Nobody has any money, no matter what Reagan says. Departments have no money, schools have no money, and what are you supposed to do if you have only $300 to rent films for a semester-long course? Or if your dependable $1,500 can't be stretched to keep up with the higher costs of film rental and postage? Or if the 16mm print you do rent turns out to be missing the first five minutes and the distributor refuses to strike a new print—and a cropped but uncut video copy can be rented for just a couple of bucks?

Well, as my grandmother said, you could always read a book.

But what most teachers will do, it now seems, is rent or buy that videotape (or laserdisc, if they want the best possible video quality and know how fast a tape deteriorates) so that they can take care of their immediate pedagogical needs. Those who distribute 16mm prints have every right to feel abandoned by a vital market and do have to consider the financial risks of doing the right thing—striking a new 16mm Scope print of *2 or 3 Things I Know About Her*, for instance—if the [print] might not be rented for courses.

If these emergencies remain endemic and people keep giving in to them, 16mm prints will go out of style, and classroom showings on video will become the cheap and easy norm. Sure will be easy to analyze those single frames.

We can all yell at the distributors for sending us damaged, cut, or panned-and-scanned prints, or for having too few prints to suit our schedules, but what they send us are *films*, movies on celluloid, and without them—or an institutional library of 16mm prints—we have no way to show our students "the film version" of any movie. We need them to stay in business and to keep a vast diversity of titles on the active list.

Don't get me wrong here: I hate a bad print as much as the next obsessive-compulsive scholar, and I'm not defending the distributors of inferior product. I think we should rent, lease, or buy perfect prints and that we should pay a fair price for them. I think they're essential to the education of our students' eyes. I think deans and presidents should bend over backwards to approve huge sudden amounts of money to expand college film libraries. After all, do they buy cheap photographic copies of paintings to hang in university art galleries? Do they think that a videotaped lecture is a satisfactory substitute for one given in person?

Failing all that, I think that if you've got only $300, you should *buy* a new print of a great film and study it until it falls apart—after first showing it for admission, say to 300 people at $1 each, so that the next print would be paid for.

The next time some administrator offers you a lousy budget, refuse to be the middleman in this "we'd love to but we can't afford it" imposition of mediocrity. Tell them what you and the program and the students need, period. Be as flexible as the IRS. If film teachers cease to insist upon the *film* component of film studies, no matter how much lip service they pay it ("You really ought to see this sometime," they'll say as they "play" *Citizen Kane*), the market will dry up, and a new generation of students will encounter no major difference between a film studies course and the Late Show, except that the commercials will be different, or between *The Maltese Falcon* and *The Maltese Falcon in Jail*, Ted Turner's version of the horse of a different color.

Most film scholars got furious at Turner for killing the goose that laid the golden eggs—that is, for practically destroying MGM in the process of snatching its film library. So [he has] no taste, no film education, and no eye: fine. But just who is going to get this wonderful film education we defend and dream about if film teachers themselves are willing to spread out banquets in which every dish has been run through the electronic egg-slicer of the video eye?

A National Film Commission may be founded soon, empowered to designate 25 pictures a year as national treasures, not to be defaced, cropped, censored, or colorized—without proper labeling. Will this protect *films*, mandate the striking of new archival prints, lead to an annual traveling film program ("See the winners as they were meant to be seen!"), or merely regulate the treatment of movies on video? With the government's and the industry's and even academia's priorities, how many of those 25 would you expect to be really interesting? I'd give *Drums Along the Mohawk* and the by now unavoidable *It's A Wonderful Life* considerably better chances of making the list than Brakhage's *Anticipation of the Night* or Deren's *Meshes of the Afternoon* or Webber and Watson's *The Fall of the House of Usher* ("Why waste a 25th of our allocation on such a short film? Who would colorize it anyway?").

It's worth remembering that colorization primarily affects video copies of popular movies. It is, to be sure, a greasy form of theft and an insult to art. But the film remains, if a good print does (not if you just turn down the color dial, sorry; colorization affects the gray values and the grain), and it can be screened—if a print is available.

It should also be kept in mind that all broadcasts and most video copies crop the entire perimeter of even the 1.33:1 image. This can be explained or justified electronically in terms of image stability, but the real reason for all this bleeding, this fear of the blank rim, is TV's inferiority complex. It knows it's small, so it has to fill itself up; this lets it feel bigger, or lets the viewer more easily enter the [bourgeois] space of the [full] frame. Any inner frame, whether 1.33:1 or 2.35:1, promotes Brechtian estrangement and might let the viewer stay out, tune out, turn off.

TV also knows that it is not an electronic development of cinema but illustrated radio. TV has to force people to pay attention to it, has to grab their attention when it needs it, and is otherwise content to provide a continuous soundtrack (as Rick Altman, among others, has observed) to which one may half-attend, perhaps while doing housework or chowing down with the folks. Movies have such problems only when they are made by idiots or shown on televisions.

There is more to film studies than the study of the moving image. Nevertheless, the merge is on. Schools of cinema-television and departments of English or communication that house a few film people continue to proliferate; many new grad students report that they find television studies a more attractive and open field than film studies; and many faculty now consider it logical, realistic, and "with it" to treat film as the revered ancestor of the electronic arts rather than as the happy child of the theatrical and visual arts (and music, and dance, and literature, and history, and... —which is why a film studies major has the potential to focus a solid education in the liberal arts). All this is fine and progressive, so long as film studies retains its integrity within such programs and a few things are kept straight.

Video art and film art can both be studied as art. The television and film industries can both be analyzed as ideological cornucopias, economic and communication systems, or whatever. Television and video and film should all be celebrated and taken seriously; all are rich and relevant audiovisual and scholarly fields. To understand them *and* to interrelate them, we need [to avoid confusing] them. We need to let them be separate, to be themselves—to let cinema be cinema and television be television—as well as study their points of overlap, influence, and intersection.

All that is going wrong here is that someone is trying to *let video be film*. And the argument appears attractive to production as well as academic personnel, all of whom are feeling the squeeze and many of whom are legal residents of the state of the art.

If this trend continues, something may disappear from our classes, if not from the movies. At least the appreciation, and perhaps the very experience, of every aspect of a movie that is just not there and not happening when the "same text" is played back through a TV set: the aura of the real thing, the richness of the dyes, the dark, the silver, the quality of the light that flickers from behind you...

There is nothing wrong with providing students access to video or laserdisc uncut copies—in the library, for example, as texts on reserve—of movies that have been *projected* in class. But anyone, teacher or student, who doesn't respect the difference between a 35mm print of *The Red Shoes* and a video copy ought to get into another field. Even if a great many film students do come to us today with an education in movies acquired primarily via broadcast and cable TV as well as the ubiquitous VCR, our job remains to start with what they know and take them where they need to go: to teach them what a movie is, to excite their interest and enlarge it. To explore, among other things, the alchemy of the cinematic synthesis, as electronics, mechanics, optics, and chemistry come together as the film image—rather than to bow to the purely electronic, the convenient, the trendy.

The last time something like this video/film debacle happened was when Super8 sales went through the roof and everybody lost interest in 8mm. At the time, I was running a film studies program at Wells College on an annual budget of $500. I went down to 34th Street and bought enough 8mm equipment to run UCLA—good steel cameras with prime lenses, five bucks a pop. Hence a word to the wise: this may be a very good time to spend all the institutional money you can scare up on 16mm prints of the movies you expect to be able to continue to show in class, because they may not be around much longer.

Adam Reilly was, among other things, a brilliant, resourceful, and dedicated collector of great prints of great films. When I taught a Griffith course here at the University of Colorado at Boulder, he provided me and my 13 students with complete prints of every single extant Griffith feature (a tinted print of *Scarlet Days*, an interminable print of *One Exciting Night*, even *Lady of the Pavements*), at least half of the shorter films, and a pile of features and shorts made by Griffith's contemporaries, like *Traffic in Souls*, *The Italian*, and the amazing *Young Romance*. He threw open the doors of his Denver Center Cinema (now a memory itself [...]) to show us *The White Rose* in 35mm. When the students completed their final project—to make a 16mm film that could pass for a previously undiscovered 1911 Biograph—they struck a print of *Love's Choice* for Adam, because they understood his gift.

About six months later, he was dying young of cancer. Just over a year ago, the hour it turned out he died, I cancelled the film I'd been planning to end Film History II (Sound) with and instead showed a silent film Adam had made it possible for us to purchase for $400, a brand new 16mm tinted print of Griffith's *The Greatest Question* (1919). I can only hope you've seen it. It stars Lillian Gish and Bobby Harron, and it's as good as *True Heart Susie*.

The movie was great and the print was gorgeous: it was a brand new old thing, a marvel to unreel. It was about life after death, and everyone who worked on it except Miss Gish is dead; Bobby Harron died before he made another picture for Griffith, and Adam was expected to die that afternoon. But the film was alive, it was present; it answered the story's question. The tinting was so translucently even, the photography so sharp, and the fine-grained print so downright perfect that you could see the weave in the cloth behind the intertitles, and you could tell that what was roped around the words was a real cord, not a drawing.

20
VIDEO FRAME ENLARGEMENTS

I worked on this article, which was published in Film Quarterly *in 2008, for five years. Every time the technology advanced, I had to make new trial stills. By the time I was ready to write up the results, Snappy had gone out of business and I had to start over with a new frame grabber. The original comparison was between black-and-white and color frames, using* Citizen Kane *and* Vertigo. *When the article was completed, however, the studio refused to allow the use of the* Vertigo *frame. So I shot the frame from* Intolerance, *which is in the public domain, and rewrote the article so that the comparison was between a close-up and a long shot. Explaining how to grab a frame took me back to the year I worked at IBM while I was in college, rewriting the programmers' draft of a long technical manual.*

There used to be two ways to illustrate a book or article with pictures from a film: to photograph a frame enlargement from a 16mm or 35mm print or to select a production still that originally came from a press kit. Production stills, distributed for reproduction in magazines and newspapers, are posed and generally give sharp views of the sets and the actors in costume, and sometimes they approximate the blocking of actual scenes. For a literal view of what is onscreen for a fraction of a second, one needs a copy of an actual frame from the movie. A frame enlargement could be printed as a photograph and submitted to the publisher as an 8 × 10 or as a 35mm slide. Production stills, usually found in archives and in memorabilia stores, most often were 8 × 10s.

Now, however, fewer prints are available from which to shoot frame enlargements, and DVDs, with their tantalizing restorations, are everywhere. Schools often meet their budgets by showing films in class on DVD, in spite of the fact that students are left watching a TV. As film classes rent fewer prints, distributors have less incentive to replace scratched and faded prints; thus fewer titles remain available on film—in good shape or any shape. Frame enlargements shot from inferior prints are liable to be scratched and faded too. The very frame one wants may be a wreck. But on a DVD, the frame may be pristine. The only problem is that it is a video image, not a film image.

The frame is electronic and must be reproduced not with a camera but with a computer, yielding a digital video image rather than a photographic one. Even when the digital file is printed on photographic paper, it betrays its video origins. And press kits have gone electronic. Rather than a sheaf of 8 × 10 black-and-whites and color slides, most of them now offer production stills and the occasional frame enlargement only on a CD, in the form of high-resolution film scans. So an article or a book manuscript may now be accompanied not by a sheaf of photographs but by a disc to which frame enlargements made from video sources and production stills copied from electronic press kits have been transferred.

We may be looking at the future of frame reference. DVDs already are more widely available than celluloid prints, and the hardware and software for video frame grabbing are simple to use. The question is, how good are video frame enlargements in comparison with enlargements shot on and from film? To test this, I needed a close shot and a long shot, and I needed to be able to examine and present, to the extent possible, the identical frames on film and on video. I secured a 35mm frame from *Citizen Kane*, which I then printed as an 8 × 10, and an 8 × 10 35mm frame enlargement from *Intolerance*, then shot (or "grabbed") the same frames from VHS, laserdisc, and DVD copies of the films, both when the image was moving and when it was paused. For those first tests, I used a frame-grabbing device called Snappy, which is now available only on eBay; it was made by Play, ran only on a PC, and plugged into the parallel port. Any video source with a standard RCA jack could be connected to Snappy, while most of the products now available are designed to grab only from DVDs. Snappy got the best results with DVDs and CAV laserdiscs, and it did best when it grabbed from a moving source. Tests with color and black-and-white films—the color film used was *Vertigo*—produced nearly the same results when printed on black-and-white stock (as pictures would be in *Film Quarterly* and most books). For the final test, I grabbed the frames from a paused DVD using the VideoLAN Client (VLC) media player. The VLC player is free, runs on a PC or a Mac, and can be downloaded from http://www.videolan.org/vlc/; it also got better results than Snappy or any other frame grabber I tested. It did equally well with paused and moving sources and with color and black and white. Although I had a professional laboratory print the video frames as 8 × 10s for close study, the publisher used the electronic files to print them in this journal on glossy paper. Only the final published versions offer a rigorous example of how video enlargements really look, and how they might look in a book. On a computer monitor, of course, they look fine; their suitability for electronic publishing and distribution can be taken for granted (once one has cleared the rights if that is necessary; the same legal rules that apply to film frame enlargements apply to video frame enlargements).

There are two ways to grab a DVD frame with VLC. In Windows, Linux, or Unix, if one is playing the DVD in full-screen mode or in a smaller window, one hits Ctrl+Alt+S; on a Mac, Command+Alt+S (in Windows, hit the S key last while holding down the other two, or the program crashes). When playing the movie in a smaller window, one also has the option of going to Snapshot on the Video menu. In addition, the smaller window allows one to use the pause control, which takes a second or less (it varies) to stop the image; it helps a great deal when one is trying to grab a particular frame, even if it takes some practice. Almost immediately after one hits Snapshot with the mouse or presses the three keys, VLC presents the image of the captured frame in a small window. VLC accumulates shots sequentially in a directory the user can specify (on the Settings menu, go to Preferences and then to Video; the video snapshot directory is listed there, along with the format in which the snapshot will be saved and the aspect ratio of the source).

VLC defaults to flat settings. From the point of view of the test this was an advantage, because the idea was not to produce the best possible frame but to evaluate an unaugmented frame. Once a frame has been grabbed and saved as a file, it can be opened in a program like Adobe Photoshop and resized, brightened, and so on, augmentations and adjustments that are valid as long as the goal is to match the look of the original rather than to produce a nice new picture. VLC can grab from any source it can play; the easiest sources to use are DVDs and streaming media files. VLC can save the snapshot in a variety of formats, one of which (.png) is Photoshop-friendly and preferred by [many publishers; it also saves in .jpg, preferred by many other] publishers. The VLC grab can be made while the movie is running or paused. VLC shoots color sources in color; its other relevant default is that it grabs frames in the aspect ratio of the source. Whichever brand of frame grabber one uses, it is important to make sure that the software preserves the original aspect ratio; many such player/grabbers default to 16×9, stretching a full-frame image sideways.

Whether desktop video frame enlargements can stand up to celluloid frame enlargements in the first place appears from the comparison below.

*

Figure 20.1 was printed from a 35mm frame taken from an internegative of *Citizen Kane*, near the end of the boarding-house scene narrated by Thatcher in his memoirs. I am grateful to Robert Carringer and RKO for getting me this frame and to Warner Bros. for permission to reproduce it. On the nose of the boy (Buddy Swan as Kane) there is a dark, curled hair. This hair appears on this frame in almost every film and video print of *Kane*; the restored DVD and print have "cleaned" it away. It is a film artifact. Because the hair is positive

190   SELECTED FILM ESSAYS AND INTERVIEWS

Figure 20.1. A 35mm frame enlargement from *Citizen Kane*.
© RKO Pictures, Inc. Licensed by Warner Bros. Entertainment Inc. All Rights Reserved.

Figure 20.2. A VLC video frame enlargement from *Citizen Kane*.
© RKO Pictures, Inc. Licensed by Warner Bros. Entertainment Inc. All Rights Reserved.

on a print, it cannot have fallen on the negative; it must have fallen on the interpositive and then been copied to the internegative from which prints were struck. Every photographed hair and bit of snow is distinct, the cap has a deep texture, there is great detail in and around the eyes, and every line is smooth. The shadow at the base of the cheek and part of the neck, however blotchy it is, has many points of definition; the texture and tones of the skin vary from the bright top of the cheek to the dark lower jaw, where the sled is beginning to dissolve in. There is a flare of light in his hair and on his neck.

Figure 20.2 is a VLC snapshot, a video grab of high quality. It is not exactly the same frame as Figure 20.2, but it is close—perhaps 2 or 3 frames ahead (the dissolve [has barely] started). The image has been cropped along the perimeter, approximately 3 percent. The exposure level of the shot is dark. The eyebrow and the ends of the hairs that touch the boy's ear are fuzzier than the hairs in the film image. The tiny bits of snow above the ear, on the cheek, and on the cap are less sharply defined. The line around the boy's iris is jagged, like the cutting edge of a saw; the line has "jaggies" but should be smooth and even. There is a similar problem at the top edge of the bottom eyelid, which shows scan lines and a three-leveled blotch. The shadow on the cheek looks like a shadow rather than a skin defect (which is how it appeared in the Snappy experiments); the most difficult area of the frame to render, this shadowed part of the face is quite good. The overall quality of the skin has, however, gone a little spongy. The freckles are in focus. The hair on the nose is missing—because the frame has been restored and in any case because this is a slightly different frame; the flare and [all but a hint of] the sled are missing, too, because this is a different frame. But the cap is missing some of its texture, and the eye's line some of its smoothness, because this is a video frame.

In other words, the lower resolution and electronic nature of the video image have consequences, here seen most plainly in the skin texture and in the number of distinguishable hairs in the eyebrow. These may be considered minor differences, unless a long shot makes a face the height of that eyebrow.

Figure 20.3 is a frame enlargement made by the Museum of Modern Art from a 35mm print of *Intolerance*. The shot comes at the start of the sequence depicting Belshazzar's Feast, and it is crammed with small details that demand high resolution. Everything in this frame is distinct and in focus. One can make out the people on the top of the back central wall, who are extremely small, and the darker line running horizontally beneath them and above the line of decorations. Partway down that wall, the tops of two huge, geometrically framed doorways or openings let the sunlight through (it is cut off by another great wall in the farthest background). Through the left doorway one can see a hanging drape catch the sunlight in a bow shape, while through the right one there is a lit triangle, perhaps a staircase, one side jagged-edged and one

Figure 20.3. A 35mm frame enlargement from *Intolerance*.

Figure 20.4. A VLC video frame enlargement from *Intolerance*.

side cut off by a smooth shadow. One can make out the people on the balcony of the pillar at the upper right as well as the people on the balconies of the other three pillars. The central columns of the pillars are curved rather than straight, and one can see the lines in their sides. At the central right, the large statue of a seated goddess is easy to make out, and so is the lion near her feet. All the true horizontal and vertical lines are straight and sharp. Among the clearer smaller details are the lines on the trunks of the elephant statues in the bottom row, the alternation of dark and light areas on the bottom central steps, and the rows of lion's heads that run up the sides of those steps. Even in the case of the people who are closest to the camera it is not possible to make out any faces, but their bodies are clearly defined.

One aspect of a film frame enlargement that does not carry forward into video is that everything in this frame is definitive. This is the source, the criterion of what is meant to be readable in the original image.

Figure 20.4 is a VLC grab of a frame from a bit later—roughly a second—in the same shot. Between Figure 20.3 and Figure 20.4, the camera has moved slightly forward. The first thing one notices is that dark horizontal line at the top of the wall in the central background, for it has expanded to become a much wider band; it looks like a shadow, but in the film frame it clearly is not. I got the same dismal result using both of the currently available DVDs of *Intolerance* (Kino and Image) and shooting repeatedly, both when the movie was paused and when it was moving. The lines that are supposed to be clean, sharp verticals and horizontals are straight, however, and the bowing lines of the columns are rendered correctly. The curve of light on the hanging drape is there. One can make out the lion at the foot of the goddess if one knows it is a lion. But the alternating black and white areas on the lower central steps are not distinct, and the lion heads at the sides of the steps look at best like spherical blobs. The geometrical outlines of the rear doors are dark and sharp, as are the thick outlines around the carved figures at the lower left and right. One has no trouble making out the larger elements of the shot: the elephant statues, the pillars, the statue of the seated goddess, the walls, the steps, and if not the individual dancers, the fact that there are a lot of dancers. One can with difficulty make out the people on the balconies of the pillars, but it is clear that they are people. Those on the top of the back wall are barely visible; the people behind the left doorway are an indistinguishable mass. Despite the straightness of the lines, which VLC has rendered especially well, the lower resolution gives a fuzzy quality to the whole image. The range from black to white is reduced to a short range of grays. The hard-edged texture of the original is lost and with it some essential aspect of the grandeur of the *mise-en-scène*. Nevertheless the general outlines of the shot and the architecture of the set come across, as do details like the jagged edge of the triangle seen through

Figure 20.5. A Snappy video frame enlargement from *It's A Wonderful Life*.

the right doorway. This shot poses a very different problem from the *Citizen Kane* shot, for it is an extreme long shot full of small details rather than a close shot of a face. One must conclude that the lower resolution of the video frame enlargement, along with its tendency to flatten the lighting, made an excellent grab of this frame impossible. Then there is the matter of the spreading out of that black line into a band of shadow, the only distortion introduced by VLC that could be read as modifying the frame and introducing what looks like a different object. It is not a common problem with VLC, but it is a problem in this particular grab, making the grab unusable as well as uncharacteristically unreliable. For most video frame enlargements do convey the gist of their originals, even though they cannot convey all of their essence.

Comparing these four images, it is clear that at the current level of technology, a video frame enlargement sometimes distorts lines and curves, often fails to resolve the finest details, and has a narrower range of grays. Both film frames run from nearly white to nearly black, while the video frames run from light to medium-dark gray, giving the image a less defined and less composed look. The problematic skin texture in Figure 20.2 is found in many video frame enlargements, but VLC's results are better than others'. The obscuring of detail in Figure 20.4 is characteristic of current technology; it will take more work before those blobs on the banisters turn back into lions' heads.

In a pinch, then, in the absence of a film frame, grabbing a video frame enlargement from a DVD can yield an adequate image, though an admittedly inferior one whose details may not be clear enough to read and whose tones may be less photographic. The smaller the final picture, the better the image will look, even though it will still look like a video. But if it is small and sharp enough, it can pass not for film but for a viable reference, a reliable approximation of the frame. The reproduction is degraded in comparison with the original, and is inexpensive and ready at one's fingertips, for the same reason: that it is video. If Benjamin were writing today, he might observe that a good release print now has the aura of an original while video is the inferior but inexpensive medium of mass distribution.

Film is better, but these results are not bad. One must use film if the point is to uphold a certain technical and optical standard, if one wants every detail of the image to be readable, if one wants the absolute tones and textures of the original, and if one wants the best-looking final product. It should, however, still be possible to illustrate an article or book with video frame enlargements if one is willing to make sacrifices in the areas of detail and texture. But if the point is simply to document a reference and if convenience is a consideration, a video frame enlargement can hardly be improved on. One such reference is offered in Figure 20.5, substantiating that the title of *It's A Wonderful Life* should be spelled with a capital A by reproducing the movie's original title card.

21
THREE ENDINGS

In this article, published in 2011 by Film Quarterly, *a shot near the end of* Avatar *is compared with a shot near the end of* La Roue, *leading to observations about the contemporary viewer's willing suspension of disbelief and the changing nature of the indexical sign in cinema. (As an indexical sign, a photograph can be grounded in the reality outside the camera by the light that radiates from or bounces off whatever is being photographed and physically affects the emulsion, as Bazin argued without getting into semiotics.) Historically and technologically, this was written in the digital era, which followed the video era, which followed the film era.*

When he saw the clouds moving around the mountain like a wheel and had the cameraman take several shots of them, Abel Gance must have been ecstatic. He may have been waiting for the shot for months, or it may have been a matter of good fortune that he was presented with a real-world image that related to the symbolic core of his *La Roue* (*The Wheel*, 1922) and was fit to be part of the summing up of the whole long movie: a natural image of the wheel, defined at the end (quoting the intertitles) as an "eternal tragic dance" in which "everything turned...even the clouds," and shown in an icon in the corner of many of the intertitles as a torture wheel on which a prisoner's body is broken. Symbolically, the image of clouds around the mountain is related, however positively and transfiguratively, to the fateful, crushing wheel that is evoked throughout the movie; indexically, it is a film image taken in real time; and iconically, it is a recognizable picture of clouds and a mountain—*those* clouds, shot when they were present, intercut with intertitles and with shots of young people dancing in a circle up the mountain. In the terms posed by C. S. Peirce and examined in relation to the cinema by Peter Wollen, the shot of the clouds around the mountain is a complete cinematic sign, with iconic, indexical, and symbolic elements that are clearly expressed and plainly interdependent. And it is not an effects shot, which is one reason it compels and rewards belief. Although silent, it is a shot richly expressive of the semiotic range of the cinema.

No lucky weather was involved in catching the image of the "Toruk Makto" flying off into the sunset near the end of *Avatar* (2009): there was nothing to

Figure 21.1. Near the end of *La Roue*: The mountain and the clouds.
© 2008 Film Preservation Associates, Inc. All rights reserved. DVD © 2008 Flicker Alley, LLC. All rights reserved.

catch. There was no gigantic dragon to catch in flight, and the sky itself wasn't there. There are clouds in the shot, but we cannot tell whether they began as photographed clouds or were generated or reworked on a computer. (Would Cameron have been content with a real, untweaked sunset?) The star and the clouds, the sky itself, are not ours but are those of the fictional moon Pandora. And the Toruk Makto is a creature given form and movement by the computer. Complete with sound and color and in 3D, the shot is a representative digital composite. It is, of course, an effects shot. Iconically, it resembles the event it portrays; symbolically, it evokes Earthly images of a bat or bird flying across the moon, and the sunset and the creature's journey away from the camera imply resolution; indexically, it is nowhere.

The hero who sometimes rides this airborne reptile was never on it and was created partly by motion-capture work that yielded a photorealistic figure, one who looked as if he had been photographed although he never existed physically in that form. The photorealistic shots of the extraterrestrials and their environment, with everything sharply shot or as if sharply shot, are easy to accept on their own terms, as parts of the story and its coherent world. Audiences have no trouble suspending disbelief in the world, characters, and

Figure 21.2. *La Roue*: The accompanying intertitle.
© 2008 Film Preservation Associates, Inc. All rights reserved. DVD © 2008 Flicker Alley, LLC. All rights reserved.

Figure 21.3. Near the end of *Avatar*: Flying into the sunset.
© 2009 Twentieth Century Fox Film Corporation and Dune Entertainment III LLC. All rights reserved. DVD © 2010 Twentieth Century Fox Home Entertainment. All rights reserved.

events of *Avatar* because the effects are both photorealistic and seamless. As the Toruk Makto flies and we see the planet that Pandora orbits and the other moons—all that and the sunset create a skyscape that is utter science fiction and that appears to be present. Effects have always attempted to convince the audience that an event that could not be photographed in reality was somehow happening; all that is new about *Avatar* in this context is that it does what today's audience considers a better job—that is to say, a more credible, convincing job, while the effects shots in older films look dated. (The definitive characteristic of the digital, electronic image is that it lends itself to manipulation as the film image does not. A film image can be modified—on an optical printer, for example—but that is far more difficult and "against the grain" than revision of a digital image.) Those who saw the Red Sea part in *The Ten Commandments* (1956) may have vaguely noticed the black matte line that separates the figures on the shore from the sea; they may even have recognized it as a matte line or as something that showed up in many spectacles and science fiction films. But their primary attention would have been on the water, on the other side of the matte line, where the sea did appear to part, hold itself up, and then rush together. Today's audience sees the matte line and may be pulled out of the illusion by it. But the sunset shot in *Avatar* lives up to current expectations, and most audiences are conscious less of a digital composite than of an extraterrestrial sky.

There are clouds in the sky, but they are not in *that* sky if they were ever anywhere at all, and in spite of the willing suspension of disbelief, we know it. We also know that the image was imagined and then made, not captured in a fortunate moment, and in this respect the shot is representative of another aspect of digital cinema: that its essential, originating space can be found on a monitor more often than in a viewfinder.

It is a sky in which we believe only for the purposes of fiction. The shot in *La Roue* offers a skyscape in which we can and do believe not only as part of the fiction, but also as a real mountain and sky that existed in front of the camera long enough to be photographed. The *Avatar* sunset looks like a sunset and could even have been photographed, though probably not in 3D (at the end of the shot there is a small lens flare that might be an artifact from that shoot or could have been added to give a sense of photographic realism). But we do not take it for a real sunset. The fact that both *Avatar* and *La Roue* are fictions is not the point. The *La Roue* shot presents itself to be believed, while the *Avatar* shot invites and depends on the willing suspension of disbelief. Both shots look photorealistic, but only one was photographed. The digital image, whether it presents a fantasy world or an everyday one, can become as convincing as photography and persuade us of the existence of its world, even on the as-if basis of fiction. But, if only because we cannot be sure to what extent it has been computer-manipulated, it will always to some degree lack the often exciting groundedness of filmed reality.

Even if a digital shot is entirely plausible, it may still strike the audience differently from a filmed shot. Part of the reason for this is that we know the digital shot or some of its details could be phony. There is an authority of reality behind the *La Roue* shot, taken on the real Mont Blanc—as in the "hypothetical experiment" cited by Siegfried Kracauer in *Theory of Film* (New York: Oxford University Press, 1960): "Blaise Cendrars...imagines two film scenes which are completely identical except for the fact that one has been shot on Mont Blanc (the highest mountain of Europe) while the other was staged in a studio. His contention is that the former has a quality not found in the latter" (35). Of course the two Mont Blanc shots cannot have different qualities from each other because they are both hypothetical. But the shots we imagine can be distinguished by the assumptions we bring to them. If we know that the real Mont Blanc was used for the first imaginary shot, we can read into it that it is more grounded and trustworthy, and we can consider or perceive the second more as an excellent artifice, even while we are considering both shots to be visually identical. But this is a matter of reading in and of imagining a valid, even obvious but invisible difference. In any case, if we now look back at images from classical cinema, whether shot on location or in a studio, we know at least that they cannot be CGI. A digital effects shot, [in] contrast, can be wonderfully plausible at the same time as it abandons the authority of reality. The folding of the street in *Inception* (2010) can be such a persuasive if fantastic experience because it looks just as it might if the event had happened in front of a camera. The only indication that it was an effect came from its physical impossibility, from our knowing it couldn't happen except in the dream terms of that movie. This may increase our willing suspension of disbelief—after all, we just saw the street fold over—but what we see is still fake, lacking in reality. In a digital film, our knowledge that anything can have been modified may keep many of us, especially those who first knew cinema before the advent of CGI and digital-image processing, from willingly suspending disbelief in the fiction.

Although I enjoy being carried along and convinced by great digital images, I will miss shots like the one from *La Roue*. I will also miss battle scenes with people rather than pixels in the extreme long shots. Developments in movie technology increasingly mean that my willing suspension of disbelief will no longer involve a complementary trust in the reality that faced the camera (which is, for example, one aspect of enjoying Buster Keaton's stunts). Digital cinema's relationship to reality is always hypothetical to some degree, uncertain—even when, in the finest high-definition work, there is as much visual detail about a physical, photographed subject as one could want. It is no secret that a Blu-ray disc can give a better image than a 16mm print and that a 4K digital master can look as good as a 35mm print, yet every one of the numerous pixels that constitute the digital image's stunning detail may have been altered.

Gance's 35mm image is rich, and I fall in readily with its representation of reality. I accept it as a true record of a few seconds in the 1920s and as a fictitious element within the story of *La Roue*. I do not see any evidence of a miniature mountain or a cloud chamber. Even if it were an image of a different mountain from where the action was set, I would still recognize a real mountain with clouds around it [...].

A shot like the one near the end of *La Roue* still could be taken, though no doubt many digital filmmakers might actually prefer what they can achieve on a computer. Such an image might look very similar to Gance's, it might even be nearly as compelling, but it would not have the same automatic claim on belief (which may be just a potential for belief, grounds for it). To make too much of this development is perhaps to indulge in nostalgia for the indexicality of the photographed image. But I [do].

The time of the pre-digital image is ending, thanks to a major shift in technology of which both filmmakers and audiences are entirely aware. Even if it had its share of effects shots and fakery, of make-up and lighting, and generated worlds that were often paradoxically both real and artificial, pre-digital cinema could shoot sheer reality if it wanted to and would find an audience willing to embrace the shot. The audience that wants digital photorealism now will find it most readily not in a narrative film but in a documentary, such as Herzog's *Cave of Forgotten Dreams* (2010), where the material is authentic and the digital 3D enhances a beautiful kind of realism whose gradual passing [is a real loss].

ACKNOWLEDGMENTS

"*Carnival of Souls*": *Carnival of Souls* (New York: The Criterion Collection, 2000). © 2000 The Criterion Collection. All rights reserved.

"Creative Remembering (and Other Perils of Film Study)": *Film Quarterly* 32, no. 1 (Fall 1978): 62–5. © 1978 by The Regents of the University of California.

"Dorothy's Dream: Mindscreen in *The Wizard of Oz*": *Film Moments: Criticism, History, Theory*, ed. Tom Brown and James Walters (London: Palgrave Macmillan/BFI, 2010), 149–51. © British Film Institute 2010. Individual essay © Bruce F. Kawin 2010. Still from *The Wizard of Oz* © 1939, 2009 Turner Entertainment Company. All rights reserved.

"*The Elephant Man*": *Film Quarterly* 34, no. 4 (Summer 1981): 21–5. © 1981 by the Regents of the University of California.

"*The Fury*": *Take One* 6, no. 6 (May 1978): 7–8. © 1978 by Unicorn Publishing Corp. All rights reserved.

"Horton Foote": © 1997 The National Film Preserve Ltd.

"Howard Hawks": Excerpts were published as "Hawks on Faulkner: Excerpts from an Interview" in *Post Script: Essays in Film and the Humanities* 22, no. 1 (Fall 2002): 3–22. © 2003 by Post Script, Inc. This is the first publication of the complete interview. I am grateful to Aladeen Smith for transcribing it.

"Late Show on the Telescreen: Film Studies and the Bottom Line": *Film Quarterly* 42, no. 2 (Winter 1988–89): 56–60. © 1989 by the Regents of the University of California.

"Lillian Gish": This is the first publication of the interview. Still from *Broken Blossoms* © 1919 D. W. Griffith.

"Me Tarzan, You Junk": *Take One* 6, no. 4 (March 1978), 29–33. © 1978 by Unicorn Publishing Corp. All rights reserved.

"The Montage Element in Faulkner's Fiction": *Faulkner, Modernism, and Film: Faulkner and Yoknapatawpha, 1978*, ed. Evans Harrington and Ann J. Abadie (Jackson: University Press of Mississippi, 1979), 103–26. © 1979 by the University Press of Mississippi. All rights reserved.

"The Mummy's Pool": *Dreamworks: An Interdisciplinary Quarterly* 1, no. 4 (Summer 1981): 291–301. © 1981 by Human Sciences Press. Revised version in *Planks of Reason: Essays on the Horror Film*, ed. Barry K. Grant (Metuchen, NJ and London: Scarecrow Press, 1984), 3–20. © 1984 by Barry Keith Grant. Still from *The Mummy* © 1932 Universal Pictures Corp. All rights reserved. From the library of the Academy of Motion Picture Arts and Sciences.

"An Outline of Film Voices": *Film Quarterly* 38, no. 2 (Winter 1984–85): 38–46. © 1985 by the Regents of the University of California.

"*Piranha*": *Take One* 6, no. 11 (November 1978): 9–11. © 1978 by Unicorn Publishing Corp. All rights reserved.

"Three Endings": *Film Quarterly* 65, no. 1 (Fall 2011): 14–16. © 2011 The Regents of the University of California. All rights reserved. Stills from *La Roue* © 2008 Film Preservation Associates, Inc. All rights reserved. DVD © 2008 Flicker Alley, LLC. All rights reserved. Still from *Avatar* © 2009 Twentieth Century Fox Film Corporation and Dune Entertainment III LLC. All rights reserved. DVD © 2010 Twentieth Century Fox Home Entertainment. All rights reserved.

"Time and Stasis in *La Jetée*": *Film Quarterly* 36, no. 1 (Fall 1982): 15–20. © 1982 by the Regents of the University of California. Still from *La Jetée* © 1963 Argos Films. All rights reserved. DVD © 2007 The Criterion Collection. All rights reserved.

"Video Frame Enlargements": *Film Quarterly* 61, no. 3 (Spring 2008): 52–7. Still from *Citizen Kane* © RKO Pictures, Inc. Licensed by Warner Bros. Entertainment Inc. All Rights Reserved.

"Violent Genres": *Violence in America: An Encyclopedia*, ed. Ronald Gottesman (New York: Scribner's, 1999), vol. I, 529–37. © 1999 by Charles Scribner's Sons. All rights reserved.

"*Welcome to L.A.*": *Take One* 5, no. 10 (July–August, 1977): 10–11. © 1977 by Unicorn Publishing Corp. All rights reserved.

"The Whole World Is Watching": *American Book Review* 9, no. 5 (November–December 1987): 3–5. © 1987 by American Book Review.

"Wild Blueberry Muffins": *Film Criticism* 17, nos. 2–3 (Winter/Spring 1993): 53–5. © 1992 Film Criticism.

INDEX OF NAMES AND TITLES

Abadie, Ann J. 131
ABC of Reading 134
Absalom, Absalom! 121, 132, 138–9, 141, 146–7, 150
Absolution 115
Act of the Heart 68
Aeneid, The 26
Aeschylus 67
Affliction 25
Aguirre the Wrath of God 67
Air Force x, 99
Alamo, The 121–2
À la recherche du temps perdu 132, 134
"Alexander's Ragtime Band" 95
Alger, Horatio 165
Alien 23, 37–8, 41, 46
All That Heaven Allows 159
"All the Dead Pilots" 136–7
All the President's Men 27
Almond, Paul 68
Alone 149–50, 152
Altman, Rick 184
Altman, Robert 9–10, 63–4
American Book Review 13
American Me 28
American Playhouse 152
Ames, Ramsay 47
Amistad 30
Anderson, Jack 89
Ankers, Evelyn 41
Annie Hall 159
Annie Laurie 85
Anthony, Joseph 152
Anticipation of the Night 183
Antonioni, Michelangelo 58, 132
Apocalypse Now 19, 23, 43–4
Aristotle 73

Arness, James 39
Arnheim, Rudolf 75
Arthur, Jean 11
As I Lay Dying 111, 137, 143, 146–7
Avatar 196–9

Baby the Rain Must Fall 150, 152
Bacall, Lauren 101–2, 114, 122
Bacchae, The 163
Badlands 24
Ball of Fire 95
Bancroft, Anne 75
"Band Played On, The" 160
Barn Burning 152
Barry Lyndon 15–16, 66
Barrymore, John 126–7
Barrymore, Lionel 106
Barthelmess, Richard 110
Battleship Potemkin 142–3, 177
Baudelaire, Charles 178
Baum, L. Frank 167
Bazin, André 74, 133, 196
Beauty and the Beast 41
Beckett, Samuel 131–2, 136, 146–7
Beery, Wallace 110
Beethoven, Ludwig van 7–8
Belasco, David 132
Bellin, Olga 150
Bellour, Raymond 178
Belson, Jordan 68
Benjamin, Walter 29, 135, 182, 195
Beowulf 39
Beresford, Bruce 152
Bergman, Ingmar 58–9, 67, 132, 160, 168
Bergren, Eric 72
Bergson, Henri 52
Bertolucci, Bernardo 68

Bey, Turhan 46
Beyond the Pleasure Principle 44
Big Parade, The 82
Big Sleep, The 89, 100–103, 118, 122, 124–5, 159
Billy Jack 3, 11–12
Billy Jack Goes to Washington 11
Birth of a Nation, The 26, 82, 84
Blake, William 152
Blandick, Clara 168
Bleak House 143
Blesh, Rudi 176
Blob, The 41, 43
Blood Feast 57
Blood of a Poet, The 59
Bloom, Harold 67
Blow Out 24, 66
Blue Angel, The 177
Blue Velvet 23
Bobker, Lee 176–7
Bogart, Humphrey 100–103, 122, 124–5
Bogdanovich, Peter 117
Bohème, La 81–3, 85, 166
Bolger, Ray 168
Bonnie and Clyde 9, 22–4
Bordwell, David 31–2
Boy With Green Hair, The 25
Boyle, Peter 12
Boys in the Band, The 117
Brackett, Charles 96
Brackett, Leigh 96, 100, 103
Brainstorm 157, 159, 166
Brakhage, Stan xi, 132, 183
Braque, Georges 134
Brazil 26
Breathless 148
Brecht, Bertolt 70, 184
Bresson, Robert 67–8
Brewster, Ben 32
Bride of Frankenstein 41, 73
Bride of the Gorilla 41
Bridge on the River Kwai, The 89, 97
Bridges at Toko-Ri, The 27
Bringing Up Baby 126, 163
Britton, Celia 32
Broken Blossoms 25–6, 85–7
Brontë, Emily 176
Brooks, Richard 8

Brown, Tom 167
Buffalo Bill and the Indians 63–4
Buñuel, Luis 68
Burke, Billie 75, 169
Burning Bed, The 25
Buster Keaton 176
Butch Cassidy and the Sundance Kid 11

Caan, James 103–4
Cabinet of Dr. Caligari, The 155, 160
Cacoullos, Ann R. 22
Cain, James M. 17
Callenbach, Ernest "Chick" v, xiv, 50
Cameron, James 197
Cantos, The 132, 134
Capra, Frank 11, 17
Carnival of Souls 57–9
Carradine, John 47
Carradine, Keith 9, 63–5
Carrie 67–8
Carringer, Robert 189
Carter family 86
Carter, Jimmy 86
Casetti, Francesco 162
Cassavetes, John 66
Castle, William 162
Cather, Willa 92
Cat People 26
Cavell, Stanley 32
Cave of Forgotten Dreams 201
Cendrars, Blaise 200
Chamberlain, Richard 43
Chandler, Raymond 100
Chaney, Lon 73
Chaney, Jr., Lon 41
Chaplin, Geraldine 64
Chaplin, Sydney 98
Charon, Rita ix
Chase, The 152
Chayefsky, Paddy 151
Chekhov, Anton 149, 151
Chienne, La 159
Chinatown 9, 11
"Cinema/Ideology/Criticism" 165
"Cinematographic Principle and the Ideogram, The" 135
Citizen Kane 32, 69–70, 89, 127–8, 132, 146–8, 163–4, 179, 183, 187–91, 194

INDEX OF NAMES AND TITLES

Citron, Michelle 166
Clifford, John 58–9
Clift, Montgomery 96
Clockwork Orange, A x, 3, 5, 7–8, 10–11, 16, 19–20, 26
Close Encounters of the Third Kind 40
Cocks, Jay 63
Cocteau, Jean 58–9
Coleridge, Samuel Taylor 164
Collins, Joan 98, 118
Collins, Shannon 69
Colman, Ronald 116–17
Color Purple, The 25
Come and Get It 95
Comolli, Jean-Luc 165
"Composition as Explanation" 11
Condemned Man has Escaped, A 67
Conformist, The 68
Conrad, Joseph 93, 165
Convicts 152
Cooper, Gary 90, 103
Coppola, Francis Ford 67, 163
Corman, Roger 69
Cornthwaite, Robert 39
Courtship 152
Coward, Noel 112–13
Crawford, Joan 90–91, 124, 141
Creature from the Black Lagoon 70
Creature Walks Among Us, The 40
Criminal Code, The 28
Cronenberg, David 23
Cronkite, Walter 14
Cronyn, Hume 149
Crowther, Bosley 15
Cukor, George 86
Cummings, Howard 152
Curse of the Cat People, The 37

Daley, Richard xii, 13
Dane, Karl 82
Dante 140–41
Dante, Joe 69–70
Daughter Rite 166
David, King 11, 146
Dawn of the Dead 43
Days of Heaven 32
Day the Earth Stood Still, The 28, 35, 38–40
Dead of Night 154, 156, 159–60

Deliverance 25
Denby, David 16, 18–20
Denver Post, The 15
De Palma, Brian 66–8
Deren, Maya 183
Derrida, Jacques 49, 76
Dersu Uzala 67
DeVore, Christopher 72
Dickens, Charles 4, 132
Dictionary of Film Makers 176
Die Hard 3 25
Dillman, Bradford 69
Displaced Person, The 152
Divine Comedy, The 141
Dmytryk, Edward 107
Dog Star Man 132
Don Quixote 142
Don't Look Now 43
Dos Passos, John 92, 132
Double Indemnity 154
Douglas, Kirk 67
Dracula 41
Dreadful Hollow 89–90, 116
Dreamworks 35
Dreyer, Carl Theodor 43, 57, 67–8, 148, 169
Dr. No 28
Dr. Strangelove 7, 14–20
Drums Along the Mohawk 183
"Dry September" 141
Duck Amuck 25
Duras, Marguerite 148
Duvall, Robert 150

Earhart, Amelia 110
Earthquake 29
Easy Rider 9, 28
Edwards, Don 15
8½ 156
Eisenstein, Sergei 74, 111, 131–6, 138, 140–42, 145, 147, 151, 162, 165
El Dorado 96, 102–4, 114
Elements of Film 176–7
Elephant Man, The xii, 72–7
Eliot, T. S. 132, 134
Eraserhead 73
Evans, Walker 152
Everitt, David 162

Exorcist, The 66
Eyes of Laura Mars 166

Faces 32
Fail-Safe 18
Fairbanks, Douglas 93
Fall of the House of Usher, The 183
Family Plot 63
Fassbinder, Rainer Werner 132
Faulkner, William x–xi, xiii–xiv, 89–93, 95–6, 98–101, 105–9, 111–18, 120–25, 127–8, 131–48, 150–52
Faulkner and Film 89, 131
"Faulkner and Yoknapatawpha" 131
Faulkner–Cowley File, The 140
Faulkner's MGM Screenplays 89
Faulkner, Modernism, and Film 131
Fellini, Federico 148
Ferber, Edna 95
Fields, W. C. 162
Fig Leaves 94
Film 131–2
Film as Art 75
Film Criticism 31
Film Moments 167
Film Quarterly xiv, 50, 72, 153, 175, 180, 187–8, 196
Film Tricks 162
First Blood 29
Fitzgerald, F. Scott 147
Flashdance 161, 165
Fleming, Victor 113, 167
Fly, The 28
Foote, Hallie 150
Foote, Horton xii, xiii, 81, 149–52
Foote, Lillian Vallish 81, 149, 151
Footloose 163
For a New Novel 143–4
Forbidden Planet 28
Ford, John 97, 113, 121–2, 157, 163
Ford, Peter 77
Foreman, Carl 97
For Whom the Bell Tolls 115
4 Little Girls 27
Francis, Freddie 72
Franco, Francisco 5, 15
Frankenstein 41, 43, 48, 73
Frazer, James xi, 37, 42, 44–5

Freaks 73
French Connection, The 117
Frenzy 27
Freud, Sigmund 35, 37, 41–4, 46, 49
Freund, Karl 36
Friday the 13th 24
Friedkin, William 117
Friendly Persuasion 6
Fuller, Samuel 17, 67
Full Metal Jacket xii–xiii, 13, 15–21
Furthman, Jules 96, 99, 113–15, 127
Fury 27
Fury, The xii, 66–8

Gabby Hayes Show, The 151
Gable, Clark 92, 108
Gance, Abel xiv, 132, 135, 142, 160, 196, 201
Garbo, Greta 67
Garland, Judy 167, 171
Genette, Gerard 153
Gentlemen Prefer Blondes 164–5
Gertrud 67
Ghost Story, A 89–90, 115–16
Ginsberg, Allen 4
Gish, Dorothy 84
Gish, Lillian x–xiv, 81–8, 149–51, 186
Gish, Mary ("Mother") 81, 84–6
Godard 176
Godard, Jean-Luc 74, 132, 148, 176, 178
Godard: Three Films 178
Godfather, The 5, 23, 163
Godfather Part II, The 23, 26, 163
Godfather Part III, The 24
Godzilla 57
Gog 29
Golden Bough, The xi, 42–5
Goldwyn, Samuel 94–5
Gone With the Wind 132
GoodFellas 30
Gottesman, Ron 22
Goya, Francisco 49
Grand amour de Beethoven, Un 160
Grant, Cary 96–7, 114, 119, 121
Grapewin, Charley 171
Gravity's Rainbow 132
Great Dictator, The 164
Greatest Question, The 186

INDEX OF NAMES AND TITLES 209

Great Gatsby, The 147
Greed 132
Green Berets, The 20
Greetings 67
Grésac, Madame de 81–2
Grey, Zane 93
Griffith, D. W. xii, 48, 68, 85–8, 132, 136, 185–6
Gulpulil 43
Gun Crazy 27
Guzmán, Patricio 55–6
Guzzetti, Alfred 32

Haley, Jack 168
Hall, James 164
Halloween 22–3, 28
Halloween II 22
Hamilton, Margaret 168
Hamlet 74, 139, 153
Hammett, Dashiell 100
Hampton, Fred 14
Harakiri 67
Harrington, Evans 131
Harrison, Ken 152
Harron, Bobby 186
Harvey, Herk 58–9
Hatari! 96, 120, 122
Hawkins, Jack 98
Hawks, Howard x, xiii–xiv, 11, 38–9, 68, 89–128, 131, 133, 136, 163, 165
Hawks, William 116–17
Hawthorne, Nathaniel 83
Hayes, Alfred 107
"Heart of Darkness" 165
Heart of Glass 67
Heaven's Gate 24
Hecht, Ben 91
Hegel, G. W. F. 132, 134, 147
Hellinger, Mark 160
Hemingway, Ernest 92, 95–6, 109, 113, 122, 127
Henderson, Brian 153–5
Henry V 72
Henry: Portrait of a Serial Killer 22, 25
Hepburn, Katherine 105
Herr, Michael 19
Herrmann, Bernard 68
Herzog, Werner 66–8, 201

High Noon x, 3, 5–7, 10, 12, 25, 103–4
Hill, The 28
Hilligoss, Candace 58–9
Hills Have Eyes, The 24
Hiroshima mon amour 111, 148, 159
His Girl Friday 89, 97, 103, 127–8
History of the Cinema, A 176
Hitchcock, Alfred 66–8, 156–7, 159
Home Alone 23, 25
"Honor" 115
Hopkins, Anthony 75
Horror and the Horror Film 35
House on 92nd Street, The 28
Howell, Michael 77
How Green Was My Valley 153–5
How to Read a Film 177
Humphrey, Hubert 14
Hunchback of Notre Dame, The 73
Hurt, John 73
Hutton, Lauren 64

I Am A Fugitive From A Chain Gang 27–8
Imaginary Signifier, The 32, 175
Ince, Thomas 82
Inception 200
Inferno 141
Internet Movie Database 175
Interpretation of Dreams, The 37, 41
Intolerance 3–4, 48, 87–8, 132, 143, 159, 187–8, 191–4
Introduction to Metaphysics, An 52
Introductory Lectures on Psycho-Analysis 41
Invasion of the Body Snatchers 8, 28, 40
Irving, Amy 67
Island of Lost Souls 73
Italian, The 185
It's A Wonderful Life 181, 183, 194–5
Ivanhoe 26
I Was a Male War Bride 89, 102, 114, 118–19

Jaffe, Sam 38
James Bond series 23
Jaws 26, 43, 45–6, 69–70, 159
Jaws 2 69–70
Jetée, La xiii, 50–56
Johann, Zita 44
Johnson, Lyndon 15, 18

Jones, Chuck 22, 25
Jones, Parnelli 117
Joyce, James 132–4, 136, 140, 146–7
Jud Süss 161, 164
Jules and Jim 177
Julia and Julia 181
Jumbo 99

Kael, Pauline 10, 16–17, 63
Karloff, Boris 44
Karlova, Irina 89
Kawin, Morris 149
Kaye, Danny 95
Keaton 176
Keaton, Buster 131–2, 169, 176, 200
Keitel, Harvey 64
Kellerman, Sally 64
Kelly, Gene 7
Kelly, Grace 6
Kennedy, John F. 15, 18
Kenner, Hugh 131
King and Country 16
King Kong 132
Kings of the Road 148
King Solomon's Mines 28
Knight, Arthur 177
Kobayashi, Masaki 67
Kracauer, Siegfried 200
Kubrick, Stanley xii, 7–8, 14–21, 132
Kurnitz, Harry 98, 118
Kurosawa, Akira 67
Kwaidan 67

Lady Eve, The 23
Lady in the Lake 154, 158
Lady of the Pavements 185
Lahr, Bert 168
Lamb, Charles 74
Land of the Pharaohs 98–9, 109, 118
Lang, Fritz 68, 132, 177
Lang, June 107
Langlois, Henri 53
Lao Tze 10
Lasker, Albert 120
Lasky, Jesse 93
Last House on the Left, The 25
Last Wave, The 35–6, 43
Last Year at Marienbad 148, 155, 164, 177

Laszlo, Ervin 143
Laughlin, Tom 4
LeBorg, Reginald 36
Ledoux, Jacques 53
Lee, Harper 150, 152
Left Hand of God, The 107, 118
Lethal Weapon 22–3
Life of an American Fireman 176
Life Upside Down 59, 156
Light in August 120–21, 148, 152
Lily Dale 150, 152
Lindfors, Viveca 64
Lindsay-Hogg, Michael 152
Little Big Man 4
Liveliest Art, The 177
Lolita 17
Lombard, Carole 126–7
Lonely are the Brave 9
Looking for Mr. Goodbar 8
Losey, Joseph 16, 132
Lost Highway 23
Love's Choice 185
Lowery, Robert 47
Lugosi, Bela 41
Lumière 64–5
Lumière, Louis and Auguste 163
Lynch, David 23, 58, 72–7
Lyrical Ballads 164

M 27, 177
MacArthur, Charles 91
Macbeth 137
Madame Bovary 154
Made in U.S.A 148
MAD 66–7
Mad Max 2 26
Magician, The 59
Magnificent Ambersons, The 160
Malone, Dorothy 101
Maltese Falcon, The 181, 183
Mankiewicz, Herman J. 147, 164
Mann, Thomas 92
Manners, David 45
Man Who Shot Liberty Valance, The 27, 163
Man Who Would Be King, The 28
Man with a Movie Camera, The 132
March, Fredric 106
Marker, Chris 50, 53, 55–6

INDEX OF NAMES AND TITLES

Marlowe, Hugh 38
Marriage of Kitty, The 82
Martin, Dean 96, 112
Marx, Groucho 162
Mast, Gerald xi, 175–7
Masterson, Peter 152
Maurel, Victor 82
Mayer, Louis B. xi, 81–3, 85, 124
Mayo, Virginia 95
McCabe & Mrs. Miller x, 3, 9–10
McCarthy, Joseph 6
McCarthy, Kevin 69
McGovern, George 14
McTeague 132
Medea 4
Medium Cool 9
Melville, Sam 14
Menn, Lise xiv
Men Who Made the Movies, The 125
Menzies, Heather 69–70
Merrick, John 72–7
Meshes of the Afternoon 183
Metaphors on Vision xii
Metz, Christian 32, 175
Mickey Mouse Club, The 19
Middlemarch 163
Mildred Pierce 25
Milestone, Lewis 17
Mind of the Novel, The 50, 147
Mindscreen 32, 37, 72, 77, 153, 155, 157, 167
Misfits, The 9
Mitchum, Robert 96
Moby-Dick 70, 154
Modern Times 10–11
Moir, Phyllis 84
Monaco, James 177
Moreau, Jeanne 64
Morgan, Frank 168
Morris, Peter 176
Most Dangerous Game, The 28
Mother 159
Movshovitz, Howie ix–xii, xiv
Mr. Sardonicus 162
Mr. Smith Goes to Washington 11
Mulligan, Robert 152
Mummy, The 35–6, 44–5
Mummy's Ghost, The 36, 46–9
Mummy's Hand, The 46–7

Mummy's Tomb, The 46–8
Murnau, F. W. 66
Mutiny on the Bounty 132, 164
Mystery of Kaspar Hauser, The 67
Mythical Latin-American Kingdom Story 115

Naked City, The 160
Napoléon 142
Narboni, Jean 165
Narrative Discourse 153
Nashville 64
Natural Born Killers 22–4, 26
Neal, Patricia 38
Nelson, Ricky 103
Never Give a Sucker an Even Break 162
New York 16
New Yorker, The 16, 117, 123
New York Times, The 16
Niagara 27
Nichols, Dudley 96
Night and Fog 27, 166
Nightmare on Elm Street, A 28
Night of the Hunter, The 151
Night of the Living Dead 23, 28, 59, 66
Night of the Storm 151
1918 150, 152
Nixon, Richard 6, 14
Nordhoff, Charles 164
North, Oliver 15
North by Northwest 28, 159
Nyby, Christian 38

Obsession 67–8
"Occurrence at Owl Creek Bridge, An" 58
October 132, 142, 162, 165
Of Mice and Men 152
Oglesby family 86
O'Hara, Maureen 97
Oklahoma! 22
"Old Man" 140–42, 151
Old Man 149–51
Oliver Twist 163
Olivier, Laurence 73
One Exciting Night 185
O'Neill, Eugene 150
Only Angels Have Wings x, 109–11
On the Beach 18
On Valentine's Day 152

Open City 30
Ordet 67
Oresteia, The 67
Orlean, Susan xi
Orphans' Home, The 151–2
Orpheus 58–9
Orwell, George 5, 182
Our Hospitality 176
Out of the Past 27

Page, Geraldine 149–50, 152
Paine, Thomas 14
Passion of Joan of Arc, The 67
Paths of Glory 7, 16–17, 20
Pearl 42–3
Peck, Gregory 150
Peckinpah, Sam 4, 10
Peeping Tom 57
Peirce, C. S. 196
Persona 37, 67–8, 159–60, 168
Phantom of the Paradise 67
Picasso, Pablo 109, 132, 134
Pickford, Mary 93
Pierrot le fou 148
Pinter, Harold 177
Piranha xii, 69–71
Plato 40
Platoon 19–20, 27
Playboy 116
Playhouse 90 151
Pointe-Courte, La 131, 148
Polanski, Roman 68
Pomerance, Bernard 72–4
Porter, Edwin S. 176
"Portraits and Repetition" 132
Potemkin: see *Battleship Potemkin*
Potter, Sally 166
Pound, Ezra 131–2, 134, 136
Prince of the City 26
Proust, Marcel 132, 134, 136, 143–4, 147
Psycho 22–3, 25, 28
Pudovkin, V. I. 159
Pylon 107–8, 113, 115, 141

Queen Christina 67
Quest for Failure 137
Quiet Man, The 97

Ra Expeditions, The 163
Raging Bull 30
Rains, Claude 41
Rashomon 156, 159
Rather, Dan 181
Ratoff, Gregory 106
Reagan, Ronald 13, 182
Rebecca 160
Red Planet Mars 164
Red River 96–7, 103, 117, 132
Red Shoes, The 185
Reilly, Adam xii, 185–6
Réjane 82
Rennie, James 84
Rennie, Michael 38
Republic, The 40
Resnais, Alain 131–2, 145, 148, 164, 177
Rhode, Eric 176
Ribicoff, Abraham xii, 13
Rich Man, Poor Man 112
Rio Bravo 95–6, 103, 112, 114
Rio Lobo 96, 111
River's Edge 14
Road Runner cartoons 25
Road to Glory, The 89, 106–9
Road Warrior, The 26
Robbe-Grillet, Alain 132, 143–4, 148, 164
Robinson, David 176
Robinson, Francis 82
Rocketship X-M 28
Rocky Horror Picture Show, The 162
Romeo and Juliet 75–6
Romero, George A. 23, 40, 59
Romola 85
Rooster Cogburn 105
Roots in a Parched Ground 151–2
Rose, Billy 99–100
Rose, Reginald 151
Rosemary's Baby 28, 57
Rossellini, Roberto 163
Roud, Richard 176
Roue, La xiv, 132, 142, 196–201
Rowan, Dr. 84–5
Rudolph, Alan 63–5
Rules of the Game 163
Rupture, La 68
Russell, Bertrand 14
Ruttmann, Walter 132

INDEX OF NAMES AND TITLES

Sadoul, Georges 176
Sailor who Fell from Grace with the Sea, The 11
Salt of the Earth 26
Sanctuary 92, 108–9, 121, 137, 139
Sands of Iwo Jima 97
Saturday Evening Post 91, 123
Sayles, John 70
Scarborough, Dorothy 85
Scarface 26, 127
Scarlet Days 185
Scarlet Letter, The xi, 81, 83–5
Schechter, Harold 162
Schenck, Joseph 119
Schenck, Nicholas 81
Schickel, Richard 117, 125–6
Schneider, Alan 131–2
Searchers, The 97
Secrets 90
Senise, Gary 152
Sennett, Mack 132
Serling, Rod 161
Serre, Henri 177
Servant, The 177
Se7en 23–4
Seventh Victim, The 57
Shampoo 63
Shakespeare, William 72, 137, 146
Shame 67
Shane 26
Shawshank Redemption, The 25
Shearer, Norma 90
Sheridan, Ann 107
Sherlock Jr. 169, 176
She Wore a Yellow Ribbon 97
Shining, The 15–16
Shootist, The 105
Short History of the Movies, A xi, 175–7
Silence, The 67
"Singin' In The Rain" 7
Singin' In The Rain 164
Siodmak, Curt 41
Slatoff, Walter 137
Smith, Aladeen 203
Snodgrass, Carrie 67
Snow White and the Seven Dwarfs 25
Soldiers' Pay 92
Song is Born, A 95

"Song of Myself" 132
Sound and the Fury, The 111, 127, 136–8, 143–6, 148, 150
Spartacus 7, 16
Speed 29
Spiegel, Sam 97
Spielberg, Steven 17
Spirit of the Beehive, The 43
Spy Who Came In from the Cold, The 28
Spy Who Loved Me, The 159
Stanley, Kim 150–51
Stanwyck, Barbara 95
Stark, Ray 117
Star Trek 181
Star Trek II: The Wrath of Khan 29
Steele, Barbara 69–71
Steel Helmet, The 22, 27
Steelyard Blues 12
Stein, Gertrude 11, 132, 136, 144, 147
Steiner, Max 177
Stepford Wives, The 37
Sternberg, Josef von 114
Storm Fear 152
Story of Gösta Berling, The 83
Strangers On A Train 155–6, 158, 160
Straw Dogs x, 3–5, 7, 10–11, 25
Stromboli 163
"Stuttering Sam" 89, 99–100
Styne, Jule 108
Sutherland, Donald 12
Sutter's Gold 140–41
Swan, Buddy 189–90
Swift, Jonathan 17

Take One 3, 8, 63, 66, 69
Tall Man, The 117
Tandy, Jessica 149
Tarantula 29, 43
Tatum, Art 99
Telling It Again and Again 135
Tempest, Mary 82
Ten Commandments, The 199
Tender Mercies 150–52
Texas Chain Saw Massacre, The 23, 46
Thalberg, Irving 81, 83, 85, 90–91, 93–4, 97, 123–4
Theory of Film 200
They Died with Their Boots On 182

Thing From Another World, The 31, 35, 38–40, 42–3, 46, 120
This Island Earth 28
Thompson, Jim 27
Threepenny Opera, The 14
Thriller 166
Through the Looking-Glass 159
Thulin, Ingrid 67
"Time and Description" 143–4
Time 63
Titanic 30
Tobey, Kenneth 39
Today We Live 89–91, 109, 115
To Have and Have Not 89, 96, 99–100, 114, 122, 177
To Kill a Mockingbird 27, 149–50, 152
Tol'able David 11, 24
Toland, Gregg 107
Tolstoy, Leo 9
Tom Jones 177
"Tomorrow" 150–51
Tomorrow 149–52
Tone, Franchot 90
To the Lighthouse 20
Tout va bien 159
Traffic in Souls 185
Trapeze 108
Treves, Frederick 72–7
Trial of Billy Jack, The 4
Trip to Bountiful, The 149–52
Triumph of the Will 161
True Grit 105
True Heart Susie 186
True History of the Elephant Man, The 77
True Lies 24–5
"Turn About" 89–91, 108, 123
Turn About 89–93, 124
Turner, Ted 183
Twentieth Century 126–7
Twilight Zone, The 58, 161
2 or 3 Things I Know About Her 74, 148, 160, 177–8, 182
2001: A Space Odyssey 15–17, 22
2010 17

Ulysses 132–4, 138–9, 146
"Unattainable Text, The" 178
Unforgiven 30

Uninvited, The 28
U.S.A. 132

Vampyr 43, 46, 57, 66–8, 169
Varda, Agnès 131, 148
Variety 108
Verdi, Giuseppe 82
Vertigo 22, 67–8, 157, 159, 187–8
Vidor, King 82–3
Villa, Pancho 111
Violence in America 22
Voyage in Italy 163

Waggner, George 36
Waiting for Godot 53, 132
Walcott, Charles 123
Walters, James 167
Walthall, Henry B. 83–4
War Birds 89–90, 115–16
War Game, The 15
Warner, Jack 95, 99, 102, 107
"Waste Land, The" 132, 134
Watering the Gardener 163
Watkins, Peter 15
Watson, James Sibley 183
Watt 146
Wayne, John 96–7, 103–5, 112, 121–2
Webber, Melville 183
Weekend 176–7
Weir, Peter 36, 43
Welcome to L.A. xii, xiv, 63–5
Welles, Orson 127–8, 132, 146, 160, 163–4
Wellman, William A. 116
Wenders, Wim 148
Werner, Oskar 177
West Side Story 25
What Is Cinema? 133
White Rose, The 185
White Sister, The 85
Wiene, Robert 132
Wilcox, Herbert 84
Wild At Heart 28
Wild Bunch, The 23–4
Wild Child, The 175, 179
Wilder, Billy 96
"Wild Palms" 140, 142, 151
Wild Palms, The 111, 131, 138–43, 148, 151

Wild Strawberries 59
Williams, Annwyl 32
Williams, Tennessee 150
Wind, The 81, 85
Wise, Robert 38
Wittgenstein, Ludwig 147
Wizard of Oz, The xiii, 28, 35, 37, 75, 132, 156, 159, 167–71
Wolfe, Thomas 164
Wolf Man, The 35–6, 40–42, 46
Wollen, Peter 196
Woman Under the Influence, A 5
Wonderful Wizard of Oz, The 167
Wood, Ed 58
Wood, Robin 119
Wooden Crosses 106
Wordsworth, William 164

"Work of Art in the Age of Mechanical Reproduction, The" 29, 135
Worthington, Cal 71
Wurtzel, Sol 94
Wynn, Keenan 69

Young, Loretta 118
Young, Robert 90
Youngblood, Gene 8
Young Man from Atlanta, The 150
Young Romance 185

Z 27
Zabriskie Point 66
Zanuck, Darryl F. 106–8, 118
Zoot Suit 25
Zucco, George 46–7, 49

www.ingramcontent.com/pod-product-compliance
Lightning Source LLC
Chambersburg PA
CBHW020911020526
44114CB00039B/339